NEGOTIATING **DIFFERENCE**

BLACK LITERATURE AND CULTURE
A series edited
by Houston A. Baker, Jr.

Michael Awkward

NEGOTIATING DIFFERENCE

Race, Gender, and the
Politics of Positionality

THE UNIVERSITY of CHICAGO PRESS
Chicago & London

Michael Awkward is associate professor of English and Afro-American Studies and director of the Center for Afroamerican and African Studies at the University of Michigan. He is the author of *Inspiriting Influences: Tradition, Revision, and Afro-American Women's Novels* and editor of *New Essays on "Their Eyes Were Watching God."*

The University of Chicago Press, Chicago 60637
The University of Chicago Press, Ltd., London
© 1995 by The University of Chicago
All rights reserved. Published 1995
Printed in the United States of America
03 02 01 00 99 98 97 96 95   1 2 3 4 5

ISBN: 0-226-03300-7 (cloth)
        0-226-03301-5 (paper)

Library of Congress Cataloging-in-Publication Data

Awkward, Michael.
   Negotiating difference : race, gender, and the politics of
positionality / Michael Awkward.
       p.   cm. — (Black literature and culture)
   Includes bibliographical references (p.) and index.
   1. American literature—Afro-American authors—History and
criticism—Theory, etc.   2. American literature—Women authors—
History and criticism—Theory, etc.   3. Criticism—Political
aspects—United States.   4. Feminist literary criticism—Men
authors.   5. Feminism and literature—United States.   6. Women and
literature—United States.   7. Afro-Americans in literature.
8. Afro-American men—Attitudes.   9. Sex role in literature.
10. Race in literature.   I. Title.   II. Series.
PS153.N5A943   1995
810.9'896073—dc20   94-17205

For Lauren and Camara, my fellow travelers, and
for Houston, for helping me to negotiate the way

CONTENTS

ACKNOWLEDGMENTS

The question that motivates each of the chapters of this study is: how do artists, scholars, and others concerned with representations of Afro-American life respond to views that gender, race, class, and sexuality determine or circumscribe their own and others' lives and narratives? Debates within afrocentric and feminist critical circles over, among other matters, the consequences of difference have made it possible for me to try to find answers to that question. I am particularly grateful to be participating in Afro-American expressive cultural study at a moment when so much fine, nuanced, and challenging work is being produced. While our debates and tensions—concerning the meanings of gender, race, ideology, power, and other inescapable human matters—illustrate that (comm)unity remains a perhaps not actualizable goal, these debates, when they are publicly named cogently scrutinized, can lead to a marvelously productive criticism and self-criticism. For helping me—in their clarifying work, in conversations, and/or by inviting me to write about my interpretive dilemmas—to navigate the territory explored in *Negotiating Difference,* I want especially to thank Hortense Spillers, Skip Gates, Mae Henderson, Claudine Raynaud, Kim Benston, Linda Kauffman, Wahneema Lubiano, Marcellus Blount, Robyn Wiegman, Alan Nadel, and Nellie McKay.

The University of Michigan has been a marvelous source of support and stimulation. I am indebted to friends, colleagues, and students both in English and in Afro-American and African studies, and I want especially to thank: Anne Herrmann, whose wisdom and encouragement were invaluable when I began to sketch the rough contours of this project in the summer of 1987; Martha Vicinus and Nesha Haniff, for listening on numerous occasions to my unformed ideas; and Chris Flint, Athena Vrettos, and Patsy Yaegar, all of whom helped me recognize what I was trying to accomplish in this study's final chapter. In their administrative capacities—which obligated them to feign interest in every thought I uttered—Lem Johnson, Earl Lewis, and Bob Weisbuch were incredibly support-ive, and I can only begin to understand now, after my first year as an administrator, how difficult that must have been. While I was writing this book, the Center for Afroamerican and African studies provided funds to hire Katie O'Connell, Tim Chin, Sharon Holland, and Michelle Johnson, who offered valuable research as-sistance. I am especially grateful to Michelle, who worked with me through the difficult period of the final preparation of this book, and whose enthusiasm never waned, even when mine did in the face of various frustrations.

I owe a special debt to the folks in the Afro-American Studies Program at Princeton University, in whose clean, well-lighted spaces I worked during the first half of 1992 as a President's Postdoctoral Fellow. I completed a good bit of this study during these months, which I attribute in part to the unsurpassed vitality of Afro-Americanist inquiry there.

I was invited to discuss aspects of my work by friends and colleagues at a number of universities, including the University of Pennsylvania, University of Wisconsin-Milwaukee, Rutgers, Princeton, Ohio State, and Berkeley. For mak-ing those occasions immensely productive for me, I thank David deLaura, John Roberts, Cheryl Johnson, Donald Gibson, Carol Barash, Cheryl Wall, Gayle Pemberton, Roland Williams, Steve Goldsmith, and Celeste Langan.

Also, I want to thank the folks at the University of Chicago Press, particu-larly Alan Thomas and Randy Petilos, for helping to make *Negotiating Difference* possible.

An earlier version of chapter 1 appeared in *Black American Literature Forum* 22 (1988); parts of chapter 3 appeared, in an earlier form, in *American Literary History* 2 (1990); chapter 5 appeared in *Callaloo* 13 (1990); and chapter 6 appeared in *May All Your Fences Have Gates: Essays on the Drama of August Wilson,* edited by Alan Nadel (University of Iowa Press, 1993). Permission to use this material is grate-fully acknowledged.

M. A.

Ann Arbor, MI
July 1994

NEGOTIATING **DIFFERENCE :**
Race, Gender, and the Politics of Positionality

Across the lines
Who would dare to go
Under the bridge
Over the tracks
That separates whites from blacks
Choose sides
Or run for your life
Tonight the riots begin

Tracy Chapman, "Across the Lines"

What is involved in the project of rescinding borders is a critical awareness of how borders have been (and continue to be) systematically policed and for whose ideological benefit and material profit. The way to rescind borders is of course to cross them and, in doing so, blur them, confuse them, make them permeable, open for traffic from all directions, and, as a result, realize that they have in fact been open all along, crossed by illegal traffic of all kinds—in short, that differences of the kind that do not settle down into binaries have already proliferated in our own backyards.

Vera Kutzinski, "American Literary History as Spatial Practice"

Anyone who searches for the "text itself" will find a never-ending series of construals of it.

Paul Armstrong, *Conflicting Readings*

Reading across the Lines

According to the lyrics of Tracy Chapman's prophetic song, of which I make epigraphic use here, interracial travel is a daring, potentially life-threatening activity. For Chapman, heretofore available—if not necessarily free—avenues of travel "across the lines" of difference ("the bridge," "tracks") have ceased to serve as means of traversing dangerous terrain.[1] Because these avenues of mediation are currently so inaccessible (closed, in no small way, by battles for cultural power) people "separate[d]" by a late twentieth-century manifestation of the color line are now adversaries whose differences include the production of disparate, intensely self-interested readings of the means to eliminate American racial antagonisms.

Despite her presentation of race as an impenetrable boundary dividing "whites from blacks," Chapman's persona insists on the possibility of choosing sides, of locating one's self within racially inflected spheres of demarcation. If choice here pertains to notions of both ideological and territorial specificity, the danger for the chooser may lurk not merely in the form of the adversarial racial other but in the form of occupants of a common geography who regard the chooser's racial(ized) performance as inadequate. In this reading, "riots" may arise not only from border disputes but also as intraterritorial responses to the adoption of behaviors, worldviews, and methods of interrogation which those who seek to determine racial meaning assume are not endemic to their specific cultural place.[2] Black discourse is filled with scores of examples. Two recent ones, which were motivated by assumptions of what constituted righteous and, conversely, treacherous black behavior, are the efforts to *pinpoint* the ideological effects of Clarence Thomas's rural black southern roots upon his judicial decisions, and Joyce Joyce's condemnation of Afro-American practitioners of contemporary critical theory.[3]

This reading of Chapman's lyrics challenges the utopian fantasy that the essential meanings of race can be transcended in America, a fantasy that others have argued seems to motivate, for example, Michael Jackson's explorations of what it signifies to be marked as "black or white." It is not my intention in this Introduction to plunge further into an inquiry of figurations of race in black popular music, though the final chapter of this study does explore Jackson's putative efforts to achieve in his person a literal erasure of racial origin. Using formulations applicable to this mass cultural subject, I hope instead to examine academic discourse in the humanities within which employment of a politics of positionality has become a significant aspect of our critical behaviors. My emphasis is the putative or actual interpretive consequences of race, gender, class, and sexual orientation, among other characteristics. To use Nancy Miller's phrase, many of us have been "getting personal"[4] in our writings, have been locating ourselves publicly along a series of identity axes, to the extent that the question, "How does your work reflect the politics of your (racial/gendered/sexual) positionality?" may have overtaken the inquiry, "What is your theoretical approach?" as the most popular conversational gambit at conferences and other sites of professional interaction. Indeed, we might say that sincere responses to the injunction, "Critic, position thyself," are seen by many as among the most effectively moral and significant gestures of our current age, protecting us from, among other sins, fictions of critical objectivity that marred previous interpretive regimes.

Whatever we feel about this trend, it is indisputable that boundary transgression—interpretive movement across putatively fixed biological, cultural, or ideological lines in order to explore, in a word, difference—has come to require either extreme theoretical naiveté or perhaps unprecedented scholarly daring. The sense of risk in such transgressions is made no less significant by the fact that interpretive journeys are not nearly as dangerous as the literal crossing of geographical borders between communities can be. References to places like Central Park, South Central L.A., Detroit, Crown Heights, Bensonhurst, and urban America have come to symbolize for many the danger of interterritorial travel, but this should not dissuade academics from attempting to explore the areas surrounding our relatively safe professional environs. Rather, this knowledge ought to encourage in us a judicious examination of these spaces and their sometimes seemingly minimal relation to one another. Any such examination on my part must begin with an acknowledgment that, perhaps because I grew up in a South Philadelphia ghetto where the threat of organized violence against my person (from without and within, from whites and blacks) seemed, frankly, omnipresent, I am well aware—especially when engaging (in) academic discourse which examines the implications of writing from the borders—of the protections I enjoy during even the most energetic, ideologically charged academic battles.

A number of scholars have begun to interrogate American subjectivities in ways that disrupt facile equations between real ghetto and marginal academic space. To cite one example, Hortense Spillers begins her essay, "Mama's Baby, Papa's Maybe: An American Grammar Book," with a catalog of designations of a specifically gendered and racialized presence—a catalog attentive to the sources and consequences of the marginal identities she is believed to occupy. Spillers offers a discourse that is explicitly both self-referential and critical of others' acts of group designation:

> Let's face it. I am a marked woman, but not everybody knows my name. "Peaches" and "Brown Sugar," "Sapphire" and "Earth Mother," "Aunty," "Granny," God's "Holy Fool," a "Miss Ebony First," or "Black Woman at the Podium": I describe a locus of confounded identities, a meeting ground of investments and privations in the national treasury of rhetorical wealth. My country needs me, and if I were not here, I would have to be invented.[5]

Spillers interrogates the fact of being "marked," of being assigned a series of conflicting social meanings by advocates of both white and black power, and seeks to intervene in her audience's readings of her body, soul, and flesh. If the conflicting identities are, by their very nature, irreconcilable, Spillers—an objectified subject placed in the unenviable position of representing a complex social body—is admittedly also "confounded" by her position, and she seeks to "invent" a discourse capable of rewriting the historical record and describing heretofore generally unrecognized nuances that characterize black (especially black female) participation in an American "meeting ground."

I appropriate Spillers's formulations here to help create rhetorical space among provocative discursive stylings for my own versions of that "meeting ground." In part, Spillers's work—and Chapman's—serves as a means of initiating my discourse's "beginnings" in Edward Said's sense of that term. According to Said, "beginning is making or producing difference," which is "the result of combining the already-familiar with . . . fertile novelty."[6] In keeping with Said's view that beginning requires the production of a state of complementarity between "the new and the customary" (xiii), I am striving in this study to produce a self-consciously black male inquiry that as often as possible considers its terms as categories to be examined rather than as mere confirmation of "the already-familiar." Like Spillers, I want to assess ways in which signifiers inundated with cultural meaning such as the at least oxymoronic formulation "black male feminist" might be "marked" both by conceptual limitations and possibilities of "rhetorical wealth," by disabling blindness and enabling insight. The status "Black Woman on the Podium" encourages the beginnings of Spillers's journey through the discursive muck of historical, autobiographical, mythic, and sociological narratives in order to propel us toward more liberating acts of naming. It is my hope that a similarly self-conscious inscription of one scholar's sense of the interpretive possibilities of black maleness might help, however minimally, to dislodge some of the limiting misnomers which have calcified around that complex positionality.

Rather than, like Spillers, seeking to effect this end by producing a revisionary historical analysis, I explore largely contemporary Afro-American sitings—fictive, filmic, scholarly—wherein (to borrow an image from Cornel West) ghosts of a nostalgic essentialism continue to haunt interrogations of gender and race. Given postmodernism's interpretive cachet within the academy, it is certainly now customary for scholars to assert the arbitrariness, the culturally constructed nature, of race, gender, class, and nation, and by and large my treatment of these matters is necessarily derivative, "already-familiar," patently unoriginal. What is, I believe, novel about my project is my willingness to push the critical possibilities suggested by my gendered and racial positions to what I hope are fruitful, clarifying ends. This project's value, as I see it, will be determined by its success in surveying relevant discursive meeting grounds and demonstrating that race and gender represent negotiable (albeit dangerous) terrain that can be traversed with the help of tools drawn from Afro-American literary theory, feminism, and postmodernist cultural studies. Rather than emphasizing the impossibilities of reading across man-made and, hence, fundamentally arbitrary lines, I posit that a willingness to acknowledge that race and gender are constructed can enable rather than disable provocative journeys. I do not attempt a Hurstonian "standing off" from or Gatesian interpretive "defamiliarization" of cultural materials, but an exploration of some of the analytical consequences of being positioned at this particular historical moment, both in gendered space and in what we might call, following Hurston, "the crib of negroism."[7]

Location within a geography of difference contributes to its inhabitants not essential being and insight, but strategies of racial, gendered, class, and sexual performance that, like all forms of human behavior, can be accepted or rejected, in part or in full.[8] Lest we wish to leave our discourses vulnerable to subversive threats, we must be ever attentive to the ideological implications of moving across the lines, though doing so may open us up to allegations of boundary policing even as we chart the partly fictive nature of such boundaries. Further, we must be able to distinguish between politics and poetics, between a desire to see representatives of the borders gain access to mainstream power and an impulse to suggest that only those markedly affiliated with "minority" space can persuasively read the expressivity which derives from that space. The arguments over just what constitutes adequate expressions of difference are so hotly contested that, if we are forthright in our investigations of criteria used to determine artistic or interpretive "authenticity," we must acknowledge that the outcome of such debates confirms merely the effectiveness of strategies to insist that these criteria are signs of indisputable truth or purity, not the existence of some irreducible essence itself.

Note, for example, the battles over qualifications that marked the Malcolm X filmic phenomenon: Spike Lee's declaration that Norman Jewison was by virtue of his race ideologically unsuited to the task; Amiri Baraka's insistence that Lee was, because of his work's general failure to "support . . . the Black Movement," similarly unqualified; Lee's acknowledgment that, since blacks held so many competing views about who and what Malcolm was (his acknowledgment, in other words, that no single community vision existed), his racial responsibility was to film his own, necessarily limited perspectives; and Lee's request, on completing the film, that print media executives assign black reporters to interview him because "black writers . . . have more insight about Malcolm than white writers." When confronted with discourse of this sort, we also confront the slipperiness of the meanings of blackness at the borders between blacks and whites as well as within Afro-American cultural spaces.[9] Until we are able, if not to resolve the tensions between reading and politics, at least to push energetically to understand their strategic motivations and implications, critics on the borders are in danger of employing or endorsing theoretical practices that are easily exposed as philosophically flawed and fundamentally retrograde.

Cornel West has offered perhaps the most insightful and persuasive contemporary interrogations of the consequences of this and other dilemmas that confront Afro-American academics.[10] In "The New Cultural Politics of Difference," for example, West urges black scholars to explore the significance of the historical fact of "the assault on Black humanity" that has characterized our new world placement in and by the West—"this state of perpetual and inheritable domination"—and that has contributed to the "*modern Black diaspora problematic of invisibility and namelessness.*"[11] A juxtaposition of Spillers's and West's formulations might encourage investigation into whether this racialist "assault" produced in black diasporic subjects a belief that we are unseen or misperceived, nameless or misnamed, placeless or misplaced. We may agree with the Baldwinian phrase, "nobody knows my name," or with Spillers's variation on his theme. But if West is correct—and I think he is—that forces still powerful within Afro-American geographies endorse as a corrective to this historical condition a search for "positive images" and a belief in the existence of a "real Black community" to which all of Africa's new world descendants essentially belong, the deconstruction of race that black scholars such as West and Spillers advocate will only very slowly come to influence the perspectives of the black masses. How we intervene successfully in this state of affairs is a question that no one, including West, has adequately addressed. In fact, in what appears to be an uncharacteristic moment, West seeks either to wish essentialist resistance away or to magnify the impact of "postmodern Black intellectuals" on the masses, claiming that "the coffin used to bury the innocent notion of the essential Black subject was nailed shut with the termination of the Black male monopoly on the construction of the Black subject" (29). While "the essential Black subject" may have been buried, as it were, by some Afro-American intellectuals, its spirit continues, especially at moments of perceived boundary transgression, to haunt the houses of the living more certainly than the Morrisonian beloved baby.

In addition to urging black scholars to move decisively beyond a preoccupation with "contesting stereotypes" and the production of "positive images of homogeneous communities," West insists that "Black cultural workers must constitute and sustain discursive and institutional networks that deconstruct earlier modern Black strategies for identity-formation, demystify power relations that incorporate class, patriarchal and homophobic biases, and construct more multi-valent and multi-dimensional responses that articulate the complexity and diversity of Black practices in the modern and postmodern world" (29). A necessary precondition to engagement in such cultural work is Afro-American intellectuals' development of "their capacity for and promotion of relentless criticism and self-criticism—be it the normative paradigms of their white colleagues that tend to leave out considerations of empire, race, gender and sexual orientation or the damaging dogmas about the homogeneous character of communities of color" (32). "Difference," in West's formulation, is constituted as primarily a "new," explicitly "moral" Afro-American cultural politics (31) that rejects the psychic protections of essentialism in favor of nuanced accounts of our complex place on the American stage. Further, he warns black intellectuals away from a view that, however strong the links forged or maintained with "demoralized, demobilized, depoliticized and disorganized people," they have escaped the transformative touch of the mainstream. Instead of propagating views of their irreducible difference, West urges black cultural workers in the academy to recognize that their status "puts them in an inescapable double bind—while linking their activities to the fundamental, structural overhaul of these institutions, they often remain financially dependent on them. . . . For these critics of culture, theirs is a gesture that is simultaneously progressive *and* co-opted" (20).

The simultaneously progressive and co-opted black man or woman at the podium who stands armed with (and perhaps disarmed by) challenging theorizing such as Spillers's and West's finds himself or herself in a somewhat daunting situation. Though liberated from the responsibilities of having to represent a homogeneous race (and to represent the race as homogeneous), the speaker is nonetheless aware that in the minds of many in the audience, he or she constitutes only a symbolic representativeness, with all of the sometimes burdensome responsibilities of membership accorded thereto. In "The Body in General," Lisa

Kennedy speaks cogently about the burdens of membership: "This is . . . a more visceral fear: will we become slaves to the collective body? Forced always to speak for it and to its needs? And scared to death that if we don't, we won't be allowed to say anything; or if we misrepresent it for the sake of ourselves we will be expelled, we will not exist? We will be 'Toms,' or 'house Negroes,' or 'not black,' when clearly we remain in our skins."[12] What Kennedy describes here is the black spokesperson's "visceral fear" of dismissive misnaming that could result in intra-territorial invisibility and exclusion. But we must learn to contain that fear and get on with our work, or we will be reduced to voicelessness not by racial adversaries but by fictive constructions of blackness. If Spillers is correct about the signifiers associated with her dark female presence, a black male cultural worker at the podium must be dedicated to producing discourse that seeks to cut through the calcified terms of signification attached to "black man anywhere," including "Buck," "Lazy, Shiftless Nigger," "Rapist," "Ghetto Blaster," and, more recently, "Affirmative Action Baby" and "Car Jacker."

As a black male scholar whose beginnings—whose entry onto the academic stage—were as a feminist with an at least gendered difference, I have been engaged to some extent in a project the educational theorist Henry Giroux terms "border crossings." According to Giroux, the act of interpretive border crossing "signals forms of transgression in which existing borders forged in domination can be challenged and redefined."[13] At a time when many in the academy hold that sophisticated knowledge production occurs in a variety of geographical sites, students of culture should engage knowledge as "border-crossers, as people moving in and out of borders constructed around coordinates of difference and power":

> These are not only physical borders, they are cultural borders historically constructed and socially organized within rules and regulations that limit and enable particular identities, individual capacities, and social forms. . . . [Students of culture] cross over into realms of meaning, maps of knowledge, social relations, and values that are increasingly being negotiated and rewritten as the codes and regulations that organize them become destabilized and reshaped. (29–30)

Giroux speaks persuasively of the necessary negotiations, destabilizations, and reshapings that are a function of conscientious, clear-sighted border crossings. He recognizes that individual and group identities are both enabled and limited by criteria "forged in domination" by the oppressor (and, I would add, the oppressed). This perception links his project to West's, who envisions a new cultural politics that substitutes for a largely defensive strategy of reverse racial hierarchies a nuanced articulation of complexity and self-difference.

As a scholar seeking to enact an alternative cultural project, Giroux insists on his own responsibility to reconstitute himself by engaging—among other realms of difference—dark, feminized borders. Consequently, he investigates black feminist criticism, but from what he speaks of as an interested ideological position. His location, he says, "as a white, academic male positions me to speak to issues of racism and gender by self-consciously recognizing my own interests in taking up these practices as part of a broader political project to expand the scope and meaning of democratic struggle and a politics of solidarity" (125). Giroux thus employs instances of black feminist criticism in order to confirm his vision of the contingencies necessary to create a truly democratic pedagogy and a postmodern America; hence, he emphasizes "the diverse voices of Afro-American feminists constituted in different relations of power" (125), all of whose strategically chosen comments support his sense of the persuasiveness of his vision.

My own "politics of location" with respect to black feminist inquiry differs from Giroux's and, for that matter, West's, both of whom use black feminism as confirmation of the larger cultural emergence of a postmodernist politics. To the extent that it is possible to codify my published reactions to black feminist literary criticism, I have been concerned with exploring the compelling struggles of that discourse with poststructuralism.[14] Consequently, our takes on black feminist discourse are quite different. While Giroux counts Barbara Christian among his allies because of her insistence on the ability of blacks "to define and express our totality rather than being defined by Others," I would note the intensity of her resistance to aspects of the project in which he grounds his work. Giroux embraces Christian without mentioning the fact that poststructuralist theory, which he insists "attempts to redraw the very maps of meaning, desire, and difference, . . . calling into question traditional forms of power and their accompanying modes of legitimation," has been termed by Christian a newly emergent hegemonic entity that has served to further subordinate emerging black female subjects. While "The Race for Theory" does confirm Giroux's (and West's) political and theoretical interests in a number of ways, including its derision of black cultural nationalism's "emphasis on *one way* to be black," Christian has asserted that, in its emphases, language, and practice, theory "mystifies rather than clarifies our condition, making it possible for a few people who know that particular language to control the critical scene—that language surfaced, interestingly enough, just when the literatures of people of color, of black women, of Latin Americans, of Africans, began to move to 'the center.' "[15] If Giroux's politics of (white/male/democratic) location facilitates his absorption of the anti-theoretical particularities of her work into his "broader political project," one of whose goals is to "further rupture a politics of historical silence and theoretical erasure" (125), what is silenced is this example of black feminist resistance to the discourse from which the new democratic postmodern order he envisions is largely derived. At best, Giroux's appropriation of Christian suggests some of the dangers that accompany "border crossings" at a time when it is still the case, as he himself acknowledges, that "theoretical cultural criticism becomes the exclusive discourse of mostly white academics, while the theoretical cultural criticism of Afro-American feminists is either ignored or marginalized" (133). In speaking for Christian, he misspeaks in order to serve the progressive ends of his democratic project.

But clearly such acts of misappropriation are possible not merely in white/male/democratic discourse but at a variety of border locations, including the one I have attempted to clear in order to do my own work. Despite my awareness of this fact, despite my sense of the strategic and distorting nature of Giroux's border crossings in this instance, I find his project personally enabling, in part because of the premium he places on the possibilities of interpretive "crossing over." In acknowledging this fact, my intent—given my own location somewhere on the borders of black feminist criticism—is to emphasize my desire to move in concert with work which seeks to refigure notions of the interpretive disposition needed to interrogate others' cultural contexts and texts. And while I run many risks—including the risk of seeming to endorse misappropriations of black feminist intellectual efforts—speaking as I have here may assist efforts to disrupt antiquated, though still powerful, views that location is destiny, that interpretive border crossings are, by definition, impossible or doomed to ideological or exegetical failure.

Like Christian, I believe that the institutional power of contemporary theory does not necessarily contribute to progressive sociopolitical transformation if that discourse is not focused upon enabling an anti-racist, anti-sexist, and anti-homophobic critical and cultural practice. And, like West, I want to insist upon the necessity of viewing all categories of human organization that originated in a caucacentric (that is, Caucasian-centered), phallocentric past—race, gender, class, and even the binary "theorist" and "non-theorist"—as "phenomena to be interrogated, and thereby [not] foreclos[ing] the very issues that should serve as the subject matter to be investigated" (28).

A text that has assisted my efforts to understand both the problems and the possibilities of boundary crossing is John Howard Griffin's discussion of his transracial experiences, *Black Like Me*.[16] This memoir chronicles the perspectives on mid-century American race relations of a white man who darkens his skin in order to gain intimate access to—*experience of*—Afro-American life in the Deep South.

Believing that "communication between the two races had simply ceased to exist," that "the Southern Negro will not tell the white man the truth [because he] long ago learned that if he speaks a truth unpleasing to the white, the white will make life miserable for him" (12–13), Griffin sets for himself the task of serving as mediator between the two races in order "to bridge the gap between us" (13) by providing, from what is for him the closest possible approximation of a black subject position, reports from an Afro-American underground.

Griffin's text is informed by two abiding beliefs about what we might call interracial epistemology: that reading across racial lines is, because of specific restrictions and a lack of access to certain kinds of knowledge, virtually impossible; and that simulating the physical surface of the other represents the only means of gaining access to that knowledge. While acknowledging the institutional patterns that render (apparent) biological difference as constitutive of vastly different sociocultural possibilities, Griffin believes that these differences are devoid of significant inherent value and thus represent arbitrary and permeable categories. Further, Griffin's text, in its insistence on the permeability of race as a consequence of the adoption of the other's surface, strongly suggests that neither race itself nor the ideologies of power that have arisen in response to it are intractable. For the purposes of this discussion, I am less interested in Griffin's actual transracial experience—that is, the specific incidents in his life "as" a black man—than in the discourse he employs to describe those experiences, as well as the motivations for and ultimate consequences of his dangerous transformation.

In order to experience blackness, Griffin feels he has to become black, an act which erases, if only temporarily, his white physicality, his racial self. Upon seeing himself in the mirror after his initial application of skin-darkening ointment, Griffin immediately senses that he has lost not only his white hue, but, more important, himself:

> In the flood of light against white tile, the face and shoulders of a stranger— a fierce, bald, very dark Negro—glared at me from the glass. He in no way resembled me.
>
> The transformation was total and shocking. I had expected to see myself disguised, but this was something else. I was imprisoned in the flesh of an utter stranger, an unsympathetic one with whom I felt no kinship. All traces of the John Griffin I had been were wiped from existence. (15)

Griffin seems to believe that his immediate experience of blackness is not a heightened awareness of the distinction between his assumed new black surface and his essential white interiority but is a total difference, the becoming of the racial other. However, his reaction to blackness on or in himself belies this representation of his response. For certainly it is not the new black self, innocent of caucacentric ideology, that experiences itself in terms of white racist equations of blackness with danger and fierceness, but rather the white Griffin underneath the darkened skin who seems to have internalized more of his society's stereotypes than he is aware. Read against the author's designs, Griffin's experience as an apparent black man holds the potential to erase not the biological but the ideological white self that has unconsciously embraced racist equations of blackness and evil.

There are many elements of Griffin's transformation and its motivations that strike me as problematic. I wonder, for example, why Griffin felt he could offer more convincing depictions of black life than those provided in the voluminous black-authored fictive, poetic, sociological, and historical texts that existed in the late 1950s. And, in these postmodern times when truth-claims are always viewed with skepticism and when claims to full comprehension and thorough understanding of undifferentiated groups are held as suspect at best, it is incontestable that Griffin's transracial act failed to provide him access to "the [transcendent] truth" of blackness. However, my interest in the explicit meaning of Griffin's no doubt courageous gesture as it relates to the interpretive process—specifically, that whites need to come as close as possible to crossing the racial divide in order to interpret blackness convincingly—permits me at certain moments to bracket these and other troubling aspects of *Black Like Me,* including the relative ease with which he believes he assumes, physically and especially psychologically, a black subject position.

In fact, Griffin's text might be seen as providing the skeletal foundations of a theory of reading across racial lines. If, as feminist theorists have argued, we become gendered in and by the reading process, if, that is, gendered roles are set in motion only when we respond to the cultural codes of our own or other geographies, then race arises as a significant consideration only as a consequence of an engagement with ideologically saturated texts and codes. Even if we reject some of the implications of Griffin's race change, which equates understanding with becoming, preserving Griffin's notions of difference as a dangerous but permeable category, as an experientially and not wholly biologically determined entity, may assist our efforts to theorize about the relationship between interpretive insight and experientially derived knowledge.

A question we have begun to ask at the present moment, when difference represents a site of materially, morally, and interpretively lucrative expressivity, is, To whom does the textual representation of border experience belong? Who has the authority to compose it, analyze it, profit from its academic and popular circulation? To the degree that our identity politics—our politics of location—determines the responses we can offer to these questions, answers might range from a view that the aesthetics and thematics derived from the cultural experiences of identifiable groups (for example, those found in rap music) "remain the property and possession of the people who develop them," to a notion that cultural forms should be utilized by people from every conceivable location who take an interest in them.[17] What insiders and outsiders, artists and scholars alike, must attend to in discussing this matter is the fact that complex cultural forms are not available to anyone simply by virtue of geographical location, gendered or racial situation, sexual orientation, or other putative marking of experience. Like all sophisticated skills, learning to produce or professionally critique cultural forms is a difficult, time-consuming process, and to the extent that we minimize the amount of work involved therein, we operate like casual observers who offer theories of innate Afro-American basketball talent in order to explain black numerical and stylistic preeminence in that sport. What critics of the American borders especially cannot lose sight of is that regardless of our origins, neither we nor the artists whose work we examine exist as reflections of untainted "whiteness," "blackness," "asian-ness," "maleness," "gaiety," or "femaleness." We are all, to some degree, formed by the cultural crisscrossings of race, gender, class, sexuality, and religion that serve, I believe, to determine much of the nature of our lives in a contemporary American "meeting ground" characterized by unprecedented access to the images, perspectives, and behaviors of locational others.

As an image of translocational influence, "crisscrossing" is not intended to suggest an America wherein each receiver passively imbibes specifiable aspects of others' culture, or "human touch," but a method of acknowledging and mapping, however imprecisely, the presence of a multicultural synchronicity in a variety of subjects. For example, my own sense of the world has been shaped, to be sure, by black folks' musical, discursive, and attitudinal stylings, with which I was happily inundated from infancy, but those often competing perspectives interacted with similarly conflicting information I learned during contacts with white elementary-school classmates and teachers, as well as with books, movies, newspapers, and especially television programs, the majority of them produced by whites. However "black" I was, and am, I can claim an untainted locational purity only by erasing facts from my autobiographical account, including my view as an adolescent that Doris Day—who is, by almost every measure I know, optic white, in Ralph Ellison's use of that term—was ideal female company. If, as I suspect, others can offer similar narratives of geographical impurity, if as adults we continue to sample texts derived from both within and outside of our own spaces of territorial origin "in order to . . . be summoned," as West eloquently puts it, "by the styles they deploy for their profound insight, pleasure and challenges" (31), then we must abandon fictions of natural affinity or unbridgeable perspectival separateness ("Don't tell me black writers don't have more insight about Malcolm than white writers"), and confront the implications of what Spillers terms our "confounded identities."

To that end, I have attempted to suspend disbelief, to interrogate actively the consequences of border crossings, including my own, rather than assume a predictably transgressive outcome to, say, black male engagement with black female expressivity or white investigation of Afro-American discursive acts and practices. I am not always successful in this regard—I am no objective arbiter of gendered matters, nor do I, as one commentator on my work correctly notes, "reside in some incontestable black authenticity or whatever."[18] I do, however, wish to test the premise that reading others' critical, fictive, and mass cultural discourse is neither an impossibility nor always a contribution to the consolidation of hegemonic power. Vera Kutzinski urges us toward "a critical awareness of how borders have been (and continue to be) systematically policed and for whose ideological benefit and material profit."[19] While I am by no means suggesting that border policing by those marginalized by caucacentric and phallocentric history evinces potentially the same broad social effects as its hegemonic counterpart, this study operates on the assumption that the powerful and less powerful alike engage in border protection, that frequently such acts are designed to gain for its subjects freedom from contamination by other cultures, and that, however differently motivated, both more and less hegemonic practices can profitably be scrutinized. On our American shores of knowing, there is no racial or gendered purity, no space to which we can go to locate an untainted state of being, no irreducible difference. It should be clear that Washingtonian notions of a strategic separateness are no longer tenable, if they ever were.

It is possible for me, as an act of autobiographical recall that would inevitably be part fiction, to trace here the genesis of my interpretive interests. However, my utilization of acts of self-referentiality—to locate origins, posit affinity, even recognize connections between my own self-embraced or other-imposed "identities" and similar acts of self-representation—ought not necessarily be deemed sufficient grounds upon which to grant me authority to speak the cultural truths of blackness (or, more precisely, black maleness). We have seen a number of recent instances in which blackness was strategically utilized for "ideological benefit and material profit." Note, for instance, such public spectacles as Clarence Thomas, Vanilla Ice, Terry McMillan, "X" marking and marketing, the desperate search of some academic departments for black faculty, the sadly overhyped black film renaissance, and the ascension of Shelby Steele to the status of the cultural elite. Given the fact of strategic uses of difference by those with inevitably interested agendas, we might begin again to inquire energetically into the persuasiveness of the critical truism that readers make textual meaning. Especially in these times of the profitability of difference within a number of cultural arenas, we might consider, once more, the degree to which texts exert control over our judgments of the range of their possible meanings. In large part because of my sense of the strategic utilizations of difference, I want to posit that texts do not serve as pliable vehicles of their readers' imaginative re-creations; in their most powerful manifestations, as we are all aware in our less public readerly moments, they help, in fact, to guide that re-creation. Paul Armstrong puts the matter this way in his discussion of textual "heteronomy":

> A heteronomous conception of the text acknowledges the paradox that interpretation is neither a total imposition of meaning nor a passive reception of it. . . . New methods of understanding may recompose a work in unexpected ways, but literary works can also react on interpretive approaches and compel them to revise their assumptions. This reciprocal interaction between text and interpretation requires a theory of understanding that sees the act of construal as both constructive and receptive, both actively formative and also open to otherness.[20]

Armstrong's effort to find a workable "meeting ground" between monist and pluralist attitudes about the process of making textual meaning is, to me, generally persuasive.[21] In positing a notion of textual heteronomy that intersects with his sense of "the paradox that interpretation is neither a total imposition of meaning nor a passive reception of it," Armstrong helps to open a critical space for interrogation of the reflection in texts of aspects of a culture and resistance to the status of unimpeachable cultural representativeness.

Armstrong utilizes the image of the field in his effort to resolve differences between readerly and textual meaning. Specifically, he posits that the heteronomous literary text is "a field of different possible meanings, each correlated to a particular method of interpretation, meanings harmonizing with each other to a greater or lesser extent (or not at all)." According to Armstrong, "A field may be multiple and various and open to new developments, but its heterogeneity is limited because not everything belongs to it. . . . A heteronomous conception of the work as a heterogeneous, bounded field . . . preserves the work's multiplicity without sacrificing its distinctness."[22] It is on this notion of the text as multiply suggestive but nonetheless limited semantic field that I wish to close my introductory formulations on the politics of location. Incontestably, for any text to be considered broadly as a significant cultural production, it must be seen as capable of transcending the provinciality of any single interpretive method and of reflecting in illuminating ways on a myriad of issues that preoccupy members of the critical community at a given historical moment. Even if Afro-American readers, privileging perspectives arising from their own geographical origins, insist that the "distinctness" or most significant element of texts such as Paule Marshall's *Praisesong for the Widow* is their compelling utilization of materials gleaned from black cultural spaces, many of those texts demand at crucial points our attention to their strategic use of European forms and of canonical white texts. No notion of an untainted black cultural space to which only Afro-Americans have access will allow us, for example, to make interpretive sense of Marshall's disruptive invocation of a well-known British romanticist formulation.

Briefly, the novel charts the journey back to cultural immersion and diasporic vision of an older, comfortably middle-class woman named Avatara (Avey) Johnson. Having been born, in her great-aunt's view, to keep alive the mythic story of a magical Ibo journey across the Atlantic Ocean from impending enslavement to African freedom, Avey learns, after her spiritual rebirth, to embrace this mission. It is at this point, when Avey begins her missionary work, that Marshall refers to Coleridge's figure of directed romanticist wanderings:

> "*It is an ancient mariner / And he stoppeth one of three.*" Like the obsessed old sailor she had read about in high school she would stop them. As they rushed blindly in and out of the glacier buildings, unaware, unprotected, lacking memory and a necessary distance of the mind (no mojo working for them!), she would stop them and before they could pull out of her grasp, tell them about the floor in Halsey Street and quote them the line from her namesake.[23]

Clearly, the gap between obsession and dementia appears to be quite narrow here—we know, though Marshall does not say so, that more than a few whom Avey petitions must have resisted energetically her anti-materialist gestures. But space does not permit a fuller inquiry into the possible meanings of her missionary zeal. What I do want to indicate is that it cannot be mere coincidence—particularly for a writer who takes such supreme care as Marshall in her uses of the symbolic—that she has "summoned" this canonical "rime" at Avey's blackest moment, as it were. Avey contextualizes her missionary act so that we cannot help noting its interterritorial resonance. If her text is indeed a field of multiple, though limited, interpretive possibilities, that field must include the Coleridgean figure, and, indeed, some of the series of Western cultural formulations that have proved valuable to scholars in explicating the poem. To grant anything less is to deny the validity and resourcefulness of Marshall's journey across cultural, national, and temporal boundaries.[22] To the extent that we repress or question the legitimacy of Marshall's reference, or, more generally, insist that using resources developed in another territorial realm amounts to an act of treason, we approach texts not as multiply suggestive fields with the potential to enliven the already familiar, but as mere confirmation of an unattainable dream of cultural and ideological stasis.

This study represents, in part, a no doubt personal attempt to stave off interpretive stasis. Each of its chapters concentrates on instances of boundary crossings and policing, on expressive cultural production and events that for a time dominated the popular imagination and that serve for others as potentially illuminating occasions to proffer defenses of or challenges to notions of the fixity of racial, gendered, and ideological difference. My interest is not in advocating an emphatic end to such interrogation, which seems to me to be the logical outcome of social constructions of difference that neither academic nor legislative acts can successfully eradicate, but in exploring its inevitably strategic motivations and some of its critical, imaginative, and political consequences.

In part 1 I survey aspects of the contemporary critical terrain in order to clarify my own notions of reading across racial and gendered lines. Chapter 1 focuses on arguments within Afro-Americanist and American feminist criticism which suggest that the scholar who occupies a subject position distinct from that of the author of counterhegemonic discourse cannot offer informed, persuasive interpretation. By exposing such suppositions as, at least in part, protectionist critical maneuvers, I insist that these discourses need to move from discussions of the authority of experience to examination of the ways in which race and gender are utilized (and at times misused) in what are, given the structures of power with which they are forced to contend, unavoidably strategic formulations of a "politics of reading."

Chapter 2 theorizes about a black male feminism, taking as its point of departure the knowledge that feminist theory is a complex, institutionally powerful, and potentially transformative discourse about whose fundamental emphases, suppositions, and goals women who consider themselves members of the "class" often disagree. This self-reflexive chapter seeks to locate a specific place for black men in this discourse and calls for the inclusion of inquiries about other forms of difference in a debate which seems too often to operate from the assumption that despite the disputes within feminism, gender is the only category that matters in our efforts to measure what is, in fact, not easily measurable—the sincerity of males' engagement with an anti-phallocentric discourse, one of whose fundamental purposes is to disempower them.

Focusing on white-authored, self-referential investigations of Afro-American literary and critical texts, chapter 3 explores the self-reflexive phenomenon in cultural and literary studies that the preceding chapter both participates in and seeks to problematize. I insist that we view this critical trend—as represented in this chapter by negotiations of hegemonic (white) racial positionality—as one strategy among others that we can deploy to inscribe our critical perceptions, and not, as it is often viewed, as a virtual guarantee that the discourse produced under its auspices will be more free of interested misreading or a will to power than analyses employing any other interpretive method.

Part 2 of this study explores imaginative texts and cultural events as investigative sites in my effort to put into practice a black male feminist discourse. Chapter 4 explores the question of rape in the context of formulations that appear in men's studies, Catharine MacKinnon's theories of sexuality, and cultural studies. Specifically, this chapter examines Mike Tyson's legal trial and Spike Lee's efforts to produce a feminist film in *She's Gotta Have It*, and it constitutes an analysis of rape as an extremely troubling form of gendered speech. A self-consciously black male feminist reading, this essay explores, along with Tyson's and Lee's phallocentric perspectives, the implications of Tyson's victim's participation in a beauty pageant, which signals the intractability of a gender hierarchy that encourages sexual violence, and Lee's generally compelling efforts to produce a feminist film.

Chapter 5 investigates the motivations for and impact of Toni Morrison's choice of a male protagonist as apparent epic hero in *Song of Solomon*. Given Morrison's focus on female characters in her earlier novels, her choice of a male protagonist is striking, particularly since much of the novel evinces her grapplings with the gendered biases and limitations of the classical form of the epic. I demonstrate that her choice offers Morrison a means of both critiquing the epic form and indicating the continuing obstacles to female engagement in heroic, fulfilling, and communally salvific activities to which even the most psychically unprepared males appear to have access by virtue of their gender.

Chapter 6 reads August Wilson's statements about cultural obstacles that would inhibit a white director from convincingly adapting his play, *Fences,* to the medium of film against the play's own strenuous critique of the erection of racial, sexual, and generational boundaries. Specifically, I look at Wilson's polemic, " 'I Want a Black Director,' " in the context of the Pulitzer Prize-winning play's more nuanced ideological stances, as well as theoretical perspectives on race, culture, and the politics of filmic adaptations of literary works. My aim is to suggest connections between Wilson's polemic and art in the light of the playwright's desire to see his work as a means to effect social change.

In the concluding chapter, I look at Michael Jackson's participation in *transraciality,* a term I use to describe the adoption of physical traits of difference for the purpose of impersonating a racial other. In this chapter, which begins with the premise that Jackson cannot be easily understood in terms of contemporary theories of multiple subjectivity, I attempt to glean what Jackson's cosmetic transmutations of his black male body—and analytical responses thereto—have to say about the continuing and changing American meanings of race and gender. Indeed,

Jackson can help us comprehend the limitations of beliefs that essentialism and constructionism exist in opposition to one another. Rather than arguing that we replace a residual essentialism with constructionist notions of social being, Jackson's example—and this study more generally—demonstrates the indissolubility of the connections of the two concepts for nations and communities structured around the belief that it is possible to ascribe fixed meanings to racial, gendered, sexual, economic, and other marked differences among its citizens.

one

Surveying the Critical Terrain

We're gonna move on up, one by one
We ain't gonna stop 'till the work gets done
Am I black enough for you?

> Billy Paul, "Am I Black Enough for You?"

To choose an attitude toward interpretation—and therefore toward language—
these days is to choose more than just an attitude: it is to choose a politics *of*
reading, it is to choose an ethics *of reading.*

> Alice Jardine, "Opaque Texts and Transparent Contexts"

1

Race, Gender, and the Politics of Reading

In my view, no single text more effectively delimits the interpretive, discursive, and ideological possibilities and dilemmas in Afro-American literary studies at the close of the twentieth century than *Black Literature and Literary Theory*. This 1984 collection, edited by Henry Louis Gates, Jr., presents not merely finely nuanced theoretical perspectives and close readings of central Afro-American literary texts by particularly insightful scholars, but also explicitly articulated and subtly encoded speculation about future directions for this field of critical inquiry. Of all its memorable moments, perhaps none stands out more vividly for me as an interpretive guidepost—both because of what it examines and what it fails to examine— than Gates's delineation of his own sense of the terms of a new critical covenant. In his characteristically rich introduction, "Criticism in the Jungle," he writes of the particular issues that must compel scholarship on black literary production at the end of the twentieth century:

> Unlike critics in almost every other literary tradition, much of what we have to say about our literature is new. What critics of the Western tradition can make an even remotely similar claim? . . . The challenge of our endeavor is to bring together, in a new fused form, the concepts of critical theory and the idiom of the Afro-American and African literary traditions. To undertake this complex process, we use Western critical theories to read black texts. The obvious question about such an intellectual activity, however, is this: does the critic of black literature acquire his or her identity parodically, as it were, in the manner of the parrot?[1]

This passage voices Gates's primary emphasis during this period: the "challenge" of investigating an increasingly institutionally central body of black literary texts in terms of interpretive technologies drawn from "Western critical theories." At a historical juncture more than a decade following Gates's initial articulation of these sentiments, the blind spots and limitations of aspects of these perspectives might be critiqued effectively.[2]

My interest in this particular passage results in large part from the signifiers Gates employs to characterize the contributors to his volume specifically and, more generally, those who hold that the academic study of Afro-American literature could develop only if its critics earnestly employed "Western critical theories to read black texts." How, precisely, does one earn the right to call one's self or be called a "critic of black literature"? How does one become one of Gates's or, for that matter, any other privileged Afro-Americanist interpretive "we"? The criteria do not necessarily include race—at least one quarter of the contributors to the collection's analyses of Afro-American literary texts are white—nor, as a quick perusal of the list of contributors indicates, is it essential to have made black literature and culture one's primary area of intellectual investigation. Further, politics or, to use a more precise term, ideology, seems not in any overt way to figure prominently in Gates's concerns, except to the extent that choosing to pursue sophisticated interrogation of non-mainstream literature potentially was (and perhaps still is) a counterhegemonic activity. What joins the diverse group of scholars who constitute his "we," beyond a common production of readings of black texts which the editor deemed intriguing, profound, and accessible, is "the methodological assumption. . . that one 'repeats' [that is, utilizes European theoretical models], as it were, in order to produce *difference*" (10). Unlike American feminist literary criticism, which in its formative moments constituted its intellectual "we" along strictly gendered (and, some would argue, class and racial) lines, the introduction to this influential collection insists that rather than a long history of demonstrated intellectual and ideological commitment, its contributors' common sense of the utility of critical theory in interrogating black texts and contexts is the determining factor in assigning membership. This is followed by Gates's intriguing call to readers concerned with both black literature and critical theory to consider the appropriateness of formulations such as Edward Said's rhetorical question: "Does this sort of repetition . . . 'enhance or degrade'" the heretofore theoretically unexplored or underexplored investigative area?

As a concept, Gates's black disciplinary "we"—critics joined by a willingness to devise readings of black texts that take into account the seemingly parodic relationship of both these texts and the critic to Western theory—is limited precisely because it does not assume that such critics need also to explore what may be their own parodic relationships to the black expressivity to which they are applying these theories. To assume, as Gates seems to, that astute employment of theory in discussions of black texts requires the development of what I term *appropriative gestures,* while making no mention of the possibility that the critic's relation to the primary texts themselves may profit from being similarly theorized, is to ignore a potentially central component of the interpretive act in this poststructuralist age. *African American Review* editor Joe Weixlmann correctly notes that little of the sophisticated theoretical energy contained in and exemplified by Gates's collection has been used to formulate reader-response approaches to the study of black literature.[3]

If "we" are to appropriate theory in the study of Afro-American literature, "we" must also be equally willing to theorize the "we" conjoined by and engaged in this project. As will become apparent, critics of black literature who differ with Gates's constitution of his critical "we" argue that such projects do not adequately examine the extent to which such interrogation will "degrade" black textual material. Given such responses to projects like those privileged in "Criticism in the Jungle," it may be necessary to consider, along with Said's question, additional ones, including the following: What is the nature of the relationship between race and reading? In other words, how does race direct, influence, or dictate the process of interpreting both black texts and Western theories? Is there a politics of interpretation that is determined or controlled by race in ways that can be compared to the ideologically informed readings of, for example, white American feminist critics? This chapter—and, indeed, this entire study—can be seen as an effort to examine a crucial issue that theoretical studies of Afro-American literature generally leave unexplored: the impact categories of difference such as race and gender can have upon the interpretive and artistic processes.

As Gayatri Spivak argues, any discussion of a politics of reading must begin with an attempt to formulate "a working notion of ideology." According to Spivak, such a notion is essential in order to "undo the oppositions between determinism and free will and between conscious choice and unconscious reflex. Ideology in action is what a group takes to be natural and self-evident, that of which the group, as a group, must deny any historical sedimentation. . . . In turn, the subject(s) of ideology are the conditions and effects of the self-identity of the group as a group."[4] Drawing upon Spivak's formulations, I want to offer my notion of an ideology of black interpretation (or what I will hereafter refer to as "afrocentric reading"). In using the term "afrocentric," my intent is not to align my project with the neo–Pan Africanist epistemology and religion of blackness advocated by African-American egyptologists such as Molefi Asante, whose goal is a black diasporic embrace of positivistic myths of Africa and wholesale philosophical rejection of the West.[5] Rather, I appropriate the term because of my interest in setting forth a potentially resonant designation to connote the myriad, often contradictory, ideological perspectives and cultural practices employed by or in the service of black people in their efforts to resist caucacentric forces.

In my use of the phrase, afrocentric reading exposes the unrelentingly caucacentric nature of the manifestations of the ethos of the white aesthetic and offers studied, corrective interpretations of the products of the black imagination. In other words, afrocentric reading attempts to counter the negative effects on the black psyche and readings of Afro-American expressive culture of caucacentric myth's of white superiority by, as Addison Gayle puts it, unearthing "the treasures of beauty lying deep in the untoured regions of the Black experience."[6]

Afro-American historical victimization at the hands of white hegemony represents the conditions that have created and serve to perpetuate a black worldview or ideology. I do not need here to trace at length such manifestations of black nationalist ideology as a shared comprehension of the white ethnocentric nature of the Western cultural aesthetic—the myriad examples in the English language that figure whiteness as purity, innocence, and goodness, and blackness as impurity and evil—and the innumerable efforts to demonstrate the beauty and strength of Afro-American culture. Many Afro-Americans interpret the world as members of a "class," in Robert Scholes's use of the word, because of "both necessity and interest."[7] They perceive a need to struggle collectively against centuries of white hegemony's devaluative figurations of blackness in order to maintain a positive self and group image.

As the formulations of Black Aestheticians make clear, nationalist, anti-hegemonic perspectives result in a politics of afrocentric reading. Too often, however, limited attention to and an undervaluing of the aesthetic properties of black texts have prevented Afro-American critics from exploring fully the discursive brilliance and hotly contested politics extant in what Houston Baker calls "the writing [of] the culturally specific" of black "ancestral faces."[8] Until recently, Afro-American criticism, because of its lack of a full commitment to energetic analysis of the art, thematic diversity, and ideological heterogeneity of Black expressive texts, has denied afrocentric reading its full complexity.

If Afro-American literary history in the twentieth century can be said to be dominated by a single issue, that issue surely is the part Afro-American literature and its criticism could and should play in the full liberation of black people in America. Following the example of "ancestral faces" such as Frederick Douglass, who declared that literacy is "the pathway from slavery to freedom,"[9] a number of Afro-American writers and critics saw black mastery of the tropes of literary expression as a means of gaining the race's liberation from the debilitating tenets of white hegemony. While the specific forms such a view has taken vary from a Harlem Renaissance representation of literature as a means of demonstrating the Afro-American's similarity to his or her white counterpart to a Black Aesthetic's celebration of black difference, Black literature served the utilitarian function in the minds of a number of its critics and creators of lighting the way to promised lands of AMERICA and/or BLACK NATIONHOOD.[10]

Gates has devoted a good deal of his critical energy to examining the historical motivations and aesthetic limitations of such interpretations of Afro-American literature. He has persuasively argued that the first black acts of writing in the West were performed as direct responses to extant racialist incredulity about black people's ability to reason. Written demonstration of Afro-American ability to reason was considered by early black writers the pathway to Afro-American liberation, but despite the lofty goals of these eighteenth- and nineteenth-century black writers, acts in demonstration of black reason and literacy failed to offer pathways to freedom. As Gates says, "Black people, we know, have not been liberated from racism by our writings. We accepted a false premise by assuming that racism would be destroyed once white racists became convinced that we were human, too."[11]

If Afro-American faith in the emancipative possibilities of the word rests on a false premise, it is one that has been accepted as the virtually undisputed raison d'être of black literary and critical discourse in this century. Whenever the question has been posed as to whether black literary expression should be analyzed in terms of its internal formal structures and attempts at aesthetic sophistication, or as, to use Richard Wright's famous autobiographical term, an extratextual "weapon" in the war against American racism, more often than not the Afro-American reader has come down on the side of weaponry. The following prescription offered to Afro-American critics by Addison Gayle stands as a representative example of a tradition of black critical attitudes about art:

> The Negro critic . . . must be guided by a temperament which allows him to explicate the work of art in terms of its contributions to the alleviation of those problems [read: racism] which have confronted humanity for too long a time. . . . [He/She must] call . . . upon the Negro writer to dedicate himself to the proposition that literature is a moral force for change as well as an aesthetic creation. . . . The Negro critic must demand that the Negro writer articulate the grievances of the Negro in moral terms.[12]

Gayle's statement, which concludes with a warning against Afro-American abandonment of socially committed creative and interpretive discourse for analyses of art for art's sake, exemplifies the critical tradition's tendency to privilege sociopolitical readings of the black text. Despite Gayle's cursory lip service to a view of black art as "aesthetic creation," it is apparent that for him the only acceptable reading of Afro-American literature is one that assesses the text's potential to increase black racial pride and transform American race relations.

I will not repeat here the statements by black critics such as Baker, Gates, Deborah McDowell, and Robert Stepto about the limitations of this traditional Afro-American critical view of supposed responsibilities of expressive art to right/write the race. Rather, I will focus on what is, for me, the most interesting interpretive implication of focusing on the accuracy of the black text's figuration of the black experience. If black expressive art is best read in terms of its representation of black reality, then it necessarily follows, some have argued, that the best readers of Afro-American literature are black critics who have firsthand knowledge of black cultural codes and the forms of racial oppression. Taking traditional readings of Afro-American literature to their logical extremes, the black experience represents the hermeneutic tie that binds together Afro-American writer, text, and critic and the hermetical seal that protects black texts from penetration both by uninformed and potentially racist white readers and by even the most insightfully appropriated versions of Western critical theories.

In the following discussion, I want to consider what constitutes "acceptable" readings of class texts such as Afro-American literature. Does the black face of the Afro-American critic actually lead to qualitatively superior or perceptively different readings of the black text than ones offered by scholars with paler faces? In what ways is Afro-American insistence on the authority of experience comparable to the similar appeals of American feminist critics who originated the phrase and made it their interpretive catchword? Can the critic of black literature, regardless of race, successfully utilize critical theory so as to "enhance" our understanding of Afro-American textual production? By comparing traditional Afro-American and white feminist appeals to the authority of experience and to the necessity of developing alternative theoretical approaches, in fact, we will be able to clearly observe the practical and philosphical limitations of a politics of reading that relies heavily upon simplistic figurations of critics' experience of difference.

In the essay that initiated the often heated discussion between herself, Baker, and Gates about the uses and misuses of poststructuralist theories in the analysis of Afro-American literature, the black critic Joyce Joyce proudly proclaims her status as inheritor of a legacy of socially committed Afro-American critics. In the conclusion of that much-discussed essay (which echoes—perhaps intentionally—Gayle's statements quoted above), Joyce argues:

> Since the Black creative writer has always used language as a means of communication to bind people together, the job of the Black literary critic should be to find a point of merger between the communal, utilitarian, phenomenal nature of Black literature and the aesthetic or linguistic—if you will—analyses that illuminate the "universality" of a literary text. . . . It should be the job of the Black literary critic to force ideas to the surface, to give them force in order to affect, to guide, to animate, and to arouse the minds and emotions of Black people.[13]

For Joyce, at odds with Gates and Baker because of their employment of poststructuralism's difficult, jargonized, "pseudoscientific language" and theories of interpretation, the role of the Afro-American literary critic is to facilitate the uninitiated black reader's journey to literacy. In other words, black critics' function is not, as Gates has argued, "to bring to bear upon their readings any 'tool' which helps us to elucidate, which enables us to see more clearly, the complexities of figuration peculiar to our literary traditions" ("Criticism in the Jungle," 4). Rather, that function is to aid the black masses' comprehension of the themes, metaphors, and messages of black texts whose subtleties, if fully understood, can lead to psychological freedom from the potentially enslaving white hegemonic "forces that attempt to subdue them."[14]

For Joyce, afrocentric critical reading uses the text as discursive key to unlock the chains of an almost timeless Afro-American psychological bondage. Baker's attempt to "move decisively beyond the inadequacies of a past historical criticism and engage[ment of] Afro-American expressive texts in their full symbolic potency" (*Blues,* 117) suggests for Joyce that the black critics who are a part of Gates's "we" have "succumbed" to what her forebear Gayle called a "sweet delirium" that influences them to shirk their larger ideological responsibilities.

Further evidence of her view of Baker's and Gates's interpretive inadequacies can be located in Joyce's reply to their venomous reactions to an essay that sees their employment of contemporary theoretical methodologies as a sign that they lack deep-felt social commitment to blacks. In this reply, Joyce suggests that Gates and Baker suffer from what we might call an interpretive disability: "A close reading of their responses reveals that neither of these men can read. . . . Perhaps, in the past few years, they have used the obfuscating language and ideas of Derrida, Barthes, Paul de Man, Foucault, Kristeva, Althusser, Bakhtin, and others to cloak their difficulties."[15] Reading between the lines of these combative remarks, we can identify Joyce's concern with a difficulty that Gates has himself discussed—how to offer competent, culturally informed readings of Afro-American literary texts by using interpretive strategies developed outside of the Afro-American hermeneutic circle.[16] Like the white feminist critic Elaine Showalter, who cautions her critical sisters against looking to the "androcentric models" of "male critical theory" for "our most basic principles,"[17] Joyce suggests that poststructuralism does not offer adequate pathways to analyses that are sufficiently afrocentric. Despite their production of studies that explore such dominant and sophisticated Black tropes of expression as signifying and the blues, the poststructuralist-informed readings of Gates and Baker are, in their apparent break with the tradition of sociopolitical Afro-American literary criticism, clearly not ideologically black enough for Joyce. She says of their break with tradition: "While Black American literature and its criticism are rooted in an allegiance to Black people, Baker and Gates have 'relinquished' that allegiance."[18]

Joyce suggests that there is a single acceptable black practice of critical reading and a single acceptable outcome. Such reading is extratextual in focus (it asks, in effect, not what the text does, but what it can do for the Afro-American reader), and is infinitely more concerned with content than with formal strategies. Scholars whose use of critical theory suggests to Joyce that they are more interested in exploring the language of the black text than in studying its potentially inspiriting content are accused of disloyalty to the cause of black liberation. Presupposing a uniform Afro-American experience of racism or, in the words (if not the precise wording) of George Kent, a singular adventure of blackness in Western culture,[19] Joyce and other traditional Afro-American critics argue that that experience ought to lead to a common, overtly political interpretation that is essentially unconcerned with the aesthetic qualities of black texts.

Joyce correctly posits that the experience or adventure of blackness can be said to constitute adequate parameters for determining what Stanley Fish has called an interpretive community. Members of such communities, according to Fish, are guided in their readings of texts by a shared "consciousness" which produces interpretive "strategies [that] exist prior to the act of reading and therefore determine the shape of what is read."[20] Membership in an Afro-American interpretive community is predicated not simply on the critic's desire to expose white hegemony but also on his or her dedication to exploring the historically unappreciated beauty and complexity of Black culture. It seems to me, however, that given the inability of even the most ideologically and aesthetically enlivened creative Afro-American texts to do so, not all the members of this community need agree that practitioners of literary criticism must see it as their role to lead uninitiated black readers to freedom.

Joyce's views to the contrary notwithstanding, the a priori assumptions of Baker and Gates, as reflected in their illuminating work on Afro-American literature, appear to me clearly in spiritual (if not discursive) harmony with the postulates of Black Aestheticians who demand that black critics "dig beneath the phrase and unearth the treasures of beauty lying deep in the untoured regions of the Black experience." The desire to actualize such goals can be said to motivate both Gates's interest in decoding signifying structures in black literary history and Baker's commitment to a Foucauldian project to "unearth" the culturally specific in Afro-American texts.

I want now to examine the motivations for Joyce's attack on Baker, Gates, and contemporary theory. Such an examination will lead to the issue I want to explore in terms of both traditional Afro-American and feminist criticism: how and why an intellectually compelling and demonstrably fluid interpretive approach such as afrocentric reading can be reduced, in the hands of critics as clearly dedicated to the celebration of their culture as Joyce and Gayle, to a blunt discursive instrument unable to perform effectively the range of tasks for which it was intended.

Afrocentric reading, like other overtly political acts of self-described interpretive communities such as American feminist criticism, holds that interpretation is a decidedly subjective and "interested" act of ideological commitment. Like many other political groups cognizant of the potential consequences of disloyalty, the afrocentric and feminist interpretive communities spend a good deal of time assessing the levels of actual ideological commitment of those who aspire to or proclaim membership. Such assessments are invariably measured in terms of the scrutinized's manifest abilities to remain pure of the ideological taint of the political other (which is, in the case of both classes, white androcentricism). When we read, for example, Joyce's doubts about Baker's and Gates's "allegiance" to Black people, or, for that matter, Elaine Showalter's view that Annette Kolodny's suggestion that feminist reading constitutes a "learned activity" is "politically suspect,"[21] we are acutely aware that the status of those under scrutiny as racial or gendered "insiders" fails to offer protection from allegations of treachery. They are unprotected precisely because "black" and "woman" are being employed as figures that define not the biological but the ideological self. In other words, black and female adventures in Western culture do not necessarily lead to what others would deem sufficiently afrocentric and/or feminist acts of reading. While I will deal later with what are, for me, the limitations of Joyce's and Showalter's perspectives on the discourses with which they are concerned, I want to emphasize at this point that their criteria for interpretive community status—race and gender respectively—are merely terms used to connote political orientation. If Baker and Gates are judged, in the words of the Billy Paul song that serve as an epigraph to this chapter, not black enough for Joyce, if Kolodny is not woman enough for Showalter, such lack results not from biology but from perceptions of insufficient ideological commitment.

In both cases, ideological lack is seen as a function of suggestions that the ideological other and/or his theories of interpretation can adequately—that is, in a non-androcentric or non-caucacentric fashion—penetrate feminist and afrocentric texts whose primary function, according to traditional class critics, is to depict, often in subtly encoded ways, the experiences of the victims of white male hegemony. Fish's discussion of the interpretive community-determined nature of textual evidence serves, I think, to illuminate the motivations for afrocentric and feminist suspicions concerning white male readings of their texts. According to Fish, there is "something very important about evidence: it is always a function of what it is to be evidence for, and is never independently available. That is, the interpretation determines what will count as evidence for it, and the evidence is able to be picked out only because the interpretation has *already* been assumed."[22] If Fish is correct, then perhaps the aesthetic standards that constitute the always already assumed of even the best intentioned white male critic render him unable to offer anything but what afrocentric and feminist critics would view as inadequate, ideologically tainted readings of black and/or feminist texts.

Major early essays by black feminists such as Barbara Smith and Deborah McDowell document the refusal of critics who are not both black and female to treat the texts of Afro-American women writers with an appropriate degree of critical seriousness and sensitivity to the implications of black female difference.[23] While the current popularity of the works of Afro-American women's literature suggests that black feminist criticism has been quite successful in its efforts to gain for the creative works of black women an important place in the Afro-American, feminist, and American literary canons, one would suspect that figures such as Smith and McDowell would not approve of the strategic distortions accompanying some of the more recent acts of canonization by gendered or racial others.

There is, in my estimation, no more troubling such act than Harold Bloom's introduction to a collection of critical essays on Zora Neale Hurston. After admitting an initial "skepticism" about Hurston—a skepticism which arises in large part because of his awareness that "contemporary work by women and by minority writers becomes esteemed on grounds other than aesthetic"—Bloom proceeds to offer a brief, uninformed reading of the black woman writer. And while it is possible to excuse his lack of serious scholarly attention to Hurston's corpus in view of his assignment to provide introductions for thousands of Chelsea House's critical series volumes, his presentation of a politically neutered version of Hurston exhausts my sympathy altogether: "Hurston herself was refreshingly free of all the ideologies that currently obscure the reception of her best book [*Their Eyes Were Watching God*]. Her sense of power has nothing in common with politics of any persuasion, with contemporary modes of feminism, or even with those questers who search for a black aesthetic."[24]

Apparently Bloom fails to understand the essential role of interpretive politics in both Hurston's rediscovery and her earlier obscurity. The always already assumed of traditional hegemonic reading—that, ultimately, art is deemed great according to timeless, fundamentally apolitical criteria—occasions a wonderfully curious canonization of Hurston, wherein the unquestionably great white male critic figuratively both submits the black female writer to a Schuylerian de-blacking machine and ungenders her. The only Hurston Bloom can welcome to his canon is a pallid, desexed version who is in an ideological sense both black and female no more.

As Bloom's reading of Hurston through clouded critical lenses demonstrates, afrocentric and feminist readers may indeed be justified in their skepticism where certain brands of critical theory and its practitioners are concerned. It is clear that Bloom (to use the phrasing Joyce chooses to describe Baker's and Gates's interpretive deficiencies) either cannot read or cannot appreciate Hurston's counterhegemonic perspectives. Bloom's intended praise of Hurston is exemplary of the limitations of analyzing gendered or racial others in a manner not sufficiently attuned to the complexities of reading across lines that demarcate cultural difference. Such acts of reading project representatives of a hegemonic (white male) order as custodians against the society's corruption by what we could call—taking our cue from Showalter's apt phrase—the wild zone of gendered and racial differences.[25]

Bloom's example of ideological reading clearly suggests some of the differences race and gender have traditionally made in the assessments of black or female texts by white male critics. Despite my use of Gates's titular phrase, however, I differ with him when he insists that race is simply "a dangerous trope" (5) because of the fact that "race, as a meaningful criterion with the biological sciences, has long been recognized to be a fiction" (4). My objections stem from Gates's failure to acknowledge here that gender is as culturally determined as race. For the purposes of this study at least, the consequence of viewing race as a trope, while simultaneously arguing that "the biological criteria used to determine 'difference' in sex simply do not hold when applied to 'race'" (5), is the suggestion that gender differences are, in considerations of culture, essentially more significant than racial difference. This is a view to which scores of feminist critics who have been energetically deconstructing what they view as overdetermined notions of sexual difference would, I believe, strenuously object. One such critic, Judith Butler, argues that "if the inner truth of gender is a fabrication, . . . a fantasy instituted and inscribed on the surfaces of bodies[,] . . . genders . . . are only produced as the truth effects of a discourse of primary and stable identity."[26]

Further, by offering such a seemingly essentialist view of female difference, Gates might be said to lend credence to the suggestions of the self-designated "downhome, downright Yankee historical" project of Showalter, who shares Joyce's belief that "male critical theory" cannot be translated across class lines.[27] Such arguments have proved so persuasive that some males openly question their right to call themselves feminist critics. In "Reading Like a Man," for example, Robert Scholes observes that a male critic "may work within the feminist paradigm but never be a full-fledged member of the class of feminists."[28]

Scholes's doubts about the possibilities of a "full-fledged" male feminist, however, are not motivated, as one might expect, by a sympathy for French feminist attempts to write the woman's body or to employ a heretofore suppressed female language (both of which men may be biologically incapable of), but rather in experience-based theories of "downhome . . . Yankee" feminism. At the conclusion of a quite provocative reading of Jonathan Culler's "Reading As a Woman," Scholes says of his difficulties with Culler's attempts to read feminism through the lens of deconstruction: "Above all, I think no man should seek in any way to diminish the authority which the experience of women gives them in speaking about that experience, and I believe that women should be very wary of critical systems that deny or diminish that authority."[29]

Scholes is referring here not to biological difference in a scientific sense, not to women's physiological otherness, which might make them write and read in a unique manner, but to the cultural consequences of being assigned to the "class" of woman. For Scholes, men cannot be totally acceptable feminist readers because they cannot experience women's oppression firsthand. But appeals to women's experience of male-"authored" oppression take us out of the realm of biology and into the world of female culture—into, in other words, a realm analogous to Gates's "race," whose coded "signifying black difference" Gates acknowledges whites can learn to read.[30]

To suggest that males are necessarily culturally inadequate readers of female texts is essentially no different than to argue, as the black critic Stephen Henderson did in 1973, that whites are experientially unsuited to offer competent readings of Afro-American literature. Henderson's views of white reading inadequacy, like those of Anglo-American feminists concerning male readers, are firmly grounded in perceptions of impenetrable class culture—in "the Black Experience"—and are most clearly manifested in his theory of textual saturation.

By saturation, Henderson means "chiefly (a) the communication of Blackness in a given situation, and (b) a sense of fidelity to the observed and intuited truth of the Black Experience."[31] Such communication is a function of "total" cultural immersion which permits the "understanding" of the discourse used to describe that experience. As Henderson insists, "Where style and subject matter are obviously Black, one may feel, for example, that a word, a phrase, a rhythm, is so *right*, so *Black*, that its employment illuminates the entire composition."[32] By virtue of their cultural experiences, blacks can, according to Henderson, recognize the rightness, the blackness, of such utterances, while experientially deprived whites cannot.

Henderson's formulations have been questioned by both Gates and Baker. Gates refers to saturation as "the ultimate tautology" that leads necessarily to unfortunate comparisons between black writers concerning their various levels of an achieved ideological blackness.[33] And Baker calls Henderson's assumptions "cultural xenophobia" because they suggest that "*only* the black imagination can experience blackness" (*Blues,* 82). For both critics, the theory of saturation is problematic because, as Baker puts it, "the creative and critical framework suggested by Henderson resembles, at times, a closed circle" from which all but blacks are forever excluded (81). But if Henderson's theories are xenophobic, they are certainly no more so than those of a faction of feminist criticism in this country represented by figures such as Showalter, who, until quite recently, seemed summarily to dismiss the possibility of adequately feminist readings by men of texts by women on the same grounds that Henderson does: cultural—experiential—difference.

If the major issue in such debates is, as I believe, whether racial and gendered experience can be adequately interpreted across "class" lines or boundaries, we find ourselves discussing matters traditionally associated not with literary interpretation but with the field of anthropology. Because of the nature of the enterprise, this field has historically had to concern itself with the question of whether it is possible for an investigator to achieve accurate analyses of alien (usually third world) cultures. In his influential essay, "Thick Description: Towards an Interpretive Theory of Culture," the cultural anthropologist Clifford Geertz argues that such analyses are possible and that their achievement is manifested as "thick description" of symbolic social action derived from an understanding of the "webs of significance" unique to the investigated culture. For Geertz, culturally informed readings of those who occupy other cultural spaces require not a shared cultural experience but rather a learned "ability to construe their modes of expression, what I call their symbol systems."[34]

Certainly one of the more satisfying appropriations of Geertzian interpretive cultural theory into the realm of literary criticism is found in Baker's *The Journey Back*. For Baker, adequate interpretation of literature, which he refers to as "a manifestation of the human capacity for symbolic behavior," requires "studied . . . attention to the methods and findings of disciplines [such as philosophy, psychology, linguistics, and phenomenology] that enable one to address such concerns as the status of the artistic object, the relationship of art to other cultural systems, and the nature and function of artistic creation and perception in a given society." An interdisciplinary "anthropology of art" provides, according to Baker, "an informed grasp—a 'thick description'—of the interrelated codes of a particular . . . culture" and "can yield the authentic 'force of meaning' of the work."[35]

Showalter also sees much to recommend in Geertz. In fact, she suggests that a cultural model offers the most "complete and satisfying way to talk about the specificity and difference of women's writing" ("Wilderness," 259). Further, she believes that a Geertzian approach offers the means of providing a "genuinely 'thick' description of women's writing [that] would insist upon gender and upon a female literary tradition among the multiple strata that make up the force of meaning in a text" ("Wilderness," 266).

Despite their similar employment of Geertz to suggest adequate means of decoding what both critics refer to as the "force of meaning" in literary texts, Baker and Showalter reach much different conclusions about the interpretive potential of cultural analysis across class lines. Already we have seen part of Baker's condemnatory response to the suggestion that only the cultural insider can adequately read Afro-American texts. While Baker grants that Stephen Henderson is correct when he argues that Afro-American expressive culture had long been "under siege . . . [by] . . . white critical condescension and snobbery, and . . .

outright pathological ignorance and fear" (quoted in *Blues,* 84), the last decade's production of some informed, white-authored readings of black literature caused Baker to reevaluate statements he had made in *The Journey Back* about the competence of whites to interpret Afro-American texts.[36] Such studies have convinced Baker that "through their own investigations of the 'forms of things unknown' in recent years, some white critics have been able to enter a black critical circle. They entered, however, not as superordinate authorities, but as scholars working in harmony with fundamental postulates of the Black Aesthetic" (*Blues,* 84).

While Baker has welcomed a few well-informed white critics into the black critical circle, Showalter, as her review essay "Critical Cross-Dressing: Male Feminists and the Woman of the Year" makes clear, has until recently maintained considerable skepticism about the success of male attempts to enter the feminist interpretive circle. For her, men's failure to produce adequately feminist readings results from their inability to confront successfully the inherent difficulties of their positions. Showalter suggests that "the way into feminist criticism, for the male theorist, must involve a confrontation with what might be implied by reading as a man, and with a questioning or surrender of paternal privileges." According to Showalter, successful "male feminist" texts such as Culler's "Reading As a Woman" and Terry Eagleton's *Literary Theory* are evidence that the male critic has read "consciously from his own gender experience, with an ironic sense of its ideological bounds. That is to say that he has read not as a *woman,* but as a man and a feminist."[37] He must be aware at all times, in other words, of his status as gendered Outsider.

While she expresses a view that men can indeed become feminist readers, however, Showalter clearly implies that the efforts of male critics generally fail because of their difficulty with the acts of "confrontation" and "surrender" necessary for this critical competence. Typically, she says, male feminist readings evince the male critic's failure "to consider his own ideological dilemma"—that is, as a privileged member of patriarchy employing feminist interpretive models which energetically critique that empowering system—and consequently what results is "phallic feminism [that] seems like another raid on the resources of the feminine in order to modernize male dominance."[38]

To return to the subject of Showalter's difficulties with Annette Kolodny's suggestion that men can learn to read in a feminist-approved fashion, the suggestion strikes Showalter as politically suspect because it fails to insist on male confrontation of patriarchal privileges. Even a cursory look at the essay in which this statement appears, however, clearly demonstrates that Kolodny's views about the interpretation of women's texts are in harmony with the cultural anthropological model embraced by Showalter.

In "Dancing through the Minefield," Kolodny offers what might be viewed as a best-case scenario concerning why women's texts had not heretofore been included in the male-controlled Western literary canon. Kolodny suggests that "the most recent feminist re-readings of women writers allows the conclusion that where [female-authored texts] have dropped out of sight, it may be due not to any lack of merit in the work but, instead, to an incapacity of predominantly male readers to properly interpret and appreciate women's texts—due, in large part, to a lack of prior acquaintance."[39] While she misses a clear opportunity to offer more biting criticism of patriarchy, Kolodny's argument is certainly in agreement with Showalter's stated belief that women's culture provides the only adequate matrix for the analysis of women's literature. In Kolodny's formulation, men could not previously read women's texts because they did not possess a sufficient analytical grasp of the codes that inform women's experiences. According to Kolodny, however, provocative feminist studies by such scholars as Patricia Meyer Spacks, Ellen Moers, Sandra Gilbert, Susan Gubar, and Showalter herself, provide the means for men to comprehend the previously elusive " 'codes of custom, of society, and of conceptions of the world' " that inform women's texts.[40]

Kolodny's views, again, are obviously consistent with the Geertzian/symbolic cultural anthropological model that Showalter embraces in "Wilderness." Further, recent developments in the universe of feminist discourse such as Alice Jardine and Paul Smith's *Men in Feminism* and what Showalter celebrates as the "genuinely exciting, serious, and provocative" involvement of some male theorists serve to substantiate Kolodny's claim that men can be and have been taught to read the codes of women's creative and critical texts.[41] Still, however, such developments do not seem to please Showalter, who is infinitely more concerned with elaborating what she views as males' failure to produce sufficiently feminist readings than she is in acknowledging and applauding the beginnings—although in her view problematic ones—of serious male attention to feminist concerns.[42]

Faced, like Joyce Joyce, with applications of so-called white male poststructuralist theory in analyses of Black literary texts, Showalter accuses Kolodny of treachery when Kolodny allegedly oversimplifies the nature of the obstacles to male analytical competence vis-à-vis feminist texts. For both critics, the corruptive potential of white male hegemony's introduction into their respective discourses far outweighs whatever explicative benefits that might obtain from such introduction. What both Showalter and Joyce fear is the neutralizing of the political possibilities of their analytical systems suggested in what are, for them, the most vexing instances of the invasion of the ideological other. Joyce fears that a poststructuralist-informed emphasis on the language of the text will seduce black critics to cease serious analysis of black literature's liberating themes, while Showalter is concerned that the reduction of feminist reading to the status of learned (but not necessarily also *lived*) activity encourages the type of "phallic 'feminist' criticism" that she quite effectively criticizes in her discussion of Eagleton's study of Richardson.

The feminist critic Mary Jacobus says of Showalter's desire to protect feminist criticism from potential corruption from white male poststructuralist critics and their misguided female feminist converts: "Showalter's energetic polemic is fueled by understandable professional anxiety about preserving an area in criticism that is specific to women."[43] This conservative impulse, motivated in part by the justifiable suspicion concerning patriarchy's historically insatiable desire to control the female, must also, I think, be viewed in connection with Showalter's definite hope that women will maintain an indisputable institutional control of feminism. Showalter's differences with "male critical theory" and with the influence of continental theory on feminist critics have as a primary source, it would appear, a desire for women to exclude male participation, to maintain, in other words, a feminist discourse of and for their own.

Showalter seems to advocate the establishment of feminist criticism as a female-controlled, adversarial equivalent of the historically androcentric Western critical canon. Even an exclusively female participation, however, would prove problematic, in view of the serious disagreements among feminist critics about the value of contemporary critical theory. Such an exclusively female membership as Showalter desires would, ironically, serve to clarify the accuracy of deconstructionists' views that the differences within a term such as *feminism* are perhaps more analytically compelling than the differences between binary opposites such as masculinist and feminist.

Many American feminist critics share Showalter's view that "the feminist obsession with . . . male critical theory keeps us dependent upon it and retards our progress in solving our own theoretical problems" ("Wilderness," 247). It is certainly the case that one of these theoretical problems—the place in feminist criticism of the poststructuralist theories developed by prominent male scholars—has caused seemingly irreparable divisions within feminist criticism. The socialist feminist critic Jane Marcus argues, for example, that relying so heavily on male theorists encourages the betrayal of the general postulates of feminist criticism. Marcus says of Peggy Kamuf's and Gayatri Spivak's readings of *A Room of One's Own* and *To the Lighthouse* respectively:

> By taking father-guides to map the labyrinth of the female text, they deny the motherhood of the author of the text. These readings reinforce patriarchal authority. By reading [Virginia] Woolf through Foucault, Kamuf names Foucault's critique of the history of sexuality as more powerful than Woolf's. Reading Woolf through Derrida, Spivak serves patriarchy by insisting on a heterosexuality which the novel attacks by privileging chastity in the woman artist. The critic takes a position which is daughter to the father, not daughter to the mother.[44]

By explicitly contrasting her own leftist, separatist interpretive politics with what one could call a New Feminist agenda that problematizes gender differences by foregrounding male theorists' notions (including those of the infamous misogynist Freud), Marcus suggests that critics such as Spivak and Kamuf have exposed both themselves and feminist criticism to the corrupting and anti-female taint of masculinist values.

Marcus's sentiments are echoed in an essay Nina Baym writes in part to clarify, as its subtitle suggests, "Why I Don't Do Feminist Literary Theory." Baym argues that the attachment of feminist theorists to the work of Freud and Lacan is motivated by what could best be described as unresolved Electra complexes, by the desire, in other words, to be " 'daddy's girl.' "[45] According to Baym, feminist theory's misogynist foundations, in addition to encouraging its practitioners to "excoriate their deviating sisters," serve also to minimize its members' ideological commitment to the class of woman itself: "Today's feminist literary theory . . . is finally more concerned to be theoretical than to be feminist. It speaks from the position of the *castrata.*"[46]

At this point, the similarities between the neo–Black Aesthetician and the down-home Yankee attacks on poststructuralism should be clear. Because traditional feminist and afrocentric reading both take as their fundamental strategy of class empowerment forceful and continued criticism of the products of the white male imagination, they view adoption of the analytical assumptions of a white male-authored contemporary critical theory as signs of treason. This becomes especially true when these theories are used in discussions of such matters as the limitations of the historical practice of these interpretive traditions. But just as critics such as Baker and Gates appropriate poststructuralism in order to allow afrocentric reading to pursue its full potential, a close reading of Jacobus's discussion of Showalter's "Critical Cross-Dressing" demonstrates that poststructuralist feminist theory, instead of being at odds with the postulates of feminism, insists that the class discourse take its critique of phallogocentricism to its most radical extreme.

Early in *Reading Woman,* Mary Jacobus provides what serves the present discussion as an explanation for her reliance on psychoanalytic theory. While she would applaud Showalter's rejection of the attempts of feminist biocriticism to write the female body because, as Showalter puts it, "there can be no expression of the body which is unmediated by linguistic, social and literary structures" ("Wilderness," 252), Jacobus disagrees with Showalter's views about how best to discuss women's culturally produced differences. For Jacobus, it is psychoanalytic theory, not down-home Yankee historical feminism, that provides the most suggestive point of entry to fruitful, nonessentialist discussions of culturally-constructed gender differences:

If there is no literal referent to start with, no identity or essence, the production of sexual difference can be viewed as textual, like the production of meaning. Once we cease to see the origin of gender identity as biological or anatomical—as given—but rather as instituted by and in language, "reading woman" can be posed as a process of differentiation for which psychoanalysis provides a model. (4)

Employing a psychoanalytical model, Jacobus is able to examine "Critical Cross-Dressing" in the context of a question that dominated feminist discourse during the 1980s: "Is 'reading as a woman' fundamentally differentiated from 'reading as a man,' and if so, by what (political, sociological, or ideological) differences?" (9). If, as Showalter and many others have argued, culture, and not nature, is the source of interpretive differences between women and men, no amount of attention to biology will aid our comprehension of such differences. Despite her avowed anti-essentialist views concerning difference, however, Showalter's essay evinces a persistent "preoccupation with legitimacy and illegitimacy, a . . . preference for unambiguous meanings and stable origins" (12) which keeps her from following her stated opposition to essentializing to its (for Jacobus) logical, psychoanalytical ends.

Despite agreeing with Jonathan Culler's view of the "difficulties in the feminist appeal to the woman reader's experience, an identity which is always constructed rather than given" ("Cross-Dressing," 139), Showalter resorts to a discourse of essentialism when she suggests that feminist critical theories are "proved on our [women's] pulses."[47] As a consequence, instead of questioning the veracity of the sign "woman" itself, Showalter "comes dangerously close to endorsing a position she has earlier derided"—the maintenance of what Jacobus calls "a gender hierarchy" that assesses suitability for membership in the circle of feminist critics solely on the basis of biology.

What critiques such as Jacobus's enable, then, is a dismantling of traditional feminist criticism's appeals to an authority of female experience, an exposure of the neither biologically nor culturally justified nature of a feminist critical advocacy of strictly gendered criteria. To simply reverse the binary opposition man/woman, when we are painfully aware of its phallocentric origins, is to suggest complicity with phallocentric fictions of history. No feminist should be comfortable with such a suggestion, despite the potential institutional gains adhering to such a strategy can provide.

As the examples of Baker, Gates, and Jacobus suggest, contemporary critical theory can enhance our comprehension of non-hegemonic class texts, if for no other reason than it demands that we continually reevaluate our critical suppositions.

Afrocentric and feminist critics whose work is informed by poststructuralism have, I believe, successfully demonstrated its usefulness in their explorations of, among other areas, the philosophical limitations of approaches to non-hegemonic literary study which insist that positivistic, sociopolitical readings constitute the only ideologically compelling means of engaging texts with which we are concerned.

Surely our understanding of the texts of the female and the Afro-American traditions can profit greatly from such less overtly laudatory forms of analysis encouraged by appropriative versions of Western critical theories. At this point in the literary history of both of the class discourses examined in this chapter, positivistic reading reduces analysis to what Fredric Jameson calls "cut-and-dried" formulas as unimaginative, stereotypical, and unworthy of the traditions they serve as predictable caucacentric male perspectives on Zora Neale Hurston.[48] For an ideology to remain vibrant and useful over time as a means of access to literary texts, it must allow for the reinvention of the nature of the issues it addresses and must present fruitful opportunities for what Adrienne Rich, in perhaps the most widely quoted single passage in American feminist criticism, calls "re-vision—the act of looking back, of seeing with fresh eyes, of entering an old text from a new critical direction."[49] This revisionary process is imperative not only in the early formulations of class methods of reading, but also when these early methods themselves become so firmly established as to become obstacles to illuminating interpretations.

But while it helps to open up fresh interpretive spaces, theory, notwithstanding strategic efforts at times by both its practitioners and detractors alike to reduce its complex urgings to a single principle or set of principles, is a multiply inflected entity whose self-difference is manifested in its practitioners' disagreements about the exegetical and ideological consequences of a clearly articulated politics of positionality. Seeking, over the space of the next two chapters, to resist cut-and-dried views of the meanings of difference, I want to use two clearly identified instances of border crossing—specifically, self-reflexive forays by men into feminism and by whites into Afro-American literary criticism—to demonstrate our need to develop a revisionary politics of reading that will allow us to examine, in a manner as devoid as possible of the conservative, protectionist impulses that mark the traditional afrocentric and feminist projects as I have identified them here, both the liberating and the potentially hazardous consequences of our attempts to dismantle the racial and gendered hierarchies by which our society has been structured.

The main theoretical task for male feminists, then, is to develop an analysis of their own position, and a strategy for how their awareness of their difficult and contradictory position in relation to feminism can be made explicit in discourse and practice.

Toril Moi, "Men against Patriarchy"

She had been looking all along for a friend, and it took her a while to discover that a [male] lover was not a comrade and could never be—for a woman.

Toni Morrison, *Sula*

Critics eternally become and embody the generative myths of their culture by half-perceiving and half-inventing their culture, their myths, and themselves.

Houston A. Baker, Jr., *Afro-American Poetics*

Nor is any theorizing of feminism adequate without some positioning of the person who is doing the theorizing.

Cary Nelson, "Men, Feminism: The Materiality of Discourse"

2

A Black Man's Place in Black Feminist Criticism

Many essays by male and female scholars devoted to exploring the subject of male critics' place in feminism generally agree about the uses and usefulness of the autobiographical male "I." Such essays suggest that citing the male critical self reflects a response to (apparent) self-difference, an exploration of the disparities between the masculine's antagonistic position in feminist discourse on the one hand and, on the other, the desire of the individual male critic to represent his difference with and from the traditional androcentric perspectives of his gender and culture. Put another way, in male feminist acts, to identify the writing self as biologically male is to emphasize the desire not to be ideologically male; it is to explore the process of rejecting the phallocentric perspectives by which men traditionally have justified the subjugation of women.[1]

In what strikes me as a particularly suggestive theoretical formulation, Joseph Boone articulates his sense of the goals of such male feminist autobiographical acts:

> In exposing the latent multiplicity and difference in the word "me(n)," we can perhaps open up a space within the discourse of feminism where a male feminist voice *can* have something to say beyond impossibilities and apologies and unresolved ire. Indeed, if the male feminist can discover a position *from which* to speak that neither elides the importance of feminism to his work nor ignores the specificity of his gender, his voice may also find that it no longer exists as an abstraction . . . but that it in fact inhabits a body: its own sexual/textual body.[2]

Because of an awareness that androcentric perspectives are learned, are transmitted by means of specific sociocultural practices in such effective ways that they come to appear natural, male feminists such as Boone believe that, through an informed investigation of androcentric and feminist ideologies, individual men can work to resist the lure of the normatively masculine. That resistance for the aspiring male feminist requires, he says, exposing "the latent multiplicity and difference in the word 'men,'" in other words, disrupting both ideologies' unproblematized perceptions of monolithic and/or normative maleness (as villainous, antagonistic "other" for feminism, and, for androcentricism, powerful, domineering patriarch). At this early stage of male feminism's development, to speak self-consciously—autobiographically—is to explore, implicitly or explicitly, why and how the individual male experience (the "me" in men) has diverged from, has created possibilities for a rejection of, the androcentric norm.

And while there is not yet agreement as to what constitutes an identifiably male feminist act of criticism or about the usefulness of such acts for the general advancement of the feminist project, at least one possible explanation for a male critic's self-referential discourse is that it is a response to palpable mistrust—emanating from some female participants in feminism and perhaps from the writing male subject himself—about his motives. A skeptical strand of opinion with regard to male feminism is represented by Alice Jardine's "Men in Feminism: Odor di Uomo Or Campagnons de Route?" Having determined that the most useful measure of an adequately feminist text is its "*inscription of struggle—even of pain*"—an inscription of a struggle against patriarchy which Jardine finds absent from most male feminist acts, perhaps because "the historical fact that is the oppression of women [is] . . . one of their favorite blind spots"—she admits to some confusion as to the motivations for males' willing participation: "Why . . . would men want to be in feminism if it's about struggle? What do men want to be in—in pain?"[3]

In addition to seeking to cure its blindness where the history of female oppression is concerned, a male feminism must explore the motivations for its participation in what we might call, in keeping with Jardine's formulations, a discourse of (en)gendered pain. If one of the goals of male feminist self-referentiality is to demonstrate to females that individual males can indeed serve as allies in efforts to undermine androcentric power—and it seems that this is invariably the case—the necessary trust cannot be gained by insisting that motivation as such does not represent a crucial area that must be carefully negotiated. For example, I accept as accurate and, indeed, reflective of my own situation Andrew Ross's assertion that "there are those [men] for whom the *facticity* of feminism, for the most part, goes without saying . . . , who are young enough for feminism to have been a primary component of their intellectual formation."[4] However, in discussions whose apparent function is a foregrounding of both obstacles to and possibilities of a male feminism, men's relation(s) to the discourse can never go "without saying"; for the foreseeable future at least, this relation needs necessarily to be rigorously and judiciously theorized, and grounded explicitly in the experiential realm of the writing male subject.

But no matter how illuminating and exemplary one finds self-referential inscriptions of a male feminist critical self, if current views of the impossibility of a consistently truthful autobiographical act are correct, there are difficulties implicit in any such attempt to situate or inscribe that male self. Because, as recent theorizing on the subject of autobiography has demonstrated, acts of discursive self-rendering unavoidably involve the creation of an idealized version of a unified or unifiable self, we can be certain only of the fact that the autobiographical impulse yields but some of the truths of the male feminist critic's experiences.[5] As is also the case for female participants, a male can never possess or be able to tell the whole truth and nothing but the truth about his relationship to feminist discourse and praxis.

But while autobiographical criticism, like the genre of autobiography itself, is poised tenuously between the poles of closure and disclosure, between representation and re-presentation, between a lived life and an invented one, I believe that even in the recoverable half-truths of my life are some of the materials that have shaped my perceptions, my beliefs, the self or selves that I bring to the interpretive act. In these half-truths is the source of my desire both to inscribe a black male feminism and to inscribe myself as a self-consciously racialized version of what Jardine considers a potentially oxymoronic entity—"male feminist"—whose literal, if not ideological or performative "blackness" is indisputable, and whose adequacy vis-à-vis feminism others must determine. By examining discussions of the phenomenon of the male feminist—that is to say, by reading male and female explorations of men's places in feminist criticism—and exploring responses of others to my own professional and personal relationships to feminism, I will identify autobiographically and textually grounded sources for my belief that while gendered difference might be said to complicate the prospect of a non-phallocentric black male feminism, it does not render such a project impossible.

At the outset, I acknowledge that mine is a necessary participation with regard to black feminist criticism in the half-invention, half-perception which, in Houston Baker's compelling formulation, represents every scholar's relationship to cultural criticism.[6] Such an acknowledgment is not intended to indicate that my male relationship to feminism is that of an illegitimate child, as it were. Rather, it is meant to suggest, like Elizabeth Weed's insistence on "the impossibility" of both men's and women's "relationship to feminism," my belief that while feminism represents a complex, sometimes self-contradictory "utopian vision" which no one can fully possess, a biological male can "develop political, theoretical [and, more generally, interpretive] strategies" which, though at most perhaps half-true to all that feminist ideologies are, nevertheless can assist in a movement toward actualizing the goals of feminism.[7]

I have been forced to think in especially serious ways about my own relationship to feminist criticism since I completed the first drafts of *Inspiriting Influences,* my study of Afro-American women novelists.[8] I have questioned neither the explanatory power of feminism nor the essential importance of developing models adequate to the analysis of black female-authored texts, as my book—in harmony, I believe, with the black feminist project concerned with recovering and uncovering an Afro-American female literary tradition—attempts to provide on a limited scale. Instead, I have been confronted with suspicion about my gendered suitability for the task of explicating Afro-American women's texts, suspicion which has been manifested in the form of both specific responses to my project and general inquiries within literary studies into the phenomenon of the male feminist.

For example, a white female reader of the manuscript asserted—with undisguised surprise—that my work was "so feminist" and asked how I'd managed to offer such ideologically informed readings. Another scholar, a black feminist literary critic, recorded with no discernible hesitation her unease with my "male readings" of the texts of Zora Neale Hurston, Toni Morrison, Gloria Naylor, and Alice Walker. I wondered about the possibility of my being simultaneously "so feminist" and not so feminist (i.e., so "male"), about the meanings of these terms both for these scholars and for the larger interpretive communities in which they participate. Consequently, in what was perhaps initially an act of psychic self-protection, I began to formulate questions for which I still have found no consistently satisfactory answers. Were the differences in the readers' perceptions of the ideological adequacy of my study a function of their own views of feminist criticism, a product, in other words, of the differences not simply *within me* but *within feminism itself?* And if the differences within feminism are so significant, could I possibly satisfy everybody with "legitimate" interests in the texts of Hurston et al. by means of my own appropriated versions of black feminist discourse, my unavoidably half-true myth of what that discourse is, means, and does? Should my myth of feminism and its mobilization in critical texts be considered naturally less analytically compelling than that of a female scholar simply as a function of my biological maleness? And how could what I took to be a useful self-reflexivity avoid becoming a debilitating inquiry into a process that has come to seem for me, if not "natural," as Cary Nelson views his relationship to feminism, at least *necessary?*[9]

Compelled, and, to be frank, disturbed by such questions, I searched for answers in others' words, others' work. I purchased a copy of *Men in Feminism,* a collection which examines the possibility of men's participation as "comrades" (to use Toni Morrison's term) in feminist criticism and theory. Gratified by the appearance of such a volume, I became dismayed upon reading the editors' introductory remarks, which noted their difficulty in "locating intellectuals, who, having shown interest in the question, would offer, for instance, a gay or a black perspective on the problem."[10] While a self-consciously "gay . . . perspective" does find its way into the collection, the insights of nonwhite males and females are conspicuously absent.[11]

Even more troubling for me than the absence of black voices or, for that matter, of general inquiries into the effects of racial, cultural, and class differences on males' relationship to feminism, was the sense shared by many contributors of insurmountable obstacles to male feminism. In fact, the first essay, Stephen Heath's "Male Feminism," begins by insisting that "men's relation to feminism is an impossible one."[12] For me, Heath's formulations are insightful and provocative, if not always persuasive, as when he claims: "This is, I believe, the most any man can do today: to learn and so to try to write and talk or act in response to feminism, and so to try not in any way to be anti-feminist, supportive of the old oppressive structures. Any more, any notion of writing a feminist book or being a feminist, is a myth, a male imaginary with the reality of appropriation and domination right behind."[13] Is male participation in feminism restricted to being either appropriative and domineering or not antifeminist? Must we necessarily agree with Heath and others who claim that men cannot be feminists? To put the matter differently, is gender really an adequate determinant of "class" position?

Despite the poststructuralist tenor of Heath's work generally and of many of his perspectives here, his is an easily problematized essentialist claim—that, in effect, biology determines destiny and, therefore, one's relationship to feminist ideology, that womanhood allows one to become feminist at the same time that manhood necessarily denies that status to men. And while Heath embraces its notions of history as a narrative of male "appropriation and domination" of gendered others, he appears resistant at this point in his discourse to evidence of a powerful feminist institutional *present* and *presence*. I believe that we must acknowledge that feminism represents, at least in areas of the American academy, an incomparably productive, influential, and resilient ideology and institution that men, no matter how cunning, duplicitous, or culturally powerful, will neither control nor overthrow in the foreseeable future, one whose perspectives have proved and might continue to prove convincing even to biological males. In surveying the potential implications of the participation of biological men in feminism, we must therefore be honest about feminism's current persuasiveness and indomitability, about its clarifying, transformative potential, and about the fact that the corruptive possibility of both the purposefully treacherous and the only half-convinced male is, for today at least, slight indeed. Surely it is neither naive, presumptuous, nor premature to suggest that feminism as ideology and reading strategy has assumed a position of exegetical and institutional strength capable of withstanding even the most energetically masculinist acts of subversion.

Below I want to focus specifically on the question of a black male feminism. Rather than seeing it as an impossibility or as a subtle new manifestation of and attempt at androcentric domination, I want to show that certain instances of afrocentric feminism provide Afro-American men with an invaluable means of rewriting—of *re-vis(ion)ing*—our selves, our history and literary tradition, and our future.

Few would deny that black feminist literary criticism is an oppositional discourse constituted in large part as a response against black male participation in the subjugation of Afro-American women. From Barbara Smith's castigation of black male critics for their "virulently sexist . . . treatment" of black women writers and her insistence that they are "hampered by an inability to comprehend Black women's experience in sexual as well as racial terms" to Michele Wallace's characterization of the "black male Afro-Americanists who make pivotal use of Hurston's work" as "a gang," Afro-American men are generally perceived as nonallied others of black feminist discourse.[14] And, as is evident in Wallace's figuration of male Hurston scholars as intraracial street warriors, they are viewed at times as always already damned and unredeemable, even when they appear to take black women's writing seriously. We—I—must accept the fact that black male investigations informed by feminist principles, including this one, may never be good enough or ideologically correct enough for some black women who are feminists.

This sense of an unredeemable black male critic/reader is in stark contrast to perspectives offered in such texts as Sherley Anne Williams's "Some Implications of Womanist Theory." In her essay, she embraces Alice Walker's term "womanist"—which, according to Williams, connotes a commitment "to the survival and wholeness of an entire people, female and male, as well as a valorization of women's works in all their varieties and multitudes"—because she considers the black feminist project to be separatist in "its tendency to see not only a distinct black female culture but to see that culture as a separate cultural form" from "the facticity of Afro-American life."[15]

I believe that a black male feminism, whatever its connections to critical theory or its specific areas of concern, can profit immensely from what female feminists have to say about male participation. For example, Valerie Smith's suggestion in "Gender and Afro-Americanist Literary Theory and Criticism" that "Black male critics and theorists might explore the nature of the contradictions that arise when they undertake black feminist projects"[16] seems to me quite useful, as does Alice Jardine's advice to male feminists. Speaking for white female feminists, Jardine addresses white males who consider themselves to be feminists: "We do not want you to *mimic* us, to become the same as us; we don't want your pathos or your guilt; and we don't even want your admiration (even if it's nice to get it once in a while). What we want, I would even say what we need, is your *work*. We need you to get down to serious work. And like all serious work, that involves struggle and pain."[17] The womanist theoretical project that has been adopted by Williams, Smith, and others provides aspiring Afro-American male feminists with a useful model for the type of self-exploration that Smith and Jardine advocate. What Williams terms "womanist theory" is especially suggestive for Afro-American men because, while it calls for feminist discussions of black women's texts and for critiques of black androcentrism, womanism foregrounds a general black psychic health as a primary objective. Williams argues that "what is needed is a thoroughgoing examination of male images in the works of black male writers"; her womanism, then, aims at "ending the separatist tendency in Afro-American criticism," at leading black feminism away from "the same hole The Brother has dug for himself—narcissism, isolation, inarticulation, obscurity," at the creation and/ or continuation of black "community and dialogue."[18]

If a black man is to become a useful contributor to black feminism, he must, as Boone argues, "discover a position *from which* to speak that neither elides the importance of feminism to his work nor ignores the specificity of his gender." However multiply split we perceive the subject to be, however deeply felt our sense of "maleness" and "femaleness" as social constructions, however heightened our sense of the historical consequences and current dangers of black androcentrism, a black male feminism cannot contribute to the continuation and expansion of the black feminist project by being so identified against or out of touch with itself as to fail to be both self-reflective and at least minimally self-interested. A black male feminist self-reflectivity of the type I have in mind necessarily would include examination of both the benefits and the dangers of a situatedness in feminist discourse. The self-interestedness of a black male feminist would be manifested in part by his concern with exploring a man's place. Clearly if convincing mimicry of female-authored concerns and interpretive strategies— speaking *like* a female feminist—is not in and of itself an appropriate goal for aspiring male participants, then a male feminism necessarily must explore males' various situations in the contexts and texts of history and the present.

Perhaps the most difficult task for a black male feminist is striking a workable balance between male self-inquiry/interest and an adequately feminist critique of patriarchy. To this point, especially in response to the commercial and critical success of contemporary Afro-American women's literature, scores of black men have proved unsuccessful in this regard. As black feminist critics such as Valerie Smith and Deborah McDowell have argued, the contemporary moment of black feminist literature has been greeted by many Afro-American males with hostility, self-interested misrepresentation, and a lack of honest intellectual introspection.

In "Reading Family Matters," a useful discussion for black male feminism primarily as an exploration of what such a discourse ought not do and be, McDowell speaks of widely circulated androcentric male analyses of Afro-American feminist texts by writers such as Toni Morrison and Alice Walker:

> Critics leading the debate [about the representation of black men in black women's texts] have lumped all black women writers together and have focused on one tiny aspect of their immensely complex and diverse project—the image of black men—despite the fact that, if we can claim a center for these texts, it is located in the complexities of black female subjectivity and experience. In other words, though black women writers have made black women the subjects of their own family stories, these male readers/critics are attempting to usurp that place for themselves and place it at the center of critical inquiry.[19]

Although I do not believe that "the image of black men" is as microscopic an element in Afro-American women's texts as McDowell claims, I agree with her about the reprehensible nature of unabashed androcentricism found in formulations she cites by such writers as Robert Staples, Mel Watkins, and Darryl Pinckney. Nevertheless, in relation to the potential development of a black male feminism, I am troubled by what appears to be a surprisingly explicit determination to protect turf. In their unwillingness to grant that exploration of how Afro-American males are delineated by contemporary black female novelists is a legitimate concern that might produce illuminating analyses, McDowell's formulations echo in unfortunate ways those of antifeminist male critics, white and black, who consider feminism to be an unredeemably myopic and unyielding interpretive strategy incapable of offering subtle readings of canonical, largely male-authored texts. Despite the circulation of reprehensibly masculinist responses to Afro-American women's literature, black feminist literary critics do not best serve the discourses that concern them by setting into motion homeostatic maneuvers intended to devalue all forms of inquiry except for those they hold to be most valuable (in this particular case, a female-authored scholarship that emphasizes Afro-American women's writings of black female subjectivity). If the Afro-American women's literary project is indeed "immensely complex and diverse," as McDowell claims, bringing to bear other angles of vision, including antipatriarchal male ones, can assist in analyzing aspects of that complexity.

While the views of Staples and others are clearly problematic, those problems do not arise specifically from their efforts to place males "at the center of critical inquiry" any more than feminism is implicitly flawed because it insists, in some of its manifestations, on a gynocritical foregrounding of representations of women.

Rather, these problems appear to result from the fact that the particular readers who produce these perspectives do not seem sufficiently to be, in Toril Moi's titular phrase, "men against patriarchy."[20] Certainly, in an age when both gender studies and Afro-American women's literature have achieved a degree of legitimacy within the academy and outside of it, it is unreasonable for black women either to demand that black men not be concerned with the ways in which they are depicted by Afro-American women writers, or to see that concern as intrinsically troubling in feminist terms. If female feminist calls for a non-mimicking male feminism are indeed persuasive, then black men will have very little of substance to say about contemporary Afro-American women's literature, especially if we are also to consider as transgressive any attention to figurations of black manhood. It seems to me that the most black females in feminism can insist upon in this regard is that examinations which focus on male characters treat the complexity of contemporary Afro-American women novelists' delineations of black manhood with an antipatriarchal seriousness which the essays McDowell cites clearly lack.

From my perspective, what is potentially most valuable about the development of a black male feminism is not its capacity to reproduce black feminism as practiced by black females who focus primarily on "the complexities of black female subjectivity and experience."[21] Rather, its potential value lies in the possibility that, in being antipatriarchal and as self-inquiring about their relationship(s) to feminism as Afro-American women have been, black men can expand the range and utilization of feminist inquiry and explore other fruitful applications for feminist perspectives, including such topics as obstacles to a black male feminist project itself and new figurations of "family matters" and black male sexuality.

For the purpose of theorizing about a black male feminism, perhaps the most provocative, enlightening, and inviting moment in feminist or in "womanist" scholarship occurs in Hortense Spillers's "Mama's Baby, Papa's Maybe: An American Grammar Book." Indeed, Spillers's essay represents a fruitful starting point for new, potentially nonpatriarchal figurations of family and of black males' relationship to the female. Toward the end of this illuminating theoretical text, which concerns itself with slavery's debilitating effects on the Afro-American family's constitution, Spillers envisions black male identity formation as a process whose movement toward successful resolution seems to require a serious engagement of black feminist principles and perspectives. Spillers asserts that as a result of those specific familial patterns which functioned during American slavery and beyond and "removed the African-American male not so much from sight as from *mimetic* view as a partner in the prevailing social fiction of the Father's name, the Father's law," the African-American male "has been touched . . . by the *mother, handed* by her in ways that he cannot escape." Because of separation from traditional American paternal name and law, "the black American male embodies the *only* American community of males which has had the specific occasion to learn *who* the female is within itself. . . . It is the heritage of the *mother* that the African-American male must regain as an aspect of his own personhood—the power of 'yes' to the 'female' within."[22]

Rather than seeing the "female" strictly as other for the Afro-American male, Spillers's afrocentric revisioning of psychoanalytic theory insists that we consider it an important aspect of the repressed in the black male self.[23] Employing Spillers's analyses as a starting point, we might regard Afro-American males' potential "in-ness" vis-à-vis feminism not, as Paul Smith insists in *Men in Feminism,* as a representation of male heterosexual desires to penetrate and violate female spaces[24] but rather as an acknowledgment of what Spillers considers the distinctive nature of the Afro-American male's connection to the "female." If Afro-American males are ever to have anything to say about or to black feminism beyond the types of reflex-action devaluations and diatribes about divisiveness that critics such as McDowell and Valerie Smith rightly decry, the investigative process of which womanist acts by Spillers and Williams speak is indispensable. Such a process, if pursued in an intellectually rigorous manner, offers a means by which black men can participate usefully in and contribute productively to the black feminist project.

Black womanism demands neither the erasure of the black gendered other's subjectivity, as have male movements to regain a putatively lost Afro-American manhood, nor the relegation of males to prone, domestic, or other limiting positions. What it does require, if it is indeed to become an ideology with widespread cultural impact, is a recognition on the part of both black females and males of the nature of the gendered inequities that have marked our past and present, and a resolute commitment to work for change. In that sense, black feminist criticism has not only created a space for an informed Afro-American male participation, but it heartily welcomes—in fact, insists upon—the joint participation of black males and females as *comrades,* to invoke, with a difference, this paper's epigraphic reference to *Sula.*

Reading "Mama's Baby, Papa's Maybe" was of special importance to me in part because it helped me to clarify and articulate my belief that my relationship to feminism need not mark me necessarily as a debilitatingly split subject. The source of that relationship can only be traced autobiographically, if at all. Having been raised by a mother who, like too many women of too many generations, was the victim of male physical and psychological brutality—a brutality which, according to my mother, resulted in large part from my father's frustrations about his inability to partake in what Spillers calls masculinity's "prevailing social fiction"—my earliest stories, my familial narratives, as it were, figured "maleness" in quite troubling terms. My mother told me horrific stories, one of which I was, in a sense, immediately involved in: my father—who left us before I was one year old and whom I never knew—kicked her in the stomach when my fetal presence swelled her body, because he believed she'd been unfaithful to him and that I was only "maybe" his baby.

As a youth, I pondered this and other such stories often and deeply, in part because of the pain I knew these incidents caused my mother, in part because, as someone without a consistent male familial role model, I actively sought a way to achieve a gendered self-definition. As one for whom maleness as manifested in the surrounding inner city culture seemed to be represented only by violence, familial abandonment, and the certainty of imprisonment, I found that I was able to define myself with regard to my gender primarily in oppositional ways. I had internalized the cautionary intent of my mother's narratives, which also served as her dearest wish for me: that I not grow up to be like my father, that I not adopt the definitions of "maleness" represented by his example and in the culture generally. Because the scars of male brutality were visibly etched—literally marked, as it were—on my mother's flesh and on her psyche, "maleness," as figured both in her stories and in my environment, seemed to me not to be a viable mimetic option. I grew up, then, not always sure of what or who I was with respect to prevailing social definitions of gender but generally quite painfully aware of what I could not become.

In order to begin to understand who my mother was, perhaps also who my father was, what "maleness" was and what extra-biological relationship I could hope to have to it, I needed answers that my mother was unable to provide. I found little of value in the black masculinist discourse of the time, which spoke endlessly of the dehumanization and castration of the Afro-American male by white men and black women—our central social narrative for too long—for this rhetoric seemed simplistic and unself-consciously concerned with justifying domestic violence and other forms of black male brutality.

Afro-American women's literature, to which I was introduced along with black feminism in 1977 as a sophomore at Brandeis University, helped me move toward a comprehension of the world, of aspects of my mother's life, and of what a man against patriarchy could be and do. These discourses provided me with answers, nowhere else available, to what had been largely unresolvable mysteries. I work within the paradigm of black feminist literary criticism because it explains elements of the world about which I care most deeply. I write and read what and as I do because I am incapable of escaping the meanings of my mother's narratives for my own life, because the pain and, in the fact of their enunciation to the next generation, the sense of hope for better days that characterizes these familial texts are illuminatingly explored in many narratives by black women. Afro-American women's literature has given me parts of myself that—incapable of a (biological) "fatherly reprieve"—I would not otherwise have had.

I have decided that it is ultimately irrelevant whether these autobiographical facts, which, of course, are not, and can never be, the whole story, are deemed by others sufficient to permit me to call myself "feminist." Like Toril Moi, I have come to believe that "the important thing for men is not to spend their time worrying about definitions and essences ('am I *really* a feminist?'), but to take up a recognizable anti-patriarchal position."[25] What is most important to me is that my work contribute, in however small a way, to the project whose goal is the dismantling of the phallocentric rule by which black females and, I am sure, countless other Afro-American sons have been injuriously "touched."

My indebtedness to Spillers's and other womanist perspectives is, then, great indeed, as is my sense of their potential as illuminating moments for a newborn—or not-yet-born—black male feminist discourse. But to utilize these perspectives requires that we be more inquiring than Spillers is in her formulations, not in envisioning liberating possibilities of an acknowledgment of the "female" within the black community and the male subject, but in noting potential dangers inherent in such an attempted adoption by historically brutalized Afro-American men whose relationship to a repressed "female" is not painstakingly (re)defined.

Clearly, more thinking is necessary not only about what the female within is but about what it can be said to represent for black males, as well as serious analysis of useful means and methods of interacting with a repressed female interiority and subject. Spillers's theorizing does not perform this task, in part because it has other, more compelling interests and emphases—among which is the righting/(re)writing of definitions of "woman" so that they will reflect Afro-American women's particular, historically conditioned "female social subject" status—but a black male feminism must be especially focused on exploring such issues if it is to mobilize Spillers's suggestive remarks as a means of developing a fuller understanding of the complex formulations of black manhood found in many texts and contexts, including Afro-American women's narratives.

I want to build briefly on Spillers's provocative theorizing about the Afro-American male's maturational process and situation on American shores. To this end, I will look at an illuminating moment in Toni Morrison's *Sula,* a text that is, to my mind, not only an unparalleled Afro-American woman's writing of the complexities of black female subjectivity and experience but also of black males' relationship to the female within as a consequence of their limited access to "the prevailing social fiction" of masculinity. In this novel, the difficulty of negotiating the spaces between black male lack and black female presence is plainly manifested in such figures as the undifferentiatable deweys; BoyBoy, whose name, in contrast to most of the authorial designations in *Sula,* speaks unambiguously for him; and Jude, whose difficulty in assuming the mantle of male provider leads him to view his union with Nel as that which "would make one Jude."[26]

The response of Plum, the most tragic of *Sula's* unsuccessful negotiators of the so-called white man's world, vividly represents for me some of the contemporary dangers of black male "in-ness" vis-à-vis the "female." Despite a childhood which included "float[ing] in a constant swaddle of love and affection" and his mother's intention to follow the Father's law by bequeathing "everything" to him (38), Plum appears incapable of embracing hegemonic notions of masculinity. Instead, he returns from World War I spiritually fractured but, unlike a similarly devastated Shadrack, lacking the imaginative wherewithal to begin to theorize or ritualize a new relationship to his world. He turns to drugs as a method of anesthetizing himself from the horrors of his devastation and, in his mother's view, seeks to compel her resumption of familiar/familial patterns of caretaking. In the following passage, Eva explains to Hannah her perception of Plum's desires, as well as the motivation for her participation in what amounts to an act of infanticide:

> When he came back from that war he wanted to git back in. After all that carryin' on, just gettin' him out and keepin' him alive, he wanted to crawl back in my womb and well . . . I ain't got the room no more even if he could do it. There wasn't space for him in my womb. And he was crawlin' back. Being helpless and thinking baby thoughts and dreaming baby dreams and messing up his pants again and smiling all the time. I had room enough in my heart, but not in my womb, got no more. I birthed him once. I couldn't do it again. He was growed, a big old thing. Godhavemercy, I couldn't birth him twice. . . . A big man can't be a baby all wrapped up inside his mamma no more; he suffocate. I done everything I could to make him leave me and go on and live and be a man but he wouldn't and I had to keep him out so I just thought of a way he could die like a man not all scrunched up inside my womb, but like a man. (62)[27]

What is significant about this passage for an analysis of the possibilities of a non-oppressive black male relationship to feminism—to female experience characterized by a refusal to be subjugated to androcentric desires—is its suggestiveness for our understanding of the obstacles to a revised male view of the repressed "female," obstacles which result in large part from black males' relative social powerlessness. If black feminism is persuasive in its analysis of the limitations of Afro-American masculinist ideology, emphasizing as it does achievement of black manhood at the expense of black female subjectivity, and if we can best describe an overwhelming number of Africa's American male descendants as males-in-crisis, the question a black male feminism must ask itself is, On what basis, according to what ideological perspective, can an Afro-American heterosexual male ground his notions of the female? Beyond its heterosexual dimension, can the "female" truly come to represent for a traditional black male-in-crisis more than a protective maternal womb from which he seeks to be "birthed" again? Can it serve as more than a site on which to find relief from or locate frustrations caused by an inability to achieve putatively normative American male socioeconomic status? If embracing normative masculinity requires an escape from the protection and life-sustaining aspects symbolized by maternal umbilical cords and apron strings and an achievement of an economic situation wherein the male provides domestic space and material sustenance for his dependents (including "his woman"), black manhood generally is, like Plum, in desperate trouble. And if, as has often been the case, a black female can be seen by an Afro-American male-in-crisis only if she has been emptied of subjectivity and selfhood, if she becomes visible for the male only when she is subsumed by male desire(s), then the types of refiguration and redefinition of black male subjectivity and engagement with the "female" central to Spillers's formulations are highly unlikely.

This question of seeing and not seeing, of the male gaze's erasure and re-creation of the female, is crucial to *Sula*'s general thematics. It seems to me that in all of her novels Morrison's figuration of black female subjectivity is largely incomprehensible without some serious attention both to her representation of black manhood and to her exploration of the relationships between socially constructed gendered (and racial) positions. To return explicitly to the case of Eva: What Eva fears, what appears to be a self-interested motivation for her killing of her intended male heir, is that Plum's pitiful, infantile state has the potential to reduce *her* to a static female function of self-sacrificing mother, which, according to Bottom legend, had already provoked her decision to lose a leg in order to collect insurance money with which to provide for her children. Having personally lost so much already, Eva chooses, instead of sacrificing other essential parts of her self, to take the life of her self-described male heir. And if Plum dies "like a man" in Eva's estimation, his achievement of manhood has nothing to do with an assumption of traditional masculine traits, nothing to do with strength, courage, and a refusal to cry in the face of death. Instead, that achievement results from Eva's creation of conditions that have become essential components of her definition of manhood: death forces him to "leave" her and to "keep . . . out" of her womb. It would appear that manhood is defined here not as presence as typically represented in Western thought, but—by and for Eva at least—as liberating (domestic and uterine) absence.

One of the intentions of this chapter is to suggest that feminism represents a fruitful and potentially not oppressive means of reconceptualizing, of figuratively birthing twice, the black male subject. But, as a close reading of the aforementioned passage from *Sula* suggests, interactions between men and women motivated by male self-interest such as necessarily characterizes an aspect of male participation in feminism are fraught with possible dangers for the biological/ideological female body of an enactment of or a capitulation to hegemonic male power. Indeed, if it is the case that, as Spillers has argued in another context, "the woman who stays in man's company keeps alive the possibility of having, one day, an unwanted guest, or the guest, deciding 'to hump the hostess,' whose intentions turn homicidal," then male proximity to feminism generally creates the threat of a specifically masculinist violation.[28] If, as I noted earlier, the dangers of a hegemonic, heterosexual Euro-American male's "in-ness" vis-à-vis feminism include (sexualized) penetration and domination, then those associated with a heterosexual black male's interactions with the ideological female body are at least doubled, and potentially involve an envisioning of the black female body as self-sacrificingly maternal or self-sacrificingly sexual. Because of a general lack of access to the full force of hegemonic male power, Afro-American men could see in increasingly influential black female texts not only serious challenges to black male fictions of the self but also an appropriate location for masculine desires for control of the types of valuable resources that the discourses of black womanhood currently represent.

But a rigorous, conscientious black male feminism need not give in to traditional patriarchal desires for control and erasure of the female. To be of any sustained value to the feminist project, a discourse must provide illuminating and persuasive readings of gender as it is constituted for blacks in America and sophisticated, informed, contentious critiques of phallocentric practices in an effort to redefine our notions of black male and female textuality and subjectivity. And in its differences from black feminist texts that are produced by individual Afro-American women, a black male feminism must be both rigorous in engaging these texts and self-reflective enough to avoid, at all costs, the types of patronizing, marginalizing gestures that have traditionally characterized Afro-American male intellectuals' response to black womanhood. What a black male feminism must strive for, above all else, is to envision and enact the possibilities signaled by the differences feminism has exposed and created. In black feminist criticism, being an Afro-American male does not mean attempting to invade an/other political body like a lascivious soul snatcher or striving to erase its essence in order to replace it with one's own myth of what the discourse should be. Such a position for black men means, above all else, an acknowledgment and celebration of the incontrovertible fact that "the Father's law" is no longer the only law of the land.

I searched for an opening, a way to enter the world of the Negro, some contact perhaps. As yet, it was a blank to me. My greatest preoccupation was that moment of transition where I would "pass over." Where and how would I do it. To get from the white world into the Negro world is a complex matter.

John Howard Griffin, *Black Like Me*

The glass through which black life is viewed by white Americans is, inescapably, . . . befogged by the hot breath of history. True "objectivity" where race is concerned is as rare as a necklace of Hope diamonds.

Hoyt Fuller, "Towards a Black Aesthetic"

3

Negotiations of Power: White Critics, Black Texts, and the Self-Referential Impulse

In the heyday of the Black Aesthetic, many of its theorists believed that there existed an "irreconcilable conflict between the black writer and the white critic."[1] Afro-Americanist cultural criticism generally has remained unwilling to theorize about or examine in any depth the interpretive effects of racial difference on white-authored analyses of black literary texts. Unlike American feminist criticism, whose energetic articulation of its positions on males' participation in feminism has made the issue a topic of serious discussion within the literary academy, Afro-Americanist scholarship has allowed the possible consequences of a socially privileged whiteness to become, in Toni Morrison's phrase, one of the discourse's "unspeakable things unspoken."[2]

The general impression that might be gained from this silence is that race—in this case, whiteness—has come to possess little or no significance in black textual analysis. But if gender and race as we have traditionally perceived them are both by and large socially constructed, then whiteness as dominant position in the Western racial hierarchy is potentially as formidable an obstacle to interpretive competence vis-à-vis black texts and contexts as maleness is to persuasive feminist exegesis. As a black male scholar who has learned to be more conscientious in my own critical practice as a consequence of debates about possible nonpatriarchal places for males within feminist discourse, I feel that novice white scholars attracted to Afro-American literature might similarly profit from extended investigations of questions of race and textual reading. Even at the close of the twentieth century when Afro-American literature has achieved an unprecedented canonical presence, race may still matter in a white critic's investigation of black expressivity. I believe that black literary studies can examine interpretive consequences of racial otherness without necessarily resorting to, or being unfairly accused of, xenophobic paranoia.

Interestingly, to begin to discuss this issue, it is most profitable to look at what white critics themselves have said about the effect of racial difference on their interpretations of Afro-American cultural materials. In fact, there is a growing body of analyses, several examples of which I will concentrate on below, in which white critics, rather than attempting to adopt either a black, racially neutral, or objective reading position, use the occasion of an analysis of Afro-American texts to discuss their own racial positionality's effects upon the process of interpretation. Lacking the more easily available means of locating the texts of racial others that the male signature provides for feminist inquiry, the afrocentric project benefits from the appearance of such analyses in part because, in addition to offering self-reflexive investigations of the implications of their authors' race, these texts provide an occasion for non-essentializing discussions of relationships between whiteness and reading.

My goal here is not to judge the exegetical benefits of biologically or experientially motivated investment—I am not asserting, nor do I believe, that the possession of a black physicality is necessary for the creation of engaging and provocative critical texts on Afro-American literature—but rather to examine some of the differences race can make in the interpretation of black texts. I believe we must concede that a white critic is differently invested in Afro-American texts than a black critic because of what Sue-Ellen Case terms "racial privilege," which is characterized by a lack of "experience of racial oppression."[3] This chapter's primary intent is not to erect racial boundaries around Afro-Americanist discourse, but to insist that when there are manifest consequences of "racial privilege" in white-authored analyses which are not consonant with what might be perceived from a variety of vantage points as the interests of the discourse, it is the responsibility of Afro-Americanist scholars to examine and expose these consequences. Even in self-reflexive white critical acts, racial privilege may create interpretive obstacles or, more important, points of resistance that color, in racially motivated ways, the effects of an exploration of blackness. In other words, white reading can mean the adoption of a posture that can be demonstrated to be antithetical to black interests.

Before considering self-referential acts of white reading, I want to emphasize my belief that neither a view of an essential incompatibility between black literature and white critics nor of whites as always already dismissive and unsophisticated in their analyses of the products of the Afro-American imagination is still tenable. Indeed, the last two decades have witnessed the production by such figures as William Andrews, Kimberly Benston, Robert Hemenway, and Jean Yellin of exemplary instances of what Afro-American critic Larry Neal refers to as "a welcome criticism." Neal uses this phrase during a 1974 interview to describe interpretive acts by whites that reflect "some understanding of [black] cultural source and . . . of the development of a critique that allows you to discuss your

[Afro-American] literature and to move it forward, to a higher level . . . , a more serious level on its own terms . . . , on terms that are fresh, that are new."[4]

While he acknowledges that the white critic has often approached Afro-American literature with "the glib assumption that he can come to the culture without taking the culture seriously enough to study the sources from which this literature springs" (22), Neal rejects the notion that whiteness necessarily presents an insurmountable obstacle to critical competence where the black text is concerned. To assume that whites cannot learn to read Afro-American literature in an informed manner because of the many acts of white critical pontification that display an observable ignorance of black culture is, for Neal, to "*a priori* condemn a white critic before I see what he has written" (23). According to Neal, the sign of critical competence lies not in the race or face of the critic but rather in the work he or she produces. Noting the existence of both persuasive, informed, white-authored criticism and fatally misinformed black analyses of Afro-American expressivity, Neal offers his view of how critical competence is generally achieved and how it must be measured in evaluations of analyses of Afro-American literature: "Doing the work means you know something. It means you have your skills, it means you have your resources, it means you know what's being written and being published and being studied about certain subjects and you come to it. It also means you have some style. It means you're informed. Now as far as I know, you get these things by studying" (25).

For Neal, critical competence with respect to Afro-American expressivity is determined not by tribal connections into which one is born; rather, it is gained by academic activity—"by studying"—in the same way that one achieves comprehension of the cultural matrices that inform the work of writers like Joyce, Yeats, and e. e. cummings. Demystifying the process of acquiring an informed knowledge of Afro-American expressivity, Neal insists that the means of access for all critics, regardless of race, is an energetic investigation of the cultural situation and the emerging critical tradition.

According to Neal, the emergence of a body of challenging and highly informed black-authored interpretive acts will inspire a sounder white critical practice:

> Instead of having the white critic get out of his area, the black critic is supposed to take upon himself the job of writing strong criticism and establishing the pace. When the white critic goes to discuss black literature—if there's a high standard laid out there for him—he'll have to meet that standard. The reason there's been such poor criticism by white critics about black literature is that there hasn't been a good standard laid out there. (24)

Part of the leadership role Neal envisions for Afro-American scholars is censuring "obnoxious white critics" who approach Afro-American texts without a requisite "sympathy for the culture" (24). But, more important, Neal advocates the development of a creative, conceptually and theoretically challenging Afro-American literary criticism that will respond in sophisticated ways to what he regards as an aesthetically and intellectually challenging body of texts.

While it is clear that Neal's "welcome [white] criticism" is now being produced in part as a result of the emergence of a theoretically sophisticated body of black critical texts, white-authored interpretive acts continue to be produced which, for a variety of reasons, might be said to be causes for concern for Afro-American critics, even when their authors adopt racially self-reflective postures. The following sections will demonstrate some of the illuminating possibilities and problems of white critical self-reflexivity. Where the problems are concerned, I want to show that these texts are flawed in large part as the result of the trajectory of their participation in turf or race wars; these essays are, in other words, resistant responses of white critics to the formulations and the very fact of black critical leadership itself.

While most of the texts explored in this chapter were written after 1980, two extended self-reflexive discussions of the place of whites in the analysis of Afro-American literature were published between 1965 and 1970, the period that witnessed the production of the most influential Black Aesthetic perspectives. These two texts, David Littlejohn's *Black on White: A Critical Survey of Writing by American Negroes* (1966) and Catharine Stimpson's "Black Culture/White Teacher" (1970), both theorize about the nature of white readerly engagement with black literary texts, although from wildly divergent directions and with diametrically opposed conclusions.[5] While Littlejohn holds that such reading constitutes an especially painful experience for whites, he asserts that white engagement with Afro-American literature must constitute a self-interested attempt to develop an understanding of the black situation in America. Conversely, Stimpson, less convinced that whites allow themselves to become sufficiently involved in black-authored texts either to feel pain or to test the accuracy of their preconceptions about Afro-American life, argues that members of her race ought to get out of the business altogether of offering pronouncements about the aesthetic complexity, thematic sophistication, or discursive power of black literary texts.

Littlejohn's introduction to *Black on White* offers what is essentially a theory of white readers' engagement with Afro-American literature, one expressly intended as a method of resistance—what we might call, following Michel Foucault, a "strategy of struggle"—to the designs of black texts.[6] Accepting Black

Aesthetician foregroundings of a more self-consciously militant and thematically transgressive art as an accurate means by which to characterize the entire literary tradition, Littlejohn regards Afro-American texts as "high explosives, racial text-books, and not [as] *objets d'art,*" only a few of which may have been "written specifically for other Negroes" (16). Consequently, Littlejohn argues that white readers—the primary audience of this literature in his view—need to develop interpretive strategies which allow them to respond effectively to these military acts and to protect themselves from the guilt and pain that result as a necessary consequence of interactions with black literature. In fact, Littlejohn characterizes Afro-American texts in terms of national practices of self-protection from or in response to intraterritorial and interterritorial transgressive behavior; according to him, black texts "convey heavily to a white reader the sense of the 'prison' of the debasing life sentence that being a Negro can mean in America" (3–4), and represent preliminary artillery strikes in a "still . . . undeclared race war in which all Americans are, by definition, involved" (4).

What for Littlejohn distinguishes Afro-American literature from more aesthetically compelling texts—from great works of Western literature—is not its production of pain in the engaged reader but rather its refusal or inability to provide the (white) reader with a means of assimilating and usefully transforming that pain. "Now a great deal of literature will give pain, will disconcert and unbalance—momentarily. But as the product of integrated imaginations, more or less at peace, it will provide the reader with a means of digesting the pain, of attaining a new and better balance. . . . The pain in most Negro literature of the American race war, however, remains solid and undigestable. It juts up, it rankles, it rubs raw like an ulcer. As it is meant to" (4). For Littlejohn, the artlessness of black literature results from a lack in the Afro-American imagination—its non-"integrated" nature—that has made the creation of a sophisticated Afro-American art virtually impossible. Extending his arsenal of war imagery, Littlejohn insists that black writers have been infinitely more concerned with minor artillery strikes than with the more important task of creating major works of art:

> Writing is one way of getting back at the enemy. The Negro's satisfaction will be doubled, of course, if his foolish white reader can be made to pay for and to praise the materials of his own discomfort. . . .
>
> Such works are designed, with more or less open intent . . . , to assert the moral superiority of the oppressed, and to force the unoppressed to grovel in guilt and fear. . . .
>
> From his supposedly comfortable position, the white reader, however pure of heart, may find it absurdly difficult to ward off the blow, to say no to the Joneses and Baldwins. He is forced, in a marvelous turnabout of tradi-

tional roles, to assume ridiculous poses and postures. Typically . . . he relinquishes moral and critical clarity in the anxious effort to jump on some pro-Negro bandwagon he has made. He may even (as in Norman Mailer's "The White Negro") plead that he is really, at heart, a Negro himself. The contemplation of such moral contortions must provide Negro observers with at least partial revenge. (4–6)

Rather than allowing white readers to continue to experience such moral or spiritual "contortions," Littlejohn composes his own "racial textbook"—a survival guide for white readers of Afro-American literature. Instead of succumbing to what he considers the sadistic designs of vengeful black writers, instead of accepting their assertions of moral superiority and the concomitant guilt and pain, Littlejohn instructs fellow white sufferers to read Afro-American literature in a strategically self-interested way. They should not attempt to identify with the Afro-American experience as delineated in black literary texts, where the white reader, trying to put himself in the skin of the black American, experiences an immediate "shudder of gratitude that he is not" black (14). Nor should they internalize potentially self-destructive guilt in response to centuries of white mistreatment of Afro-Americans. Rather, his fellow white foot-soldiers ought to read black literature with the purpose of gaining a better tactical understanding of the enemy:

> The creative writing of American Negroes *can* begin to lead outsiders to an understanding of "what Negroes are like." It will never make a Negro of one born white. However vivid the experience of reading, a white reader will always retreat into his profitable whiteness when the reading is done. Still, the good book, the powerful poem *will* change the reader somehow; he will carry away some portion of Negro experience, now made a part of his own.
>
> And the truths will not be simply learned, as from interviews or sociological texts, but coexperienced, borne "alive into the heart with passion." Here is reason enough for reading this disturbing collection. If it turns out as well to be good, if purely literary, extraracial benefits accrue in the meanwhile, of course so much the better. (15)

While this passage seems to indicate Littlejohn's sense of the possibility of an empathetic white reading of Afro-American literature, what it offers is in actuality little more than justification for white readers' resistance to any significant socially or personally motivated change whatsoever.[7] Imagining an ignorant but essentially benign white reader/soldier not prone to engaging in racist behavior,

Littlejohn instructs this figure to explore Afro-American literature strictly as a means of "self-examination."

What becomes clear from the body of Littlejohn's study—his cursory, hesitant survey of Afro-American literature published before 1965—is his own energetic employment of the strategy of struggle he articulates for other white readers, his own racially motivated resistance to and general antipathy toward Afro-American literature.[8] Clearly, we should not expect a sensitive and cogent analysis of the Afro-American literary project from a critic as poorly informed (and proudly uninformed) about that project as Littlejohn, who, for example, admits with no self-consciousness that "I had not heard of [Paul Laurence Dunbar] until last year" (67) and who argues that the prominence of black autobiographical works within the tradition reflects a "locked-in-the-self imprisonment [which] suggests that, for most American Negroes, the day of artistic objectivity and detachment has not yet arrived" (167). Imagining, despite indisputable evidence to the contrary, an American "race war" in which whites and blacks are "equal adversaries" (66), Littlejohn's goal is to fortify the white American flank. In response to what he perceives as artillery strikes from an equally well-armed troop of Afro-American writers against white forces within the society, Littlejohn responds with strategically placed volleys of his own. While his strikes against black adversaries take the form of statements such as "Gwendolyn Brooks is . . . far more a poet than a Negro" (89) and "There is something very dutiful and serious about the work of all three [Zora Hurston, George Wylie Henderson, and William Attaway], and I suspect the writing of them to have been as joyless as the reading" (64), he also attempts to encourage similar acts of resistance in whites who seem to him too sympathetic to Afro-American fictive and social constructions, too responsive to insistent black calls for power.

Finally, what Littlejohn considers as most problematic about Afro-American literary texts is their inability to provide the white reader with the only important information that such texts really hold during a national race war: what it is like to be black. Despite his admission that "there is, obviously, no 'Negro experience' in America" (157), his goal of acquiring "a good deal of inside information about Negro life" (159) apparently minimizes the import of insights concerning the lack of a monolithic black subjectivity. Littlejohn's study concludes, even after its positive assessments of the works of Ralph Ellison, Ann Petry, and Langston Hughes, that "we wait, still, for a Negro writer who can tell us, truly, what it is like to be a Negro" (170), for "no Negro yet has achieved sufficient stability and content to write fully and comfortably of Negro life" (169). While Ellison's work suggests that he has "come of this stage of self-acceptance [and] self-contentment" necessary, in Littlejohn's estimation, for the creation of great Afro-

American art, Ellison's "protest [that he is not maladjusted, self-hating, or devoid of race pride] is so exceptional that one tends (unfairly) to doubt" (169).

Black on White, a self-admitted text of white warfare, needs simplistic, self-hating Afro-Americans, needs the lesser achievements of black writers in order to provide ammunition for its purportedly beseiged ideal white readers in a changing racial climate whose real-world complexities appear to be of little concern to its author. Littlejohn imagines black adversaries significantly more powerful than they actually are, damns even the most compelling of his foes' literary acts with faint and often self-contradictory praise, arguing, for instance, both that Jean Toomer's *Cane* "should really be allowed to come back into print" and that "the book, finally . . . , is too insubstantial to be remembered" (60), and in essence dismissing the literary achievements of an entire race. Further, his perspectives on what constitute a successful black writer creates for Afro-Americans an untenable position of striving to tell the truth of blackness when there is no single, unitary truth to tell. To fail in this regard is to be condemned always to the status of psychically unhealthy nonartist. And to succeed is to separate one's self utterly from one's maladjusted race and, in addition, to encourage doubts about the extent to which you are indeed engaged in truth-telling. Surely it is not unproblematic to leave assessments about the truth-value of black literary utterances in the hands of the white warrior-critic.

If *Black on White* represents one white critic's self-interested resistance to the movement for racial justice in American society represented by the 1960s, Stimpson's "Black Culture/White Teacher" is a text that welcomes these changes in part because of their potential both to revise Afro-American literary history in constructive ways and to provide more informed analyses of that body of texts. A response to a history of pejorative and dismissive white critical acts like Littlejohn's, "Black Culture/White Teacher" is as skeptical as many Black Aesthetician writings about white interpretive competence vis-à-vis black texts. Some opening sentences of this essay—an essay which, among other things, describes Stimpson's own difficulties as a white teacher of Afro-American literature during the period of awakened black consciousness in the 1960s—clearly express the source of her skepticism: "Most white people misread black literature, if they read it at all. Their critical twistings are still another symptom of the dominant attitude toward black people and black culture in America. The white ego insists upon control. Not only do white readers demand that black literature satisfy their needs and notions, but they read it according to them" (1).

For Stimpson, Afro-American literature serves many white readers as an arena in which, as in *Invisible Man's* battle royal episode, whites manipulate black behavior in order to discover evidence for their preconceptions concerning Afro-

American inferiority. And while in Stimpson's estimation there are other reasons for white interest in Afro-American literature—"to earn credit from a would-be revolutionary future," to experience vicariously "a 'primitive' energy lost or missing from their own lives," "evidence that an alien culture supports the ideas and values of the dominant culture" (1)—exchanges between white readers and black texts cannot escape the dialectics of race that have colored the history of Africa's descendants in Western society.

Despite these somewhat varied interests, Stimpson believes that it is possible to theorize about a general white reader. According to Stimpson, "white readers of black literature have a good deal in common. The pressure of the past, fear, and vanity make them like protest fiction, which, no matter how grim or didactic, appeals to them. It says that to be black is to be miserable: being black is worse than being white. Protest fiction massages guilt" (2). As a consequence of desires for "control" and confirmation of feelings of racial superiority that are inescapable in white encounters with black texts, Stimpson—whose own interest in Afro-American literature led her to teach a course entitled "Books and the Black Experience of America" and fuels her intention "to keep reading black literature"—calls for at least a temporary abandonment by white critics of the area of Afro-American literature: "White people at the moment have neither the intellectual skill nor the emotional clarity nor the moral authority to lead the pursuit of black studies. Race, to the dismay of many, to the relief of others, has become a proper test for deciding who is best at certain intellectual, as well as political, activities, and teaching black literature is one of them" (2). Insisting that "we already had enough formal, impersonal white authorities on black literature" in print (7), Stimpson believes that whites' "biases, like rodents on the ropes between ship and pier, run up and down their statements about value" with regard to Afro-American texts (6).

Stimpson observes a need for two different theoretical projects before whites can learn to read black literature "accurately": the development of "a new, practical, literary theory for white people" that would both expose and suggest ways of overcoming white critical biases (2); and the creation of a "vocabulary . . . to describe black literature . . . , a body of theory, one which is neither adventitious nor malign, that might give order to [black literature's] contradictions and subtleties and flux" (7). Where the latter project is concerned, Stimpson calls for the development of strategies of reading derived, it would seem, from Afro-American expressive cultural practices, for methodologies that encourage an informed examination of what we might call, using Richard Wright's term, "the forms of things unknown" in black expressivity. This theoretical project—which had begun to develop in the form of the Black Aesthetic when Stimpson published her essay—is the responsibility of black critics knowledgeable about black culture, for the participation of such critics in that culture provides them with an interpretive competence with respect to black texts that white critics generally lack. And white readers, whose egos predispose them to value cognitive superiority and control over the discourse of blackness, "must also accept black authority of interpretation" (7).

While its generalizations about white and black interpretive behavior are, in several respects, debatable, "Black Culture / White Teacher" is a novel text in part because of its insistence that whites transfer institutional control of the criticism of Afro-American literature to blacks. I find Stimpson's essay particularly striking because her gesture is made despite her manifestation of perspectives sufficiently informed by afrocentric principles to provide a compelling account of the history of white reading of Afro-American literature. Note, for example, Stimpson's examination of white patron William Dean Howells's evaluation of Paul Laurence Dunbar's poetry:

> Many of Howells's phrases, such as "our tongue," are beguiling. Big Massa will bless Emerging Talent, if the price is right. Howells was perhaps the first to make a black writer a "vogue," to borrow a term from Langston Hughes. Ironically, some of the most insidious harm white readers have done to black literature has been through excessive praise of one person. Nearly every decade has had one (and rarely more than one) house nigger in the library of art. To him all praises flow. *Look,* white readers say, *that boy sure can write.* (5)

In her discussion of the white critical establishment's habitual privileging of a single Afro-American writer and her sense of the racism inherent in Howells's equation of whiteness and Standard English, Stimpson demonstrates a comprehension of essential features of Afro-American literary history. But her strategy of white self-denial—her insistence on white marginality within Afro-American literary studies despite a demonstrated comprehension of issues important to her vision of a black theoretical project—is meant to suggest that until the motivations for white participation in the criticism of Afro-American literary texts can be thoroughly investigated and adequately theorized, white participation—regardless of the extent of the white critic's comprehension of the cultural contexts out of which Afro-American literature springs—cannot escape the possibilities and accusations of racial self-interest. Because the conditions of racism have influenced both white discourse about black texts and the possibilities of developing an afrocentric black-authored discourse, white critics should feel a moral obligation to cease participating in the analysis of Afro-American literature so as to bring to a close racist and dictatorial white control over its explication and evaluation.

Clearly, knowledge of the formulations of such esteemed Afro-American writers as James Baldwin, Richard Wright, and Ralph Ellison, of black expressive practices such as call and response, of the complicated structures of address in Afro-American literature, is not enough for Stimpson. In her view of the interpretive process, race is everything, not because whites ultimately cannot learn to read black texts, but because "white people, if they read black literature properly, must eventually rebel against their own world, the world which the books reveal: to do nothing but read is to be evasive, to do nothing but speak is to be unspeakable. The end of theory is the call to practice" (10). Stimpson's form of rebellion, her move from theory to practice, is represented by her willingness to act on her recognition that social change requires the redistribution of power. Her essay demands an end to white theorizing about black expressive culture as a consequence of its author's sense of the harm whites had done and continued to do to this project. Further, Stimpson's position reflects her understanding of the difficulties an emerging afrocentric criticism would encounter in competition with privileged white voices, and faith in the evaluative complexity and insight Afro-Americans could and had begun to bring to bear in explications of their own culture. Hers is an essay that, while as essentially concerned with the question of power as Littlejohn's study, seeks—rather than the empowerment of always already enfranchised members of her own race—the empowerment of (black) others.

An important transitional point in the recent history of white engagement in Afro-American literature is represented by Robert Hemenway's 1977 study, *Zora Neale Hurston: A Literary Biography*.[9] It is the work of a white critic who, while not interested as is Stimpson in white flight from the analysis of Afro-American texts, remains as acutely aware as Stimpson of the traditional dynamics of power where white critics and black texts are concerned and who is committed to producing a discourse that does not replicate the work of this tradition. It is a superb, unquestionably afrocentric literary biography, which places Hurston's literary career illuminating within an Afro-American cultural context, one which few literary studies have matched in its informed and sensitive portrait of black literature and of Afro-American culture. Hemenway's study, of which no less an authority in the area of Afro-American literary biography than Arnold Rampersad has said that "we are unlikely to see a better book on Hurston in our time," is prefaced by remarks Rampersad characterizes as Hemenway's apology for not having "written the 'definitive' book on Hurston."[10] In the prefatory passage in question, Hemenway writes:

> My intention has always been simple. Zora Neale Hurston is a literary artist of sufficient talent to deserve intensive study, both as an artist and as an in-

tellect. She deserves an important place in American literary history. I have tried to demonstrate why this is so, not in the interests of producing a "definitive" book—that book remains to be written, and by a black woman—but in order to contribute to a new, closer examination of the unusual career of this complex author. This book provides an order to Hurston's life and interpretation of her art; there are more biographical facts to be discovered, different interpretations to come.[11]

Rather than seeing Hemenway's statement of intention strictly as an apology, I believe that, like Stimpson's abnegation of involvement in the criticism of Afro-American literature, Hemenway's is a racially motivated and strategic text quite self-conscious, for historically justifiable reasons, about its operation within a discourse intent on determining racial (and gendered) empowerment and disempowerment, on policing the boundaries, as it were, of difference. The white male biographer refuses to produce a text which, by virtue of his own racial and gendered ties to sources of institutional power, appears to connect his project with authoritarian white male critical acts, with readings characterized, in Afro-American critic Stephen Henderson's phrase, by "white critical condescension and snobbery, and . . . outright pathological ignorance and fear."[12]

The achievement of *Zora Neale Hurston: A Literary Biography* is in no way compromised by its author's self-referential strategy. Rather than undermining the effectiveness of Hemenway's study, this strategy provides—in fact *enables*—possibilities for the actualization of one of the text's stated goals: encouragement of a continued exploration of the corpus of this previously neglected black female writer. The generally positive response of Afro-American scholars to Hemenway's biography is a reflection of its success in avoiding caucacentric interactions with blackness. For example, bell hooks says about Hemenway's self-reflexive act: "As a black feminist literary critic, I have always appreciated this statement. . . . By actively refusing the position of 'authority,' Hemenway encourages black women to participate in the making of Hurston scholarship and allows for the possibility that a black woman writing about Hurston may have special insight."[13] And Houston Baker, who earlier expressed doubts about the ability of white critics to read Afro-American literature in informed and nonracist ways, cites Hemenway's text as one signal of a transformed relationship of some white critics to the Afro-American literary tradition. He says of exemplary white-authored works like Hemenway's: "Through their own investigations of the 'forms of things unknown' in recent years, some white critics have been able to enter a black critical circle. They entered, however, not as superordinate authorities, but as scholars working in harmony with fundamental postulates of the Black Aesthetic."[14] Hemenway's study is exemplary evidence of the possibilities of cross-racial American reading, of what I call reading across the lines.

I want to begin the examination of contemporary white self-referential critical acts by looking closely at Donald Wesling's self-described novice Afro-Americanist endeavor, "Writing as Power in the Slave Narrative of the Early Republic." I focus at some length on this essay because, despite its attempt to challenge received notions of American race relations in a conscientious manner, it exemplifies the virtually unshakable hold that hegemony's construction of whites, blacks, and power seems to maintain on white critics for whom, to cite Toni Morrison's provocative analysis of Afro-American presence, "the study of Afro-American literature is . . . a crash course in neighborliness and tolerance, [or] an infant to be carried, instructed or chastised or even whipped like a child."[15] While no doubt motivated by neighborly intentions, Wesling's essay is, finally, poignant evidence of the need for Afro-Americanists to be attentive to the subtle and seductive lure for white critics of socially sanctioned power.

Twice in his essay, Wesling declares his status as white outsider; these declarations correspond to his general concern with race and power as they affect the interpretive act. In fact, he begins by arguing against what he feels is a prevailing belief among nonspecialists that slave narratives are "subliterary": "Let me at the outset reject the position that these life-histories, which had such a remarkable popular success in their day, are subliterary; no narrative of recall or discovery, no narrative of the realized self *that enables the reader to live in the skin of another,* should be exiled from the sphere of the literary" (emphasis added).[16] Despite his anachronistic perspective on textual power—that is, the ability of the effective narrative to allow a reader briefly to become one with its characters, "to live in the skin of another"—Wesling goes to great lengths to emphasize his whiteness, the *difference* of his "skin" from those of the black slaves whose lives he wants to believe *Narrative of the Life of Frederick Douglass* accurately and convincingly represents. Yet Wesling's essay, which strives, at some points mightily, to transcend the West's dialectical opposition white/black, ultimately is as caught up in a hegemonic privileging of "white power" and "white thought" as the Western philosophical and social systems it strenuously critiques.

After working over Hegel's view of lordship and bondage (460–61), Wesling argues that it is only through a refusal to blacks of "the word"—the vehicle through which human identity is said to be achieved in the logocentric West— that whites were able themselves to believe and to create in others the perception of an absent black subjectivity. Employing Henry Louis Gates, Jr.'s discussion of a caucacentric West's "use of writing as a commodity to confine and delimit a culture of color" (462), Wesling argues that slave narrators such as Douglass write themselves into being as acts of "empowerment," as efforts to counter extant racist notions of black inhumanity and cognitive inferiority.

Perhaps consistent with Wesling's efforts to refute Hegel's view of lords and bondspersons and with Western culture's general privileging of whiteness is his first reference to his own white "skin." Citing the works of the two most widely respected Afro-American literary theorists, Gates and Houston Baker, both of whom have "insisted on the 'unique semantic fields, foregroundings, auto-biographical acts, and functional oppositions' of Black culture" (463), Wesling phrases his discussion of their influence on his thinking specifically in terms of a discourse of "power" which insists that, to a certain extent, race continues to de-termine hierarchical privilege. Note the language of the following sentence in which Wesling expresses his willingness to follow these black critics' interpretive approaches:

> Since one who is not black (or not American) can *follow the lead of black* *scholars* in this [insistence on black discursive and cultural difference], I would take further my earlier adjectives, *surprising* and *disruptive,* by look-ing at the semantic fields that govern meaning in the antebellum slave narratives; specifically, by suggesting differentials between their black American discourse and the three other discourses of fiction, auto-biography as a system of genre, and deconstructive hermeneutics. (463, emphasis added)

Wesling's racial markers are not without interpretive significance. They have *everything* to do with the self-consciousness of a white "alien" or outsider entering into a black field of inquiry and not wanting to impose himself as all-knowing white authority in a discourse that constitutes for (black) others a primary field of inquiry. Unwilling to project "white thought" as determinative of all meaning or to attribute to white (critical) "lords" a timeless cognitive superiority, Wesling insists upon the potentially fruitful interdependence of black and white minds. Perhaps even more "surprising" and "disruptive" to our society's traditional hier-archical figurations of black and white, he emphasizes the priority of black critical thought, and he notes its influential and clarifying effects on his own (white) thinking about slave narratives. Wesling intentionally subverts the power which the West has bequeathed him as a birthright in order to exemplify the fallacious nature of racism's informing beliefs—put simply, that "white is right" and "black is lack"—and, at least temporarily, he reverses the racist hierarchy by placing blackness in the privileged position in the binary construction.

But Wesling's radical act is undermined by his more extended discussion of race and the politics of reading. For, after offering what are, for the Afro-

Americanist critic, largely compelling readings of the "disruptive" nature of slave narratives where "the canon of Nineteenth Century Fiction" and "Tenets Concerning Autobiography as Genre" are concerned, Wesling turns to the subject of slave narratives' "Disruption of/by Deconstructive Hermeneutics."[17] In this concluding section, he returns, albeit cautiously, to traditional notions of power and racial difference, to the seemingly safer side of the interpretive Mason-Dixon line wherein white "power"—no longer universalist but deconstructionist— suggests the limitations of Afro-Americanist scholarly thought.

In the beginning of this final section, Wesling declares his unwillingness to "retract . . . a word" of the comments he has offered that reflect the influence of black critics on his thinking, including earlier suggestions about "the causally intimate connection between literacy, identity, and freedom," a connection he believes "ought not to be reduced in its human dignity, its heroism in the slave narratives, by being called an indeterminate *écriture*" (468). Despite this acknowledgment, he invokes deconstruction, whose primary goal is "the dismantling of a concept's truth-claims when it is perceived that no original moment exists that would ground truth" (467), as the most fruitful means of addressing what he considers the crucial "gap [in slave narratives] between experience and its representation" (468). Such issues include the motivations for the use of standard English in slave narratives; the "disproportionate number of . . . slave narrators [who] are mulattos"; and the "degree of inauthentic subjectivity in a life that must represent the Negro race to whites."[18]

Wesling identifies Douglass's figuration of Sandy's folk magic root as a possible site to locate a distinctively black vernacular voice and a privileged orality— that is, a black voice, expressed in written form, which demonstrates its resistance to Western hegemonic influence in its privileging of "speech over writing." Soon after Sandy gives him this root, about whose powers Douglass initially is skeptical, the young slave engages in battle with Mr. Covey, whose previous acts of brutality had succeeded in breaking Douglass's spirit. This battle, in which "the virtue of the root was fully tested," begins because "at this moment—from whence came the spirit I don't know—I resolved to fight; and suiting my action to the resolution, I seized Covey hard by the throat; and as I did so, I rose."[19]

This scene has been read by many (including Wesling, before a "rescension" motivated by his deconstructive conversion) as evidence of Douglass's belief in the prevailing strength of black oral traditions and cultural practices. But ultimately Wesling rejects this reading of the scene, encouraged by certain emphases of two respondents to an earlier version of his essay. As Wesling reports, one of these respondents, Werner Sollors, suggests that Wesling had "skimmed over the highly relevant fact that Douglass was a mulatto" (470). Sollors's comment leads Wesling to what appears to be a severe crisis of faith in his analysis:

SURVEYING THE CRITICAL TERRAIN

He touched what was for me the most vulnerable point in the paper: I had not wished to raise a thought highly inconvenient for a white critic who is commenting on black writing, namely the possibility that the mixing-in of white blood might have been one (albeit very distant) determinant of Douglass's literacy, escape from slavery, and decision to write his own story and that of the black race. A white critic who moved that way would be perhaps on the path to his or her own form of racism, a privileging of white blood, an equating of whiteness and writing. (470)

While one goal of Wesling's act clearly is to defend the *Narrative* from formerly prevalent associations of "whiteness and writing," another surely is to protect himself from charges that his own readings are influenced by caucacentric assumptions. Further, Wesling's failure to consider either Sollors's reasons for assuming that Douglass's "white blood" represented a "highly relevant fact" or his respondent's readiness to point to matters that, in Wesling's view, place a white critic potentially "on the path to his or her own form of racism," is quite striking, and is essential to our comprehension of the author's maneuvers late in the essay.

Wesling's second influential respondent is H. Porter Abbott, who informs him that "Douglass enlarged the battle with Mr. Covey in *My Bondage and [My] Freedom*." For Abbott, this enlargement evinces Douglass's "recension," his attempt to set aside "the business with the root": "I now forgot my roots, and remembered my pledge to stand up in my own defense" (470). Abbott insists that Douglass never meant to present himself as intricately tied to black folk culture, even in the initial depiction of "the business with the root." Wesling writes that "Abbott sees that stress on Douglass's own existential condition as implicit in the first, 1845 version, too, and argues that this is reinforced by the fact that the narrator is a mulatto, and not, as Douglass wrote of his friend Sandy, 'a genuine African'" (470).

In transferring his allegiance from Baker and Gates to Sollors and Abbott, from black critics to white, Wesling embraces—on faith alone, it appears, and not as a consequence of a serious investigation of the validity of Abbott's readings—a view of Douglass as existentialist mulatto emotionally unattached to the expressive traditions of his mother's people. Wesling's essay does not reexamine Douglass's text after its introduction of white skepticism in order to demonstrate *how* the slave narrator's dual ancestry has affected his connections to black orality, nor does it seek to *prove*—by offering more than Abbott's statement that it is so—that the *Narrative's* depiction of Douglass's relationship to black folk "roots" (in both senses of the word) is fraught with ultimately unreconcilable difficulties. In his movement away from Baker and Gates, in his "distancing from the black critics who have formed by thinking about Douglass and the slave narrative" (470–71), Wesling abandons the thorough, textually grounded, and rhetorically persuasive methods of inquiry that have characterized his examinations to that point. The simple declaration of "truth" by white voices of authority apparently is enough to convince Wesling and, he assumes, the readers of his essay.

Wesling's "distancing" from Baker and Gates is accompanied by his adoption of what Stimpson identifies as a more traditional position for the white investigator of blackness. While employing rhetorical gestures that seek to deny what appears to be his clear intent, Wesling moves from his early willingness to "follow the lead of black scholars" in the analysis of black texts to a posture of instructing Afro-American scholars precisely how to offer more sophisticated, less self-delusionary insights: "It is not for me to work out the moral and formal complexities of the mulatto narrative; enough for me, here, to see the abyss of that topic open out at my feet. It is enough to note the moral, and historical, complexities of a narrative such as Douglass's—for example, the black/white, speaking/writing oppositions on display here" (471). Here Wesling uses race as justification for his own failure to offer a detailed, coherent theory of "the mulatto narrative," a tradition of self-portraiture he believes is distinct in significant ways from the auto-biographical traditions of both "pure African" Americans and "pure white" Americans. Further, since Wesling has himself made such an issue of race (except in his introduction of Sollors's and Abbott's readings of Douglass, which he seems to view as unconnected to their race), what appears to disqualify him from offering a sound theory of "the mulatto narrative" is his whiteness. Apparently the task of devising such a theory falls to nonwhite critics—to black scholars like Gates and Baker—despite the fact that their "biological" difference from mulatto narrators may be no less great than Wesling's.

Having established his position as a voice of white authority, having deemed current black critical formulations insufficient to explain "the mulatto narrative," Wesling cites in his concluding paragraph another white authority whose discussion of the *Narrative* is introduced in order to confirm his own sense of Douglass's biracial and bicultural status. Specifically, he draws on "Sacvan Bercovitch's recent summary paragraph on the *Narrative,* where he argues that Douglass embraces both Afro-American forms of expression and the free-enterprise ideology of his historical moment " 'in such a way as simultaneously to deflect radical energies and to inspire the work of art' " (471). Wesling's choice provides us with the means of demonstrating the problems implicit in his distinctions between black and white perspectives concerning "the business with the roots" in Douglass's *Narrative,* and perhaps in his reading of the slave narrative tradition generally.

In the *Critical Inquiry* essay Wesling draws from, Bercovitch refers to a collection he edited with Myra Jehlen, *Ideology and Classic American Literature,* in which is reprinted Baker's materialist analysis of Douglass's *Narrative* that first appeared in *Blues, Ideology, and Afro-American Literature.*[20] Wesling's opposition of white and black scholars notwithstanding, Baker's examination of Douglass's contribution to the establishment of an "'economics of slavery' and 'commercial deportation' as governing statements in Afro-American discourse" (31) serves to complement Bercovitch's discussion of Douglass's engagement of American free-enterprise ideology. Bercovitch argues that Douglass's text evidences a deep ambivalence about America, the narrator's recognition of "the *liberating* appeal . . . of free-enterprise ideology—the rhetoric of equal opportunity, contract society, upward mobility, free trade, and the sanctity of private property" and of the fact "that on another, perhaps deeper level he was being manipulated in turn by those cultural keywords *and energized by them.*"[21]

Bercovitch's discussion suggests that whatever the extent of his ties to black belief systems, Douglass—legislatively denied full access to the promises implicit in "those cultural keywords," but thoroughly engaged in and by them—experiences a specifically American dilemma. Similarly, Baker explores Douglass's "americanness," his comprehension of the quintessentially American equation of freedom and economics. Baker notes the initially limited benefits of literacy for Douglass, including the fact that, during the attempt of a group of male slaves to escape, "the slave does, indeed, write his 'own pass' and the passes of his fellows, but the Sabbath school assembled group is no match for the enemy within" (47). Consequently, instead of locating as the liberating moment Douglass's revelation concerning "the pathway from slavery to freedom" (49)—the young slave's rejection of his slavemaster's views on the dangers of literacy for the black bondsman—Baker insists that the slave's freedom results from his arriving at "a fully commercial view of his situation" just before he escapes to the North. Douglass "removes (in his own person) the master's property. . . . By 'stealing away,' Douglass not only steals the fruits of his own labor . . . but also liberates the laborer—the chattel who works profitlessly in the garden" (48).

Bercovitch's and Baker's identification of the americanness of Douglass's response to his situation suggests the problems inherent in Wesling's trumpeted "distancing from . . . black critics." For Baker's analysis reads the differences between Douglass and Sandy as being more pronounced than do either Sollors or Abbott:

> In contrast to a resolved young Douglass . . . stands Sandy Jenkins. . . .
> Sandy offers Douglass a folk means of negotiating his crisis at Covey's, providing him with a "certain *root*," which, carried "*always on* . . . [the] right side, would render it impossible for Mr. Covey or any other white man" to

whip the slave. What is represented by the introduction of Sandy Jenkins is a displacement of Christian metaphysics by Afro-American "superstition." Ultimately, this displacement reveals the inefficacy of trusting solely to any form of extrasecular aid for relief (or release) from slavery.

The root does not work. The physical controntation does. . . . Jenkins's mode of negotiating the economics of slavery, the *Narrative* implies, is not *a man's way,* since the narrator claims that his combat with Covey converted him, ipso facto, into *a man.* (46–47)

Baker views Sandy's limited utilization of black belief as a sign of his complete capitulation to white power. According to Baker, Sandy's selective employment of forms of blackness is not accompanied by a concomitant internalization of an integrity of black difference that motivates his responses to blacks and whites. In his status as what Baker calls "the pure, negative product of an economics of slavery"—one assumes that he indeed profits from his acts of treason—Sandy has access to little but the forms of blackness. He appears unconcerned about the subversive potential offered by an energetically practiced black difference, and is protected not by his root—Douglass implies, in fact, that Sandy's roots (his connections to Africa) have been irreparably severed—but by a white hegemony-approved and enforced passivity that stands "in clear and monumental . . . contrast to . . . Douglass" (47).

Wesling's deconstructive "distancing" from "black critics" is motivated not by a fundamental "difference" so much as by a refusal to explore, in energetic and useful ways, the points of similarity between "black" and "white" thought. While "difference" in the preceding examples between black thought (Baker) and white (Sollors and Abbott) is perhaps marked by their sense of the importance of Douglass's mulatto status—his (racial) self-difference—clearly his white and black authorities would all identify Wesling's investment of Sandy and his root with anti-hegemonic power as thoroughly unconvincing. At the point at which he is forced to deal with the inadequacy of his formulations with respect to the *Narrative's* inscription of America's "cultural keywords" as the "first principles" of Douglass's formation of self, Wesling resorts to sloppy analytical practice, invokes the tenets of white authority figures without offering even a modicum of evidence to support their (and *his own*) claims, and insists that Afro-American criticism needs to alter the contours of hits investigation.

At this point it is useful to explore the formulations on American "ethnic" differences of one of Wesling's white authorities, the German-born Werner Sollors. The essay I want to discuss, "A Critique of Pure Pluralism," is, unlike the other texts I am concerned with in this chapter, not an overtly self-referential white critical act. But because he insists that black scholars, in creating critical texts which foreground their own subjectivity, have formulated a critical discourse incapable of illuminating the very texts they are dealing with Sollors comments implicitly on the general advisability of critical self-referentiality itself. In arguing that the race of the Afro-American critic should not be taken into account in his or her consideration of black texts, Sollors implies that white investigators of blackness need not be even minimally self-conscious about the effects of their racial positionality on the reading process. While welcoming changes in the academy that have created spaces in curricula for minority discourses, Sollors asserts that there is—or, in the best of all worlds, *should be*—no connection between *who* reads these recovered, explicitly racial texts, and *how* they are read.

Sollors begins by attempting to dispute the claims of the cultural left concerning the traditional, white male-dominated, Western literary canon. He argues that this canon has been reduced to the status of "contemporary scapegoat" by minority and feminist critics who mistakenly characterize its former exclusivity as the product of "a rather malicious white male imagination."[22] Further, Sollors bemoans the fact that the examination of ethnic and women's literary traditions "has tended to produce sectarian and fragmented histories of American literatures (in the plural) instead of American literary history" (251–52).

Sollors's fundamentally conservative comments beg the question of whether it is advisable to attempt to produce a single "American literary history," and reflect a willful blindness both to the ideological factors that drive canon inclusion/exclusion and to the sophisticated insights that have resulted in the last two decades from these "sectarian and fragmented histories."[23] In fact, Sollors expresses a deep disdain for culturally specific interpretive acts of "ethnic" scholars, a disdain reflected in his evaluation of critical strategies used to explore forms of American difference.

"A Critique of Pure Pluralism" allows us to see that Sollors's comments with regard to Wesling's reading of Douglass's *Narrative* are indisputably informed by his desire for critical power, by his interest in persuading others of the fruitfulness of his figuration of a unified, "polyethnic" literary America and American literary history. Sollors is engaged in a struggle for the authority to determine what constitutes the most correct goals of Afro-American (or, more broadly, American) literary studies. The seriousness of the threat of an increasingly embraced privileging and exploration of difference to Sollors's project to reestablish an American "literary-historical consensus"[24]—a consensus previously made possible by white male scholars' virtual erasure of ethnic, gendered, and certain other forms of ideological difference—is reflected in Sollors's rancorous, simplistic, and dismissive description of what he holds as the fundamental flaws in recent efforts of ethnic and feminist scholars to delineate their literary traditions. He says of these emerging forms of inquiry:

> What is often called "the ethnic perspective"—which often means, in literary history, the emphasis on a writer's *descent*—all but annihilates polyethnic art movements, moments of cultural interaction, and the pervasiveness of cultural syncretism in America. The widespread acceptance of group-by-group approach has not only led to unhistorical accounts held together by static notions of rather abstractly and homogeneously conceived ethnic groups, but has also weakened the comparative and critical skills of increasingly timid interpreters who sometimes choose to speak with the authority of ethnic insiders rather than that of readers of texts. (256)

After this effort to virtually erase the gains that have been made in ethnic minority literary studies, Sollors offers what are, according to him, more sound, more *american* interpretive goals: "If anything, ethnic literary history ought to *increase* our understanding of the cultural interplays and contacts among writers of different backgrounds, the ethnic innovations and cultural mergers that took place in America" (256).

An emphasis on difference, on that which has been the primary justification throughout American history for mistreatment of millions of ethnic, racial, and gendered others, is appalling to the white critic who insists that an understanding of American cultural consensus is the only valid goal of ethnic literary history. The examples Sollors employs in his discussion of ethnic literary inheritance (or what he calls "the construction of diachronic 'descent lines'"), however, leave no doubt that his venom is directed primarily at the especially problematic critical practices of Afro-American literary scholars:

> Do we have to believe in a filiation from Mark Twain to Ernest Hemingway, but not to Ralph Ellison (who is supposedly descended from James Weldon Johnson and Richard Wright)? Can Gertrude Stein be discussed with Richard Wright or only with white women expatriate German-Jewish writers? Is there a link from the autobiography of Benjamin Franklin to those of Frederick Douglass and Mary Antin, or must we see Douglass exclusively as a version of Olaudah Equiano and a precursor to Malcom X? Is Zora Neale Hurston only Alice Walker's foremother? (257)

Sollors's remarks are not easily dismissed, for they come from a white institutional insider who has served as chair of Afro-American studies at Harvard University. Moreover, they attack the basic premise of Afro-American and other "minority" studies. That premise, simply stated, is that these areas represent sophisticated traditions of thought that can effectively illuminate the political, cultural, and economic history of non-European and/or nonwhite male descendants in America, provided its central texts are examined in a thoughtfully intertextual manner.

If Sollors's goal is not the dismantling of Afro-American Studies as practiced for the last two decades, it is certainly the problematizing of essential aspects of that practice. Left to Sollors's design, Afro-American studies generally would become a mere subset of, would be methodologically indistinguishable from, American studies (except, perhaps, for its focus on texts composed by Africa's new world descendants). Since analyses of cross-cultural American connections represent the purpose of Sollors's version of Afro-American studies, the elements of black subjectivity—of black difference—which fueled Afro-American struggles to institutionalize and sustain such programs at American colleges and universities and which continue to motivate black critical interest in Afro-American texts, Sollors considers to be disruptive of the more pristine goals of American investigative objectivity. In his advocacy of an objectivity and an AMERICA in which many in academia have lost faith, Sollors refuses even to examine his potentially self-interested motivation for minimizing the possible interpretive benefits of black critical subjectivity, or for asserting that attention to a critic's race is, at best, irrelevant, and at worst disastrous to his or her investigations of blackness. In arguing that blackness makes no (interpretive) difference whatsoever, Sollors appears to be attempting to justify a belief that his own racial positionality is in no way in conflict with his administrative and intellectual situations.

Sollors's figuration of black literary criticism is neither a sensitive effort to move beyond what Bercovitch calls "dissensus" nor an example of Neal's "welcome criticism." Rather, it is a bold attempt to invalidate the advances of an ntire black scholarly tradition and, hence, to gain for himself as white insider the same kind of power to determine the future direction of Afro-American cultural studies on a national level that he has enjoyed at America's most prestigious university.[25]

While Sollors's point of entry into the discourse of blackness is his privileged insider's position in Black Studies, Harold Fromm's is the "discussion" between Joyce Joyce, Houston Baker, and Henry Louis Gates on the pages of *New Literary History* about the usefulness of contemporary critical theory in analyses of Afro-American texts. Among other issues, Fromm's essay, "Real Life, Literary Criticism, and the Perils of Bourgeoisfication," addresses, as do the Joyce pieces, what he perceives to be the insufficient ideological blackness of Baker and Gates. While I will avoid extended comment here on the exchange, aspects of which I have examined in chapter 1, I want to explore the essentially personal nature of Fromm's attacks on Baker and Gates.[26] These attacks issue both from Fromm's interest in generally condemning what he considers a narcissistic poststructuralist critical project by which Baker and Gates have been influenced and, most important, from his static and simplistic notions of black and white differences.

What matters to me here about Fromm's formulations is that his representation of a blissfully self-interested critical project treats Baker and Gates as representative examples. Fromm characterizes these scholars as charlatans burdened by theory and driven not by a concern for the black race but by "careerism . . . and the marketplace."[27] While "Real Life" is not the first instance of Fromm's venomous response to what he perceives to be an increasingly decadent literary academy, this essay is disturbing in its attempt at wholesale character assassination.[28] I will address Fromm's assessment of Gates primarily because, while his mean-spirited and dismissive remarks about Baker provide much ground for discussion, it is in his reaction to Gates that the essay focuses most precisely on the issue of race: on Gates's blackness, on what Fromm considers his transracial skills, and, briefly, on Fromm's own racial subjectivity.

Fromm grants that Gates is "a gifted, sometimes brilliant intellectual: rhetorical, pugnacious, relentless, engaged in conducting a twenty-ring circus all at once and with considerable skill." Still, Fromm considers Gates "a paradigmatic exemplar of what I have come to call 'academic capitalism,' an enterprise that is complicated in his case by an admixture of self-righteous obsession with race, from which he is nonetheless able to extract every known academic prerequisite" (52). Characterizing Gates's work as evidence of his self-righteous obsession with race, Fromm sees the black critic as an academic "superstar" who is able to move deftly between racial poles, between blackness and whiteness: "His most salient characteristics are his two well-worn metaphysical jumpsuits—one white, the other black—which he is able to zip on and off, sometimes in midsentence, with dizzying bravado as rhetorical needs urge him on. Although *as an intellectual he is as white and bourgeois as I,* he is nevertheless a virtuoso at exploiting white liberal guilt" (52, emphasis added).

Clearly we have come full circle from the world delineated in such white investigations of blackness as John Howard Griffin's *Black Like Me.* While racial mutability is a common concern of both texts, race has taken on for Fromm a more "metaphysical" quality than it possessed for Griffin, who feels he must darken his skin in order to gain access to the mysterious meanings of blackness. But Fromm's black transracial intellectual is capable of moving from a black subject position to a white one not by changing his appearance but by manipulating available discursive traits of racial difference. For Fromm, Gates's deft navigation between black vernacular and "high" theory, between discourses of the street and the academy, represents a transgression of firmly established racial boundaries.

Instead of the transraciality of Griffin, which appears to be a generally selfless response to white liberal guilt,[29] Gates is said to be motivated by a desire to emphasize insignificant pigmentation differences between himself and learned white academics, or what W.E.B. DuBois once termed "mere 'gross' features,"[30] so as to exploit white financiers' guilt strictly for personal gain. What makes Gates's version of academic capitalism so repugnant to Fromm is the fact that despite Gates's constant emphasis on racial difference, he is, in essence, "as white and bourgeois as I am." In other words, Gates is no more intimately connected than Fromm with the socioeconomic plight of lower class Afro-Americans who represent for Fromm what Gates (following Ralph Ellison) terms the blackness of blackness, the true participants in an authentic black culture from which the bourgeois black critic is forever estranged.

Fromm's is a jaded representation of Gates's perspectives and achievements. And while he does touch on essentially important matters where class is concerned—particularly an interrogation of the nature of the responsibility of the black middle class to aid in uplifting the race's less fortunate—he chooses to put forward caucacentric notions of black racial essence, next to which Wesling's efforts to deconstruct the West's traditional black/white dichotomy seems positively enlightened. For, in Fromm's view, Gates is "white" both because of his financial success and because of his firm possession of "the word" (his verbal acumen and mastery of the discourse of contemporary literary theory). According to Fromm, whiteness is a normative intellectual state, is always already associated with professional and financial achievement—with presence; blackness, on the other hand, is synonymous with economic and intellectual lack, with poverty and a failure to become a part of mainstream American society, with an inability to master Standard English, and an unsuitability as a proper subject of academic investigation.

Gates and Baker are no longer "black," and are, in Fromm's estimation (to invoke, with a difference, the title of Griffin's work), "white like me" because they have mastered the skills required to command respect and lucrative financial recompense in the American academic marketplace. Failing to see in the sign "blackness" anything but lack, viewing it, indeed, as representing only unmitigated suffering, Fromm associates blackness with violation on a par with "medical experiments on prisoners in concentration camps." Suffering without end, Fromm's "blackness" is the very antithesis of the sense of possibility signaled by its binary opposite, "whiteness," in American culture. Considering Afro-American life in such a limited and limiting manner, Fromm has no choice but to deride what I see as the synthetic, playful, angry, appropriative, code-switching criticism of Gates and Baker. Indeed, in a view of these scholars' work that appears to be derived almost solely from a reading of their responses to Joyce Joyce, he considers their texts to be a "betrayal, an unclean and venal act in which the suffering and blood of black Americans—as well as a liberation that is still in progress—have been turned into a market commodity not completely removed from cabbage patch dolls and rock videos" (59).

Larry Neal's attractive prophecy notwithstanding, the establishment of a black critical class/mass in the literary academy clearly has not served to eliminate the creation of boldly misinformed or malicious white analyses of the Afro-American literary enterprise. What has changed, however, is the focus of self-righteous white rancor. While David Littlejohn's infamous *Black on White,* for example, published eight years before Neal's comments, emphasized what Littlejohn considered to be a debilitating self-hatred manifested in the products of the black literary imagination, Fromm attacks the most renowned voices to have emerged from the black critical class, emphasizing, as does Littlejohn in his assessment of Afro-American creative writers, their psychologically maladjusted and divided natures. And though Afro-American creative writing itself remains securely on the periphery of Fromm's analysis—black literary texts are for him records of "the suffering and blood of black Americans," whose aesthetic qualities should not be evaluated while the black struggle for "liberation . . . is still in progress" (59)—poststructuralist black theory and its creators have, for Fromm, taken the place of the flawed literary practice of Littlejohn's perspectives. Such scholarship is the site and sign of black "minstrelsy," of a self-division or self-delusion that Fromm terms "a selective blackness" (63).

The motivation for Fromm's interest in the Joyce-Baker-Gates exchange is clearly elaborated toward the end of his essay: "This ongoing debate derives most of its interest not from the rightness or wrongness of its principals' positions so much as from its exhibition of an evolving, conflicted consciousness" (62). Fromm's attraction to the debate appears to be solely a function of his sense of its confirmation of black self-division, of a psychic split or Du Boisian double consciousness, which, despite the social, economic, political, and academic advances Afro-Americans have made over the last two decades, is no more successfully resolved, he believes, than when *Black on White* offered similar critiques of black creative writers in 1966.

For Fromm, the unity of the Afro-American critical psyche is possible only when the black critic comes to accept his belief that class is a significantly more important factor than race in the determination of one's allegiances, of one's "people." In Fromm's view, race makes no essential difference whatsoever to Gates and Baker; it offers them no crucial connections to the black masses or to their culture. Class, for Fromm, is everything, and his venomous personal attack results, in the final analysis, from their refusal or inability to recognize this fact.

This painfully limited construction of race reflects a naive conflation of class and racial states of being that a more sympathetic view of poststructuralism, for example, might have encouraged Fromm to see as fundamentally flawed. Certainly blackness—whatever we take that sign to mean—must be said to include Afro-Americans on all levels of the socioeconomic spectrum, even wildly successful professors of black literature. You don't have to be perceived as intellectually and economically impoverished in order to occupy a black subject position at the end of the twentieth century, regardless of the views of a white critic who bemoans the passing of the good old days when texts were "works," and when blackness was considered synonymous with lack in the field of literary studies.[31]

If a common element connects the essays of Wesling, Sollors, and Fromm, it is a quintessential will to power, an inability to interact as self-conscious whites with discourses of blackness except as what Baker in *Blues, Ideology and Afro-American Literature* terms "superordinate authorities" (84). In these examples, self-referentiality fails to make these scholars significantly more self-conscious in their involvement in a dialectics of race. Consequently, in these cases, self-referentiality serves to disguise their desire to dominate regions and discourses of blackness, censor what they view as insufficiently informed and seriously flawed black critical and cultural practices, and direct black natives to more enlightened modes and forms of "real life" and scholarly behavior. In my view, these examples demonstrate—for Afro-American studies specifically, but for minority discourses more generally—that self-referentiality is not necessarily a sign of the intense self-investigation that minimizes or eliminates the dangers of hegemonic self-interest. In fact, this critical practice can be used expressly to mask more sinister, more tyrannizing intentions.

What these essays demonstrate is the necessity for black critics to be attentive to the fact that what Michel Foucault calls the "operation of mechanisms of power" potentially can come into play in any white American interaction with black texts and contexts. In fact, they evidence the importance for black scholars of heeding Foucault's warnings about the constant threat of dispute implicit in any power relation. In a section entitled "How Is Power Exercised?" Foucault argues:

> In effect, between a relationship of power and a strategy of struggle there is a reciprocal appeal, a perpetual linking and a perpetual reversal. At every moment the relationship of power may become a confrontation between two

adversaries. Equally, the relationship between adversaries in society may, at every moment, give place to the putting into operation of mechanisms of power. The consequences of this instability is the ability to decipher the same events and the same transformations either from inside the history of struggle or from the standpoint of the power relationships. The interpretations which result will not consist of the same elements of meaning or the same links or the same types of intelligibility, although they refer to the same historical fabric and each of the two analyses must have reference to the other. In fact it is precisely the disparities between the two readings which make visible those fundamental phenomena of "domination" which are present in a large number of human societies.[32]

The analyses of Wesling, Sollors, and Fromm are, finally, attempts at interpretive "domination," the "putting into operation of mechanisms of power" that seek to minimize the persuasiveness of Afro-Americanist readings of texts. Ultimately, these essays, when considered in the context of Foucault's theorizing about the nature of power relations, indicate the pervasive nature of enactments of white power. In a world in which states and traits of difference "continue to matter," as Barbara Johnson argues in what I consider a welcome investigation that foregrounds the consequences of her racial difference on her reading of Zora Neale Hurston, where blackness continues to signify lack and powerlessness, Afro-American literary scholars need to be especially attentive to the nature and specifics of white disagreements with blacks in their evaluations of the significance of black difference.[33] For if, as Foucault argues, adversaries within a society tend to read the "same historical fabric" differently, until the existing power relations are no longer extant, interpretive differences between white and black critics may result, as in the preceding examples, from a desire on the part of the former to limit, circumscribe, or otherwise control the range of black discourse in order that this discourse can be made to act in accordance with existing caucacentric formulations of race and difference.

Indeed, Johnson's essay, "Thresholds of Difference: Structures of Address in Zora Neale Hurston," offers a useful, provocative alternative to the race-war dialectics that motivate many of the white critical acts under consideration here. While not innocent of what we might view as an interpretive politics—the essay emphasizes elements of Hurston's body of nonfiction that allow her to view the Afro-American writer as a (black) deconstructionist thinker par excellence— Johnson's analysis nevertheless does not seek to negate the explanatory power of afrocentric thought in order to forward her deconstructionist agenda. Johnson begins her essay with a series of interrogatives that inquire into the motivations for her interest in Hurston's nonfiction:

> It was not clear to me what I, a white deconstructor, was doing talking about Zora Neale Hurston, a black novelist and anthropologist, or to whom I was talking. Was I trying to convince white establishment scholars who long for a return to Renaissance ideals that the study of the Harlem Renaissance is not a trivialization of their humanistic pursuits? Was I trying to contribute to the attempt to adapt the textual strategies of literary theory to the analysis of Afro-American literature? Was I trying to rethink my own previous work and to re-referentialize the notion of difference so as to move the conceptual operations of deconstruction out of the realm of abstract linguistic universality? Was I talking to white critics, black critics, or myself? (172)

Johnson's deconstruction of differences between herself and Hurston, between white insider and black outsider, enables a significantly more thoughtful and illuminating investigation of the signs "white" and "black" than those of her self-referential male counterparts. While not ignoring the differences that racial difference makes—she acknowledges that binary terms such as "*black* and *white, inside* and *outside,* continue to matter" (183)—she nevertheless demonstrates the benefits of an engaged interaction with her black subject. Indeed, Johnson argues that Hurston's figurations of race and multiple implied audiences informs and deepens her own sense of the explanatory power of the deconstructive enterprise itself:

> It was as though I were asking Zora Neale Hurston for answers to questions I did not even know I was unable to formulate. I had a lot to learn, then, from Hurston's way of dealing with multiple agendas and heterogenous implied readers. . . . Hurston could be read not just as an example of the 'noncanonical' writer, but as a commentator on the dynamics of any encounter between an inside and an outside, any attempt to make a statement about difference (172–73).

Johnson's essay is proof that an analysis of racial difference can indeed produce a deeply engaged, dialogic critical discourse.

Certainly it is possible to argue that Johnson's engagement might represent only an appearance of sincerity and that we can never know with any certainty whether her "real life" relationship to blackness is actually less fraught with difficulty than we could argue Fromm's, Wesling's, and Sollors's appear to be. But it is precisely this point that Fromm's essay ignores to its own detriment: we can never know about the "real life" of scholars simply by consulting the texts which they produce to represent their thoughts and critical selves at a given moment. Critical texts, like creative ones, are performative constructions that, by their very nature, can relate only limited aspects of the totality of the self or selves. Unlike Fromm, I do not believe I know the "real life" of Baker, Gates, or Johnson any better by consulting texts written to represent their critical selves; certainly, such consultation qualifies me to measure neither Gates's and Baker's "real life" ideological blackness nor Johnson's "real life" problematization of whiteness (or, for that matter, Fromm's, even if the antipathy his essay inspires in me makes me want to believe otherwise).

In fact, this practice can get critics into traps from which they may find it impossible to extricate themselves. Consider the fact that both Fromm and Joyce Joyce view Baker's *Blues, Ideology, and Afro-American Literature* as a preeminent example of black poststructuralist self-hatred and loss of identity, as evidence of the differences between Baker's project and what Joyce considers the love-inspired creative and interpretive acts that characterize the black discursive tradition. Knowing these scholars' views, how do we respond to the fact that the esteemed biographer Arnold Rampersad believes that Baker's study, which "represents a decade of research in structuralism, post-structuralism, semiotics, philosophy, symbolic anthropology, and other related fields," is motivated by "a profound love of black people, a bristling recognition of their ongoing oppression in America, and a sense of the need to keep on with the struggle for their freedom"? Who should we believe concerning the implications and impact of Baker's theoretical education: Fromm and Joyce, or Rampersad? Does Baker love black people, or does he hate them and himself? It seems to me that the conclusions we reach about such matters reflect our feelings about poststructuralist theory itself much more accurately than they do the quality of love evident on the pages of Baker's work, or, perhaps, the quality of his work. Certainly we can—and must, considering their status in the profession and their persistent comments on the subject— energetically assess the persuasiveness of Baker's and Gates's employment of theory and readings of critical and fictive texts. But, given our general inability to define or quantify "love" in the "real life" Fromm believes contemporary criticism attempts to circumvent, it remains unclear to me how we might devise accurate measures of its manifestations in scholarship merely by surveying their use of theory or appropriations of black expressive cultural properties.[34]

Of course, this does not mean that we cannot strenuously critique critical texts, including self-referential ones, or see them as reflections of aspects of their authors' states of mind about the topics they address. But such critiques, in order to be minimally persuasive, must engage the quality of the interrogation of the dilemmas posed by interpretation "across the lines" presented in the texts in question. What strikes me as a particularly problematic instance of critical self-interrogation is offered in Sue-Ellen Case's "Women of Colour and Theatre"

(1988). Case acknowledges that her position is *outside* of the discourses she seeks both to investigate and to create. Instead of exploring her motivations for including a discussion of women of color in *Feminism and Theatre,* the book in which this essay appears, she focuses on what she considers the inherent, racially determined limitations of her analysis:

> Because this description of the position and project of women of colour has been written by a white author, the discourse is necessarily distanced from the actual experiences which shape this position. The distance is not an objective distance, but one which reflects a perspective of racial and class privilege. The white author cannot write from the experience of racial oppression, or from the perspective of the ethnic community, and must thus omit a sense of the internal composition of such a community or of its interface with the dominant white culture. Moreover, within the study of feminism and theatre, this distance creates crucial problems in research and criticism. . . . The distance of the white author from the ethnic community creates a critical absence of . . . contacts [with theatre companies of women of color] and research opportunities. This distance has influenced all of the information in this chapter, but is most evident in the restriction of its focus to examples from the United States, drawn primarily from the work of black women and Chicanas.[35]

While Case escapes the normalizing, universalizing traps that had previously characterized white feminist response to women of color—specifically, the representation of white middle-class women's lives as the standard against which all women's experience is measured—she produces instead a distanced, distractingly apologetic analysis whose attention to racial difference makes engaged interaction between critic and subject virtually impossible. Cautious about such matters to a fault—this essay, in fact, might best be seen as self-protective avoidance of the appearance of white female hegemonic imposition of its own image upon the literature of women of color—Case's essay fails to demonstrate a serious engagement with her material.

While I willingly grant that race, or cultural difference generally, can represent a significant obstacle to interpretive competence, Case's explanation of its limitations is grossly overstated. Certainly there exist enough critical, historical, and sociological studies of people of color composed by white scholars to undermine Case's claim about the impossibility of white access to nonwhite "contacts and research opportunities." (If such access was indeed impossible, how did Robert Hemenway write his biography of Hurston?) The essay's overstatement, coupled with the differences between the implicit promise of its title ("Women of

Cover of *Feminism and Theatre*, by Sue-Ellen Case.
Reprinted with permission of Donald Cooper.

Colour and Theatre") and its actual focus ("the work of black women and Chicanas" from the United States), suggests a strategic, prefunctory inclusion of nonwhite subjects.

Perhaps even more problematic than analytical failings and lame excuses is the author's inclusion, as cover art for the book, of the image of an Afro-American woman actress performing in a scene from Ntozake Shange's *for colored girls*. Given Case's view of the inadequacies of her discussions of dramas by women of color, this choice is at least curious, if not startling, for those who expect cover art generally to serve as pictorial referencing of the strengths of a book rather than its self-acknowledged weaknesses. The choice of cover art and exaggerated claims of the chapter's title, however, become comprehensible when considered in the light of Case's most direct statement about her motivation for including an essay whose limitations she continually and somewhat painfully attempts to explain in her study. Case writes that "no book of the intersection of feminism and theatre could hope to provide a relatively complete overview of the topic without some attempt to represent the position of women of colour."[36] While I am aware that surveys such as *Feminism and Theatre,* which attempt to discuss large, diverse bodies of texts, are necessarily incomplete in terms of coverage and attention paid to some of the significant texts they introduce, Case's use of racial difference as an excuse for gaps in her knowledge and the explicit focus of her study's cover seem to me at best irresponsible. If temporal or other restrictions necessitate limiting the focus of this chapter strictly to Chicana and Afro-American women playwrights of the United States, then the choice of a different title and cover photo might have been a more effective response to her critical situation than her extended, ultimately unconvincing discussion of the difficulties for white critics to gain access to materials that are certainly accessible to the diligent investigator. No matter how self-reflexive the discourse employed by the white investigator of black areas, such discourse cannot protect itself from allegations of tokenism or less than serious engagement if it appears, in fact, to manifest such qualities.

As I said at the start of this chapter, self-referential white analysis is beneficial in part because it can serve to challenge its authors and readers to move beyond essentializing discussions of the relationships between race and reading. Certainly there are numerous other possible avenues to exploring this issue than the ones I pursue in my own investigation. But until a time when racial difference can be said no longer to represent a motivating factor in a relationship of power, Americanists, especially those on the margins or writing about them, must energetically acknowledge and explore race's continuing meanings on American shores. Because racial difference still matters, we must not expect the increased visibility of blackness in American literary studies to erase the possibilities that even the most apparently self-conscious and self-referential white investigation will conclude with the advocacy of older, caucacentric orders. For the foreseeable future at least, Afro-American literary scholars would do well to maintain a degree of skepticism about and, at the very least, pay some public attention to, such critical acts.

two

Interpretation at the Borders

Force is sex, not just sexualized; force is the desire dynamic, not just a response to the desired object when desire's expression is frustrated. . . . Hostility and contempt, or arousal of master to slave, together with awe and vulnerability, or arousal of slave to master—these are the emotions of this sexuality's excitement.

Catharine MacKinnon, *Toward a Feminist Theory of the State*

Black women were and continue to be sorely in need of an antirape movement.

Angela Davis, *Women, Culture, and Politics*

To conceive of the study of men to be about liberating men is to have little interest in any area of social analysis that seriously critiques men as men, as part of the problem, not just to women and each other but to society and our continuation as a species.

Jalna Hanmer, "Men, Power and the Exploitation of Women"

"You're turning me on."

Mike Tyson, to Desiree Washington

Sex spells potential danger as well as pleasure for women. A feminist politics about sex, therefore, if it is to be credible as well as hopeful, must seek both to protect women from sexual danger and to encourage their pursuit of sexual pleasure.

Ellen Carol DuBois and Linda Gordon,
"Seeking Ecstasy on the Battlefield"

4

Representing Rape: On Spike, Iron Mike,
and the "Desire Dynamic"

In their introduction to the collection *Men, Masculinities and Social Theory,* Jeff
Hearn and David Morgan argue that a truly antipatriarchal men's studies must
investigate the complexity of men's various relationships to that pervasive system
of oppression. Rather than assume that all men respond enthusiastically or uni-
formly to inherited or newly emergent androcentric notions, they favor an interpretive model that is attentive to the effects of other features of men's subjectivities
upon their relationship to and practice of masculinity:

> Men too, within a society that may be characterized as "patriarchal," may
> experience subordinations, stigmatizations or marginalizations as a conse-
> quence of their sexuality, ethnic identity, class position, religion, or marital
> status. The interplay between hegemonic and subordinate masculinities is a
> complex one, but should serve to underline the fact that experience of mas-
> culinity and of being a man are not uniform and that we should develop
> ways of theorizing these differences.[1]

A men's studies project structured around such insights can produce multifarious
and supple analyses of men's practices of masculinity. This project offers a means
to identify more fully the factors that restrict the access of the Afro-American
male to phallic power but do not interfere systematically with the access of a
straight WASP middle-class male to that power. To recognize difference within
the class of males in this manner is to acknowledge the existence of various levels
and sites of mediation and to position the critical self to contribute to their subtle
interrogation.

One problem with their theorizing, however, is its insistence on addressing
the inadequacies of views of a monolithic male subject by polarizing (or at the

very least juxtaposing) "hegemonic and subordinate masculinities." Even as they acknowledge that the relationship between these masculinities is, in fact, "complex," Hearn and Morgan invite us to view non-hegemonic males as always distanced from the "experience of masculinity" by virtue of their being barred from partaking of all of its dimensions. If being hegemonically masculine means possessing the socioeconomic and cultural power to subjugate virtually everyone else, then "subordinate masculinity" connotes a vulnerability to the oppressive maneuverings of others, including white men. Certainly we need flexible theories of male difference—of "subordinations, stigmatizations or marginalizations"—that problematize "masculinity" by demonstrating that socially disenfranchised males cannot fully embrace all of patriarchy's features. But in addition it is crucial to its status as feminist discourse that men's studies provide as an important part of its agenda an interrogation of the manner in which marginalized men also participate in patriarchy even as (or perhaps to some extent because) aspects of its socially sanctioned and sanctioning power are denied to them.

Without such interrogation, an emphasis on the fractured nature of male subjectivity can easily become grounds upon which to argue that no man really or always occupies a hegemonic position, that, in psychoanalytical terms, no man fully embodies the phallus. Men's studies, the self-acknowledged child of feminism, can in the absence of a feminist admonition become the site of a potential derailing of one of feminisms's fundamental postulates—that men profit as a class from patriarchy—in its urgings toward a positivistic inscription of men's lives. In his capacity as editor of the series in which *Men, Masculinities and Social Theory* appears, Hearn, in fact, suggests that "an important part of an accurate study of men and masculinity is an appreciation of the positive features of men's lives."[2] Because we are aware that our gender system is structured to benefit men, it is difficult to imagine how those "positive features" would not also be implicated as mechanisms, reflections, or avenues of female oppression.[3]

It seems to me essential that analyses of Afro-American masculinity, for example, interrogate both male differences in the manner advocated by men's studies and, as feminism would insist, degrees of capitulation to patriarchal perspectives. Without a feminist imperative, an interpretation that focuses on "subordinate masculinities" is perhaps as likely as any unrepentant form of androcentrism to seek to justify, excuse, or explain away instances of male transgressions against women. Androcentrism's interpretive trajectory is manifested in an example I will discuss more fully below: the responses of many Afro-American commentators to the Mike Tyson rape trial. Evidence of black androcentrism's presence in response to this event abounds in such articulations as Ralph Wiley's comparison of Tyson's proclivities for grabbing women's breasts and buttocks in public to the behavior of putatively suave Mediterranean men and his suggestion that Tyson's conviction is evidence that—when seen in the light of William Kennedy Smith's acquittal—black men cannot get a fair trial anywhere in America; ardent black supporters' insistence that, even if Tyson had raped Desiree Washington, she should not have reported the assault because of his prominence and their common racial heritage; and, perhaps most perversely, boxing promoter Don King's argument that Washington could not have been raped because no other hotel guest heard her screaming and because Tyson's body showed no marks of struggle, such as scratches or bruises.[4] It is precisely such commentators' recognition of black males' "subordinate masculinity"—our racially-determined and often class-determined inability to embody patriarchy fully—that encourages their virtual endorsement of Tyson's wanton pursuit of satisfaction in a society that historically has attempted to repress black men's putative intellectually, sexually, and economically threatening presence.

What follows is my attempt to bring a black male feminist critique to bear upon an analysis of three acts of male sexual violence, or inscriptions thereof: an *L.A. Law* episode that aired on March 26, 1992, the day Tyson was sentenced for his rape conviction, and that focused on an athlete's sexual battery trial; the Tyson rape trial and media coverage; and Spike Lee's figuration of what his female protagonist calls her "near-rape" in *She's Gotta Have It,* his breakthrough film that inscribes into its narrative form male responses critical of unconventional expressions of female desire.

I recognize the temptation for well-intentioned but necessarily self-interested men to structure their defensiveness into analyses such as this effort to read sexual violence as a form of "gendered speech."[5] I seek to insulate my discussion as much as possible from this danger by relying heavily (though not un-critically) on feminist legal scholar and activist Catharine MacKinnon's inquiry into this issue. Her collection, *Toward a Feminist Theory of the State,* provides, in a manner approximated by no other critical text with which I am familiar, a theoretically dense and politically astute gynocentric analysis of the trajectories and consequences of a gendered hierarchy that encourages the naturalization of male objectification of the female body.

On MacKinnon, Sexuality, and
"The Eroticization of Domination"

In her theorizing about some of the contemporary meanings of gender, sexuality, and sexual violence, MacKinnon insists that no instance of sexual behavior in the West falls necessarily outside of the influence of patriarchal conditioning. MacKinnon, that is to say, sees the Western world as being structured in dominance even—*especially*—in its patterns, practices, and valuations of sexual desire.

Her rigorous, unsentimental analysis of the meanings of sex challenges readers to interrogate their own sometimes complacent thinking about patriarchy's dominion not only over traditional foci of feminist investigation such as pornography, abortion, and the workplace, but also over the politics of desire and eroticism in our own lives, over realms which we want to believe we are able to protect from the taint of hierarchal structuring.

According to MacKinnon, however, the power inequities that determine crucial aspects of the social construction of gender and sexuality are so pervasive for both men and women that to escape from their effects is virtually impossible. Arguing that an adequate definition of sexuality must acknowledge as a central facet of its general constitution "the eroticization of dominance and submission"[6]—that both subject and object are turned on, as it were, by the display of power—MacKinnon insists that feminists energetically investigate the complex ways in which these areas are deeply implicated in the patriarchal social structure. She asserts that the tendency of much feminist scholarship to avoid this type of investigation is perhaps nowhere more problematically in evidence than in the widely accepted views on rape that seek to destigmatize violation for female victims of male sexual brutality by distinguishing consensual intercourse from sexual violence. According to this view, no contiguous relation necessarily exists between phallic power and the actualizing of fantasies of nonconsensual penile penetration. Opposing this perspective, MacKinnon offers the following argument:

> To say rape is violence not sex preserves the "sex is good" norm by simply distinguishing forced sex as "not sex," whether it means sex to the perpetrator or even, later, to the victim, who has difficulty experiencing sex without reexperiencing the rape. Whatever is sex cannot be violent; whatever is violent cannot be sex. This analytic wish-fulfillment makes it possible for rape to be opposed by those who would save sexuality from the rapists while leaving the sexual fundamentals of male dominance intact. (135)

We might see MacKinnon's project as an attempt to expose "the sexual fundamentals of male dominance," even when such exposure threatens our own ability to believe that our practice of consensual sex—of lovemaking as opposed to sex taking—is untainted by manifestations of phallic power. To insist that rape is indeed sex to males and females, that what we consider consensual sex can and does often involve violence of one sort or another, and that paradigmatic dimensions of gender construction seem to encourage the use of force in situations where male desire is thwarted—this is to urge that we move to a more inclusive and systematic reading of the social meanings of sexual difference. As MacKinnon puts it interrogatively: "Is masculinity the enjoyment of violation, femininity the enjoyment of being violated? Is that the social meaning of intercourse?" (136)

These are unsettling figurations in part because they give us no license to conceive of any space, any sexual act or desire as being always already outside of these structures of dominance. If dominance, force, and control are crucial aspects of even the most standard scripts of heterosexual interaction, if the "model" articulation of sexual desire—"man proposes, woman disposes"—"does not envision a situation the woman controls being placed in, or choices she frames" (174), if the very structure of gender presents women generally with only the power of consent as though that consent is "free exercise of sexual choices under conditions of equality" when no such equality exists in fact (175)—if all these conditions obtain, how do we participate in the experience of heterosexuality in ways that do not mark our enactments of sexual desire as socially transgressive?

In her contributions to a systematic feminist theorizing of gender inequality, MacKinnon remains generally unconcerned with investigating the means by which males and females work with and around the pervasive impact of patriarchy, or fail in their efforts to do so. Because she is more interested in analyzing the structures of dominance which impinge upon women's existences than in investigating either male or female efforts to wrestle with their cultural inheritance, MacKinnon's formulations are limited as interrogations of the entirety of the culture's permissible gendered behavior. Among the matters MacKinnon fails to explore thoroughly are the possibilities of female sexual pleasure, the dynamics of female capitulation to patriarchal desires, and the attractiveness of the rewards male hegemony offers for willing (or seemingly willing) capitulation.[7] Impressed as I am by the power of MacKinnon's perspective, I believe we must also be equipped analytically to recognize and respond forcefully to the fact that certain members of non-hegemonic classes—including some who have fully internalized the putatively derogatory philosophies of patriarchy that render them mere objects of male sexual desire—seem to be faring much better psychically than members of the male ruling class who have allowed that ideology to come to represent significant aspects of their worldviews.[8] In other words, our thinking about issues from rape to representation might profit from an attempt to grapple with the fact that, as Patrick Colm Hogan argues, "there are *secondary gains* which accrue to the members of any dominated group also and thus . . . an understanding of such gains is critical for an explanation of the acceptance of dominated peoples of ideologies which preserve and extend their domination."[9]

I introduce the issue of "secondary gains" here to provide myself the analytical space to apply MacKinnon's theorizing to areas of sexual politics that include male hegemony's systematizing of mechanisms of female reward for compliance with patriarchal desire. This is not simply, then, a knee-jerk masculinist response to the perceived pleasures of female objectification, but an attempt to explore some of the ways in which the rewards for achieving patriarchy's ideals of female behavior and beauty (including the no doubt limited yet still palpable pleasure of desirability) remain so fully integrated into the structures of male dominance as to appear central to many people's sense of human existence. Surely it is ironic, for example, that at a time when some radical feminists and conservative politicians have finally found an area about which they agree—the dangers to males and especially to females of pornography—beauty contests have proliferated to the point that they are aired on television nearly as often as mass entertainment award shows.

The discussion below of figurations of Mike Tyson during his legal and media trials strives to move beyond an analysis of the convicted rapist as inevitably trapped by baneful aspects of the ethos of the street and the boxing profession in order to examine the involvement of another deeply implicated institution—the beauty contest—in this gendered drama. For if boxing represents a systematizing of cherished features of the ideal masculine portfolio, including discipline, persistence, punishment, physical and psychic strength, and most especially violence; and if the blood sport serves many spectators as a means—"sanctioned," in Joyce Carol Oates's words, "by tradition and custom"[10]—through which to channel some of our own atavistic urges, the beauty contest represents an equally powerful ritualistic realm through which we systematize the pleasures of female objectification and in which female acquiescence to masculine desire is structured and rewarded. Before tackling this subject, however, I want to turn to an *L.A. Law* episode, one which evinces both the possibilities and dangers of employing mass cultural forms as a means of seeking to change our national views about the dimensions of sexual violence.

(L.A.) Law, Rape, and the Dynamics of Ideological Contestation

Popular forms of narrative such as film and television make continual use of legal drama—especially the drama of the courtroom—because the courtroom represents a site of potentially highly charged public discursive contestation. What fictive or fictionalized legal dramas provide generally is a sense of closure, of right and wrong, an overt rendering of guilt and innocence. We typically leave contemporary legal dramas fully aware of opportunity, blame, and motive, even if the bad guys are not always punished.

But dramatic resolution is not always provided, as in the case of the episode of *L.A. Law* that aired on the very day Mike Tyson began serving his six-year sentence for raping Desiree Washington. In this episode, Grace van Owen, a partner in the show's centerpiece legal firm, defends a white major-league baseball star accused of rape. In preparing her client for his testimony with the assistance of the mock cross-examination of her colleague, Jonathan Rollins, van Owen (along with Rollins and the athlete himself) learns that he has indeed committed rape. It is not the experience of raping itself but rather the accused's unself-conscious articulation of a classic acquaintance rape scenario (male restraint of a resisting female, her clearly articulated pleas to the male for a cessation of sexual advances, and male misreading of the meanings of female resistance) that demonstrates to him—and to his various audiences—that he is a rapist.

Surprisingly, given her debilitating bouts with conscience earlier in her career, van Owen does not attempt to persuade the accused to change his plea to guilty, nor does she apparently feel deeply conflicted about her own decision not to allow her client to offer incriminating or perjurious testimony. After her admittedly less than impassioned efforts lead to the rapist's acquittal, van Owen brings to the bar in which the athlete's victory party is being held the list of mental health agencies she had promised him, from which he might choose a therapist to help him check his misogynist expressions of sexual desire. (He admits to van Owen that he has been similarly forceful with a number of other women.) When she gives him the list, however, it is clear that he has no intention of calling any of the agencies or altering his behavior significantly. The scene ends with the movement of van Owen's (as well as the camera's and, hence, our) gaze from the list stuffed casually in the rapist's back pocket to the buttocks of a female fan on which one of his hands rests. This fan, who embraced the baseball player before the attorney's arrival in a manner that could be said to reflect a degree of sexual attraction, then encourages his movement away from the somber defense attorney and toward the raucous beer-drinking celebration.

As Michael Denning notes in an analysis of the origins and trajectories of contemporary cultural studies, the exegetically compelling nature of forms of popular culture derives in part from their sometimes seemingly unself-conscious manifestations of "the dialectic of containment and resistance, of reification and utopia."[11] In other words, rather than representing a mechanism either of hegemony's control over the masses or of its forceful resistance by the masses, popular culture serves as a location of the struggle to determine the most persuasive of disputed ideological positions, among the most prominent of which are the implications and proper enactments of gender (and, to a lesser extent perhaps, race).

The L.A. Law episode evinces aspects of this struggle where the politics of sexual desire and violence are concerned. In presenting the athlete's recognition of his behavior as rape, as well as van Owen's and Rollins's cognition of that fact, the show provides a metadrama of rape education that might serve to compel the members of the audience to understand and identify the dynamics of sexual brutality in the worlds in which they live. But if popular cultural forms generally reflect both counterhegemonic utopian elements and the means of their containment, those elements are represented here in a figuration of the possibility of recognizing the dynamics of acquaintance rape and the willingness—despite the ease with which moderately competent lawyers can create reasonable doubt in the minds of the jury—if not to accept the legal consequences of that recognition, then at least to work to transform the mind-set that has made the history of sexual violation possible.

But the narrative problematizes even that somewhat compromised presentation by articulating a certainty that the unrepentant athlete will continue his pattern of brutal sexual behavior. While the fact that the rapist will continue to rape is suggested by his casual treatment of the proffered list that holds the potential for emancipation from his androcentric view of sexuality, his interaction with the female fan serves as further evidence of his lack of sincere repentance and of his inability to transform his attitudes about the expression of sexual desire. But unlike the certainty that ultimately attends a viewer's analysis of the act for which he is charged, the interchange that portends the inevitability of the athlete's future transgressions is sketched so ambiguously as to limit (if not erase completely) her or his capacity to make effective connections between the rapist's admitted transgressive behavior and his subsequent interactions with women. For it is possible to view the athlete's caressing of the fan's buttocks as a bold but not wholly unsolicited public response to an apparent indication of reciprocal female desire.

Our interrogation is further complicated by the fact that the female fan herself impels his movement from a necessarily grim space of conscience, penitence, and reformation to a more profane site of celebration, spirits, and sexuality. If we are to see the fan as representative future victim of the rapist's unchecked exercise of phallic power, as the camera's movement from redeeming list to transgressive touch would seem to indicate, why is she figured as the agent of her own victimization? As luring him away from compensatory knowledge with her shapely buttocks and apparent sexually promissory acts, including her failure to rebuff his publicly improper buttocks fondling? Because the episode investigates the propensity for male misreading of one of the most devastating consequences of hierarchical gender dynamics—sexual brutality—the fact that it concludes with a scene that brings together unrepentant rapist and lascivious temptress, and insists that we consider their inevitable off-screen sexual confrontation as a rape, is bewildering, whatever clarification its audience might have gained about some aspects of acquaintance rape. How could this temptress's interactions with the acquitted eventuate in rape if she seems at this point, in fact, to actively encourage and respond to male desire, even steering the phallic male into the place of celebration of his power? Given her participation in this gendered drama, can she then fail to consent to male urgings for penile penetration? If this fan is to be seen as representative future victim, she seems also almost literally to be asking for it.

Let me be clear about this: I am not saying that she deserves or desires her portended victimization, but that the show presents, in the space it reserves for articulating the inevitability of the athlete's continued participation in acts of sexual brutality, a scenario whose initiatory moves its viewers may be hard-pressed to see as eventuating in anything but consensual sexual intercourse. Faced with the camera's insistence on a contiguous relationship between salvific list and buttocks fondling, the viewer may be left wondering whether the athlete really needs the list, if the females with whom he comes into contact and whom he deems sexually desirable are generally as responsive to his charms as this fan; and believing that, if such seemingly reciprocal expressions of desire can eventuate in rape, it may indeed be quite difficult, given our typical puritanical reticence about speaking openly even with potentially willing sexual partners about our desires, for a fellow to know what women want sexually. Indeed, if we read this thematic muddle as resulting from a conflict between feminist pleas for an acknowledgment of acquaintance rape's devastating consequences and masculinist insistence on the near impossibility of knowing exactly what constitute transgressive behavior, we must conclude that the masculinist case is much more persuasively presented here.

Acquaintance rape happens, more often than many of us can possibly imagine, the *L.A. Law* episode seems to be suggesting. But it also implies that women's degree of sexual interest—what women want, to reference again the Freudian interrogative—is nearly impossible to know, given the contradictory messages suggested by their responses to male desire. The episode's wish to impart potentially reassuring perspectives to its viewers, then, is undermined by its presentation of female desire as thoroughly mysterious.

"You're Turning Me On": The Boxer, the Beauty Queen, and the Rituals of Gender

New York Times sports columnist Robert Lipsyte predicted two days after Mike Tyson's conviction for raping 1991 Miss Black America pageant contestant Desiree Washington that the former heavyweight boxing champion would become "a symbolic character in various morality plays, a villain-victim of the Gender War, the Race War, the Class War and the Backlash against Celebrity Excess."[12] Lipsyte's analysis was indeed prophetic, as "warrior" respondents expressed strong feelings about the relationship of the Tyson event to these individual "wars." Elements of the trial testimony—particularly recollections by defense and prosecution witnesses alike of Tyson's own words and actions—have, in fact, fueled some of these discussions. For example, according to one pageant contestant, Tyson himself tied his brazen fondling of several of the pageant entries to his celebrity: "When pageant officials introduced Tyson to the contestants during the rehearsal, he said that he wanted to have sex with all of them. 'I'm a celebrity and we do that sort of thing,' she recalled Tyson saying."[13] This statement indicates that, like many men, Tyson saw female sexual accessibility as an entitlement, as his status-conferring droit du signeur. While other issues pertaining to the Tyson event might be similarly bracketed, I believe that a truly cogent analysis of the motivations, broader social consequences, and potential interpretive ramifications of the event must begin with the premise that the wars to which Lipsyte refers are inextricably connected.

Tyson's legal and media trials have most frequently, in fact, been addressed in athletic or racial terms. This is not to suggest that social manifestations of gender relations do not figure prominently in these analyses, but that they are, according to this view, played out here in a manner unique to athletic or racially charged arenas. There is a general unwillingness on the part of investigators to see the Tyson event as an opportunity to examine the ways in which we as members of this society are deeply implicated in, and struggling with, many of the issues brought to the fore in this case. Such evasiveness is manifested, for example, in a piece Richard Corliss wrote for *Time* magazine during Tyson's trial. According to Corliss, Tyson "seems caged in his chair . . . but in his natural habitat, the boxing ring, Mike is a creature . . ." Clearly, Corliss's representation of Tyson as animalistic force has much in common, however unwittingly, with a history of caucacentric discourse about black animality. He concludes his pre-conviction analysis with the following claim: "Innocent or guilty, though, Tyson is more to be pitied than feared—not because he may lose his freedom and his livelihood, but because he seems an exemplar of all those sad studs who are prisoners of manhood."[14] Corliss seeks to contain the implications of Tyson's behavior within androcentric spaces ("prisoners of manhood") which, by and large, the general male population feels it is able to avoid rather easily. For Corliss, Tyson is uninhibited male other, the result of a palpably skewed socialization process.

Afro-American racial warriors, male and female, seem equally unconcerned about examining the sexual implications of the accusations against Tyson, or they see such implications as being at odds with intraracial imperatives. As one newspaper article, which notes the "countless debates" about his conviction, indicates, "While a number of women have been outspoken in their criticism, many others have accused Miss Washington of helping to destroy a prominent black man. Even if she was raped, these women argue, she should not have made the case public."[15] In the case of pro-Tyson female race warriors who believe that Washington might have indeed been raped, group considerations take precedence over other concerns in our never-ending struggle to forge a collective black response to caucacentric interests. Certain other Afro-Americans, particularly those whose voices are recorded in black newspapers, seem unable even to entertain the notion that

Tyson could have raped his accuser. One of the boxer's black journalist supporters, for example, argues that "Mike Tyson got jobbed" despite the fact that, as he himself notes, "the evidence, the chain of events and his less-than-adequate legal team spelled doom for him," and he insists that the "two Black jurors clearly were intimidated" by the "right-wing, ultra-conservative former marine" who "became the leader of the jury in Tyson's case." Another black newspaper columnist asserts that black male "leaders" like Tyson, "Clarence Thomas, Marion Barry, [and] Gus Savage" are accused of sexual wrongdoing by "manufactured, manipulated and manicured" Afro-American females who serve as willing pawns of a white patriarchy that seeks at all costs to undermine strong black men. Yet another columnist endorses the proclamations of a black minister who insists, "Here's another lynching of a Black man. The girl's story was rehearsed and the Whites backed the girl."[16]

Such sentiments echo the views of figures such as Al Sharpton, who promises that "no matter what, I won't turn against" Tyson, whom he thinks "may have been guilty of being very overly aggressive with his approach to women, but I do not think that Mike, by any stretch of the imagination, is guilty of rape," and street entrepreneurs who affix Tyson's visage to T-shirts that proclaim "The bitch set me up."[17] Of these responses, perhaps the most startling are the efforts of the Reverend Dr. Theodore Jemison, leader of the National Baptist Convention, who spearheaded a petition drive to collect 100,000 signatures in an attempt to "seek a suspended sentence" for Tyson, who is, in Jemison's estimation, "one of the few 'modern day African-American role models.'" According to Jemison, his activities on Tyson's behalf are justified because the boxer's legal difficulties are emblematic of the status of "the black male and his [general] plight" in American society.[18] These perspectives call to mind, all too vividly, a story Susan Brownmiller tells about an encounter with a black male librarian at the Schomburg Center while researching her seminal study of rape, *Against Our Will*. The librarian informed her that "to black people, rape has meant the lynching of the black man."[19] The librarian, a keeper of historical records on Afro-American presence, seems intent on challenging black women's status as significant sufferers in comparison to black men.

Further, figures whose work has been as focused on the consequences of the gender hierarchy as Queen Latifah and Spike Lee term what they consider his flawed trial the rape of Mike Tyson,[20] a fact which speaks volumes about the persistence of views such as those of Brownmiller's librarian that, given the choice between being attentive to allegations of black male victimization and of black female oppression, the adequately informed investigator must choose to be concerned primarily with the plight of Africa's male descendants. There are profound internal and external pressures not to pursue a course of action viewed by segments of the black population as antithetical to the struggles for social progress, as the beauty pageant sponsor who called Tyson "a serial buttocks fondler" learned when he made plans to sue the fighter. Announcing that he had abandoned the idea, the sponsor said, "I don't want to be part of an attempt to crucify a black role model."[21]

Several journalists and, indeed, at least one of the jurors in the case suggested that Tyson's own testimony and his legal team's defense strategy more generally— "depicting him as a notorious sexual predator in an attempt to persuade the jury that the accuser should have known better than to go out with him and accompany him to his room"—severely hampered his chances for acquittal.[22] Nothing Tyson or his lawyers said or failed to say during his trial more clearly indicates that he violated Miss Washington and had no understanding of the legal definitions of rape beyond the savage stranger scenario which legal scholar Susan Estrich identifies as "aggravated rape" than comments made by Tyson himself.[23] In proclaiming his innocence, he said: "I'm not guilty of this crime; there were no black eyes, no broken ribs. When I'm in the ring, I break their ribs; I break their jaws. To me that's hurting somebody."[24]

This concept demonstrates, as clearly as the view that rape is inconsequential next to our need to have inspiring black male heroes in circulation, an inability to acknowledge that nonconsensual sex can have injurious effects on the psyche of rape victims at least on a par with pugilistic beatings and racially motivated acts of injustice. Such comments, the reflections of a mentality that can conceive of sexual "hurt" only in terms of discoloring and bone-fracturing blows, leave little doubt in the minds of any but the boxer's most rabid supporters about his guilt, if we accept the legal definition of rape as "intercourse with force or coercion and without consent" (MacKinnon 173). For Tyson, who may believe wholeheartedly that he was merely "very overly aggressive" with Washington, rape appears to mean the use of a level of force on a par with that necessary to batter a highly skilled pugilistic opponent into submission.[25] Desiring Desiree, and having gained what he may have believed to be her sexual consent by virtue of her willingness to be alone with him in his hotel room, Tyson apparently initiated an episode of sexual contact that, as his accuser describes it, is consistent with a pattern of abuse rumors about which have trailed the boxer since he was a teenager.

Catharine MacKinnon's discussion of connections between the objectification of the female body and certain masculine notions of sex helps explain factors that could have contributed to Tyson's behavior: "To be sexually objectified means having a social meaning imposed on your being that defines you as to be sexually used, according to your desired uses, and then using you that way. Doing this is sex in the male system" (140). A key to successful objectification of the female body is persuading women of the benefits for them in masculinist formulations of women's erotic utility. The cultural imposition of notions of the appropriateness and inevitability of the female body's figurations as site of recreational phallic desire, in other words, depends on the success of phallocentricism's institutionalizing of its perspectives to the extent that they are unquestioned by large numbers of receptive female accomplices. Along with financial remuneration, which historically have been a major part of our sexual economy, the ability to make her want sex and to be satisfied with being the object of and receptacle for male desire—to be deemed physically worthy of inspiring that desire—has been considered by many males and females alike to be appropriate payment for services rendered.

Beauty pageants, in their unabashed reveling in the female form and their practice of rewarding the achievement of a certain measurable image of beauty, are among the most lurid sites of the practice of male objectification of women's bodies in Western societies. As an institution whose raison d'être is assessment and reward, the beauty pageant codifies and thereby legitimizes evaluative measures that, when encountered by elements of the general population, become the basis of mass vernacular practices of evaluating the female form. Recently, beauty pageant officials have sought to appease feminist groups concerned about the individual and social impact of objectification upon women by bringing to the fore the talent aspect of these undoubtedly entertaining peep shows. Nevertheless, the fact that it would be impossible to imagine a parallel mass cultural male demonstration of talent—one wherein men would be judged simultaneously on their poise in answering inane questions about the state of the world and on the aesthetic effect of their appearance in crotch-hugging bathing trunks and form-flattering evening wear—renders inescapable the phallocentric dimensions of this social practice. In fact, I would argue that such pageants serve as sites wherein some of the particulars of male hegemony are disseminated and reinforced as aspects of the eroticizing of male dominance. MacKinnon makes the pertinent distinctions:

> Dominance eroticized defines the imperatives of its masculinity, submission eroticized defines its femininity. So many distinctive features of women's status is second class—the restriction and constraint and contortion, the servility and the display, the self-mutilation and requisite presentation of self as a beautiful thing, the enforced passivity, the humiliation—are made into the content of sex for women. Being a thing for sexual use is fundamental to it. (130)

Whatever redeeming social value beauty pageants can be said to possess, we cannot ignore their role in reinforcing beliefs about women's inferiority as a consequence of their reduction of the female to the status of fetishized object. Perhaps the most detrimental aspect of that objectification is its demands for what MacKinnon calls the "requisite presentation of self as a beautiful thing," that is to say, is having one's human value assessed literally in terms of the quality of one's aesthetic self-presentation.

I introduce the subject of beauty pageants here because I believe, Tyson's history of sexual harassment and alleged acts of sexual brutality notwithstanding, we must recognize some implications of the fact that the site of the boxer's initial encounter with Washington (and, in fact, the reason for his and her presence in Indianapolis) was an activity in which such instances of female self-presentation constitute normative behavior. According to Tyson's testimony, beauty pageant officials instructed him to respond to the contestants in a visibly enthusiastic manner: "Pageant officials told me to touch, play with, and hug the contestants. I said [to the officials] . . . I like that part."[26] If MacKinnon is right in saying that such self-presentation demonstrates female adoption of the social function, "a thing for sexual use," enthusiastic male response such as Tyson's to females gathered for just such a purpose seems hardly surprising, except perhaps for its remarkable absence of tact.[27] While we must censure Tyson's phallocentric utilization of pageant contestants during the photo session as willess playthings, we might also see his behavior during the Black Expo event where he first encountered Washington as a socially conditioned reaction to women who participate so willingly in their own objectification, behavior encouraged, if his testimony is accurate, by pageant officials themselves.

Beauty pageants serve also, I believe, as sites for the projection of many of masculinity's seemingly contradictory versions of feminine desirability: virginal (or seemingly virginal—hence the emphasis on the contestant's unmarried status and apparently wholesome nature) yet sexually alluring (no more so, perhaps, than during torturous walks across stages in spike-heeled shoes and either bathing suits or form-fitting evening gowns); intelligent (all Miss America contestants, after all, are enrolled in a college or university) yet endearingly naive (forced to smile constantly while attempting to formulate answers to questions concerning the greenhouse effect or how to achieve lasting world peace); dependent yet extremely self-possessed. As such, these pageants embody seemingly contradictory aspects of male desire as well as demonstrating patriarchy's ability to disguise that desire as mere aesthetic appreciation or altruistic impulse.

Washington's participation in the Miss Black America beauty pageant, her responses to Tyson's propositions during the photo session and as a reply to what the female driver of Tyson's limousine termed his "begging" her to join him (and her eager and excited reaction to that proposition), and the rape itself—these are contiguous elements in what MacKinnon terms the "systemic context of group subjection" called patriarchy (173). Indeed, I will show that the particulars of the female state that to MacKinnon indicate facets of female capitulation to male acts of sexual objectification—the "requisite presentation of self as a beautiful thing, the enforced passivity, the humiliation"—can be said to describe Washington's self-presentation on the occasions in question.

On the sashes worn by the Miss Black America pageant contestants, there is a silhouette of a woman which represents what some hold to be a distinctly Afro-American ideal of beauty and desirability. Slim, buxom, with a rounded 1960s afro hairstyle, large buttocks, and extremely long legs, this figure stands with her right arm angled and right hand placed (rather defiantly, it would appear) on her hip. But if the defiantly placed hand is meant as a visualization of a tendency to-ward noncapitulation, self-confidence, or "attitude" (a sister who don't take no mess), that effect is undermined to some extent by her uplifted left leg whose foot points downward. At first glance, it is a leg poised to strike, a lower-bodied equiv-alent of the self-possessed and obstinately positioned right hand, but given the context in which the silhouette is offered—as the essence of black female beauty in objectifying self-display—that leg might also be seen as preparing to expose the female sex organs to a perpetual receptivity to masculine desire.

At any rate, the image is startling, not merely because of its erotic qualities or cultural encoding of black female bodies but because of the fact that it is just this pose (minus the uplifted leg, but with legs spread suggestively apart) that Washington strikes in published photos that record her participation in the swimsuit portion of the competition. In effect, she strives to personify this black masculinist fantasy, to reproduce its posture, to be, in other words, a prizewinning, real-life embodiment of this resistant, yet compliant, idealization of black male notions of black beauty. What we must recognize as part of the desirability of this fetishizing of the black woman's form is its attitudinal ambivalence, its mixed sexual signals which conform both to what is, with regard to Afro-American females, a historically resonant narrative of untraditionally resistant female behavior—the strong, self-possessed black woman to whom theories of true womanhood never adequately applied—and to male desires for erotic access to, and conquest of, this figure.[28]

While tales of Afro-American women's psychic and physical strength—myths of black superwomen, in Michelle Wallace's phrase—are legend, this strength is generally demonstrated not in or as conquest, not in an ability to con-trol or dominate others, as in the masculine ideal, but in a capacity to survive with their sanity intact the socioeconomic and sexual domination they suffer in Ameri-can society. Afro-American female strength, in other words, was and is still often seen as a function of an ability not to conquer oppression but to negotiate it suc-cessfully. Calvin Hernton presents the plight of the black woman:

> Throughout the entire span of her existence on American soil, the black
> woman has been alone and unprotected, not only socially but psycho-

logically as well. She has *had* to fend for herself as if she were a man; being black, even more so. I am not implying that the black woman has become frigid or "masculine." In fact, she is potentially, if not already, the most sexual animal on this planet. It is not frigidity that I am describing. It is *rigidity.* And it has been this quality of austerity in the Negro woman which has enabled her to survive what few other women have ever lived through.[29]

I do not endorse Hernton's perspective on black female sexuality, which, like other such generalizations in his study, is virtually impossible to verify empirically or by any other means. However, his analysis is sufficiently attentive to the socioeconomic and historical facts that accompany the mythologizing of black women's lives to stand as a representative articulation of the superwoman myth. According to this myth, to be a strong Afro-American woman historically is to participate in a tradition of endurance, is to have seen and survived horrendous troubles that would have permanently debilitated others. Their survival is generally attributed to a resilient sense of faith in God, humanity (particularly black humanity), and self, and a willingness to love others (particularly black men) who may have contributed significantly to their troubles.

I offer this simplified figuration of the important cultural myth here because it seems to me to explain a good deal about the sympathetic Afro-American mass response to Tyson and this episode in his checkered career as American citizen: the insistence of some of Tyson's black supporters that Washington should not have reported his crime; the attitudes of some black religious leaders about the allegations; and most especially the fetishized image of the black female form that adorns the Miss Black America contestants' sashes and declares Washington's suitability for entrance into this rite of objectification.[30] Because a now-celebrated history of black women surviving forms of mistreatment much more brutal and protracted than Tyson's act has led, in Hernton's view, to the development of rigidity, as well as a belief that the race war is a much higher priority than comparatively insignificant intraracial gender skirmishes, many apparently feel that Washington should have seen it as her responsibility to endure her pain in order to serve the greater good of the race. According to this view, the racial responsibility to maintain silence is especially relevant in this case because Tyson, a successful black man, gives aid to the struggle against a white hegemony that seeks to deny Afro-American people widely celebrated, unassimilated, inspiringly heroic male examples. Any other response renders Washington vulnerable to allegations of treason because of a view that Tyson's incarceration serves the interests of white hegemony more than, say, his unchecked phallic presence among the general population. Black warriors whose sensibilities are untouched by a feminist politics seem to dismiss the possibility that intraracial sexual violence can occur if

Afro-American female victims seek justice for acts alleged to have been perpetrated by prominent black men through a legal system that is demonstrably inequitable in its dealings with blacks generally, and black males in particular.

In their efforts to dictate where and how such mythic black female qualities ought to be displayed, some blacks seem to be suggesting either that prominent Afro-American men are by virtue of their status incapable of sexual harassment or rape; or sexual violence is insignificant as an issue compared to racial uplift (unless, of course, it is perpetrated by white men) and, thus, black women's historic strength is best exhibited as an ability to recognize and act in terms of this belief. Consequently, people feel justified in speaking of the rape of Mike Tyson while a young college student sits in fear that members of her race who believe that she has performed a historical wrong against black manhood will seek retribution on her person, on her already victimized body. She is said to fear a Rushdie-like sentence, to fear ostracism of the type encountered by Milton Coleman, the *Washington Post* reporter who published Jesse Jackson's putatively off-the-record "hymietown" remarks and subsequently was deemed a treacherous lackey of white male power.[31]

A *New York Times* article outlining the jury's reasons for convicting Tyson cited the following factors, among others, as contributing to the guilty verdict:

> There was her invitation to one of the roommates to join her on the date with Mr. Tyson. "She's going to bring her roommate along to watch while she has sex with him?" Mr. [Greg] Garrison asked incredulously.
>
> And . . . there was the camera that she said she brought along with her for souvenir pictures of Mr. Tyson and other celebrities she hoped to meet.[32]

These issues, however important they are in undermining the gold-digger defense strategy employed by Tyson's team of lawyers, seem infinitely less damaging to his case if considered in the light of MacKinnon's theorizing about the gender dynamics of American society that influenced the behavior of both the boxer and the beauty queen. If MacKinnon is right in her description of what our society projects generally as the ideal pattern whose object is sexual consummation— "man proposes, woman disposes"—and if women are conditioned generally not to acknowledge sexual desire even to themselves, then Washington's apparent intentions before confronting Tyson's erotic urges do not foreclose the possibility that she could have consented to having sex with the boxer. Given the non-mutuality of even the "ideal" of "female control over intercourse," what we might consider from our interpretive distance her self-evident plans are not necessarily accurate measures of her receptivity to Tyson's sexual moves. Generally, socially acceptable expressions of women's sexuality are constructed specifically as responsive to "the custom of male initiative," to articulations of male desire. For, as MacKinnon persuasively argues, "Apart from the disparate consequences of refusal, this model does not envision a situation the woman controls being placed in, or choices she frames" (174).

Washington's capitulation to this norm in other respects is demonstrated by her reactions to his expression of interest in her. As she reported in her testimony, she responded with incredulity to Tyson's inquiry about whether she and her parents "like him" (meaning, it would appear, admire his pugilistic skills and perhaps his social persona, though Tyson seems to acknowledge, as his view of celebrity entitlements indicates, no distinction between genuine affection and a fan's distanced admiration); she says that her parents "don't really know you," and that "I don't really know you either, . . . but from what I've seen, you're okay."[33] Nonetheless, she agrees, with admitted excitement, to go out with a man she doesn't really know, checks with him afterwards to make sure that "they were really going out on a date," and capitulates to his late-night "begging" that she change out of what prosecutor Garrison describes strategically as "her jammies"[34] and accompany him on a date.[34] She admits to operating in terms of this standard script of gendered behavior in her response to defense attorney Vincent Fuller's inquiry about her interest in Tyson:

> Fuller asked if she had held out any hope, when she joined Tyson in the limousine, of establishing a relationship with the 25-year-old boxer.
> "There was always the hope," she said. "But I had my camera with me. That's what I most wanted."[35]

If a desire to win Tyson's heart was, for Washington, secondary to the "hope" that he would take her to celebrity parties in order that she might capture on film images of black dignitaries (including, one would assume, Tyson himself), it was nonetheless pressing enough to encourage her to see him as an appropriate agent for achieving her primary desire. While accounts of the trial I have read do not discuss whether she could have gained entry to those parties simply by virtue of her status as beauty pageant contestant, it is certainly the case that the starstruck teenager's sense of legitimacy vis-à-vis that austere group would have been enhanced by her role as the boxer's date. To my knowledge, there was no evidence presented to suggest that Tyson ever explicitly mentioned such parties as his intended destination; she seems to have projected her desires to attend them onto his purposefully vague invitation, "We can go around Indianapolis. I want to talk to you."[36]

Tyson's attractiveness to Washington as an escort, then, was tied specifically to his celebrity status, and that status is conferred upon him literally as a consequence of his masculine power. If MacKinnon is correct that "male power takes the social form of what men as a gender want sexually, which centers on power itself, as socially defined" (131), then Tyson's assumption that female sexual availability was one of the perquisites of his social power was not his villainous phallocentric invention, or, rather, not his alone. Given characterizations of Tyson as a figure prone to adopting the views, manners of speech, and, indeed, modes of analysis of influential figures in his life, it is not surprising that he would have unselfconsciously embraced a masculinist construction that was in many respects so personally beneficial. And while we might see Tyson as a subhuman shadow upon whom we can thrust all of the negative qualities of masculinity in order to purge ourselves of the guilt of our own implication in the hierarchical structures of male dominance, what is most essential about the Tyson case for us, I believe, is that we recognize it as an occasion which screams at us to overhaul those constructs we have created, inherited, and allowed to stand as the natural constitution of gender relations.

In her status as an enthusiastic participant in a male-controlled ritual of objectification and as a figure clearly attracted to Tyson's masculine (and celebrity) power, Washington was implicated in this androcentric script before and after she encountered the boxer, as well as, clearly, during the act of sexual violence itself. To see her, in pictures taken after her encounter with Tyson, strike the pose of the self-possessed and sexually accessible black beauty queen, the very embodiment of black male desire, is to see the result of a social process that considers female objectification an unchallengeable fact of life. Hers is a pose women adopt despite the psychic and physical pain that often attends efforts to serve as fleshly embodiments of male desire. While clearly its intention is not to excuse males who victimize women, feminist theorizing of the virtual inescapability of phallocentric rule suggests that behavior such as Tyson's (and Washington's) during the 1991 Black Expo is inevitable, given our present cultural condition, and it will remain so until minds more capable of challenging the gendered status quo than his (and hers) devise mechanisms whereby to establish other modes of masculine and feminine being and action as the regulatory imperatives of the society. Without question, the outrage of many at Tyson's behavior is fully warranted. But unless we take to heart MacKinnon's view that "rape is not an isolated event or moral transgression or individual interchange gone wrong but an act of terrorism and torture within a systemic context of group subjection" (172), unless we continue to confront the meanings of these and other manifestations of androcentrism's dominion, including beauty pageants, dating rituals, and society's general tolerance of levels of sexual coercion, we can never expect that outrage to be translated into preventive social policies.[37]

Tyson's actions and post-conviction statements conform in some ways to standard scripts of sexually transgressive male behavior that MacKinnon identifies in the following way:

Rape comes to mean a strange (read Black) man who does not know his victim but does know she does not want sex with him, going ahead anyway. But men are systematically conditioned not even to notice what women want. . . . Rapists typically believe the woman loved it. "Probably the single most used cry of rapist to victim is 'You bitch . . . slut . . . you know you want it. You all want it' and afterward, 'there now, you really enjoyed it, didn't you?'" Women, as a survival strategy, must ignore or devalue or mute desires, particularly lack of them, to convey the impression that the man will get what he wants regardless of what they want. (181).

In many respects, Tyson's behavior fits this profile of a black rapist so blinded by phallocentric notions of acceptable levels of force that he does not care that he crossed what he might view as a faintly sketched line in his pursuit of sexual satisfaction.[38] In her study of convicted rapists, Diana Scully speaks of sexual criminals who proclaim their innocence of rape charges, despite their use of weapons to subdue and terrify female hitchhikers or women whose homes they had broken into, as "deniers."[39] According to Washington, Tyson—certainly the most famous denier in recent history, and a figure whose trained-for-violence body might surely have been seen by Washington to be as threatening a weapon as a knife or gun—added an improvisational twist to this standard script by asking her not whether she "loved" the sex act itself, not whether his sexual thrustings were adequately pleasurable to nullify her initial resistance and make the event physically gratifying for her also, but whether she loved *him* for his responsiveness to her expressed fears about getting pregnant. Ultimately, in response to her tortured pleas—"Please, I have a future ahead of me. . . . Please, I don't need a baby. . . . Please, I'm going to college"—he "withdrew and ejaculated. 'I told you I wouldn't come inside you,' she quoted Tyson as saying. 'Don't you love me now?'"[40]

If generally "men are systematically conditioned not even to notice what women want," then Tyson's recognition might be deemed in some minor way if not exemplary, then at least atypical. His exercise of ejaculatory control, particularly in the light of his unwillingness to check his urge to have sex with a woman who came voluntarily into his hotel room and onto his bed, demonstrates a modicum of attentiveness to the desires of his victim, a fact which perhaps suggests that he was not aware that he was raping Washington. Perhaps the fact that during his attack, according to Washington, "he started laughing like it was a game," does indeed suggest that Tyson believed that he was engaged in what is often depicted as playful acts of coercion, deception, and, finally, the mild or "aggressive" exhibitions of force men learn to employ in order to gain the appearance of consent.[41]

However easy it is for those who do not believe wholeheartedly in his innocence to vilify Tyson, we need to remember that he employed techniques he learned not via an educational curriculum restricted to male athletes and celebrities but from the larger culture in which he lived along with us. In the current state of gendered affairs, the very meanings of the term *rape* continue to be contested even by figures such as Spike Lee, who, as I will demonstrate below, spent a good deal of time productively interrogating some of the gendered behavior's more nuanced manifestations. Rather than express a utopian desire for a universal adoption of MacKinnonian definitions or perhaps an even more unrealistic hope that Tyson will abandon the rapist's strategy of denial and come to recognize the complex origins and consequences of his transgressive act, I want to advocate in this transitional critical space the more realistic goal of achieving a level of self-inquiry that encourages us to acknowledge our general complicity in a system of oppression out of which rape arises in a seemingly natural fashion. Lee's film, *She's Gotta Have It,* offers evidence that its creator has at least begun the difficult task of such an interrogation, as well a mechanism through which we might continue our ideological self-examinations.

"To Go Inside the Opposite": Gender, Sexuality, and Desire in *She's Gotta Have It*

Wendy Lesser begins *His Other Half,* an engrossing study of twentieth-century male artistic representations of female subjects, by expressing her opposition to attempts by a small segment of the feminist critical community to patrol perceived gendered boundaries to artistic expression. Reacting to the views of "some female critics who would go so far as to ban men entirely from the depiction of female experience," Lesser insists that such women misunderstand "the true implications of sexual difference":

> Any woman who has ever loved a book or a painting or a film by a man takes a part of him into her. Yet that does not mean she has become a man: one can absorb the loved one without turning into him. And the reverse is true for men: they can venture into women and still remain male. To go inside the opposite does not necessarily mean to give up the self—though it may involve risking a temporary loss of some degree of self, or, alternatively, escaping temporarily from oneself.[42]

Lesser employs images of male penetration ("takes a part of him into her," "venture into women") to wed, as it were, feminist fears of the masculinizing potential of undesired male penetration to analyses of the historical subordination of women. According to Lesser's delineation of such views, to be figured at all by the male imagination is to be violated and defeminized.

Working against perceptions of males' inevitably malevolent depiction of women, Lesser insists on the possibility of a mutually beneficial intercourse between a penetrating male pen/lens/brush and a female object of inquiry. And female receptivity to male artistic designs, while involving personal "risk," includes for Lesser the potential of abandoning the female self to benevolent male images of womanhood, a potentially self-effacing and self-erasing act. In the late 1970s Judith Fetterley was urging female readers to create disruptive interpretive strategies that could be used to resist efforts to canonical American male novels to transform them into willing, masculinized accomplices of phallic rule.[43] By 1991 Lesser was arguing that successfully adventurous canonical male artworks represent, for male artists and female observers alike, illuminating and liberating sites of engagement with female subjectivity.

Because her subject is male images of "female experience," Lesser does not examine the potential effect on males of engaging powerfully rendered, female-authored figurations of gendered relations or, more precisely, male "experience."[44] But in denying the act of reading a gendering capacity, Lesser fails in the passage cited above to leave space for a consideration of how, if not as a product of our continuous interaction with the written, filmic, and orally transmitted forms of cultural narratives, our understanding of gender expectations and roles is produced and constantly reinforced. Where else, except through reading—in the broadest sense of that term—do we learn what being male and female means to the various communities in which we participate?

Despite their observable limitations, the notions upon which Lesser's formulations depend—of reading across gendered boundaries as a potentially transgressive sexualized act; of reading affecting or even transforming our sense of gendered identity—are useful for an investigation of Spike Lee's 1986 film *She's Gotta Have It*.[45] Lee's film combines a postmodernist narrative form that challenges entrenched views of representation with an often illuminating examination of the conflicts produced by the attitudes of a black female character who, in openly maintaining sexual relationships with three men, defies societal norms of acceptable female behavior. As a self-consciously transgressive film in its form and content as well as, by Lee's own account, in the perceived incompatibility between male auteur and female-centered subject matter, *She's Gotta Have It* seeks to create cultural space for alternative visions of gender representation of black subjects. Indeed, Lee seeks to confirm the view "that experience of masculinity and of being a man are not uniform."[46]

Lee believes he can produce a feminist film; perceptions that a man cannot deal with such material are, in his view, the results of mistaken beliefs that males are incapable of creating nonsexist portraits of female subjectivity or of critiquing the system of patriarchy from which they as a class profit greatly. He expresses his determination in response to one such evaluation of his idea:

Just got a call from Lillian Jimenez at the Film Fund and she says my treatment is sexist and problematic. I'm still going to apply to them. I'll be very
surprised if I do get funded from them. They would really scream if they
knew about the Opal Gilstrap character, so I'm not counting on that
money, for sure. Spike, let's be honest. There are feminists running that
place so my chances are slim and none. . . . If the Film Fund refuses to give
me money, that's their prerogative. But, I won't compromise my script. The
film will not be sexist. It will be anything but sexist. Their problem is that a
MALE is doing a film like this.[47]

Lee's self-confidence notwithstanding, there is sufficient evidence in his
published journal, Spike Lee's Gotta Have It, to suggest that his early conceptual-
ization of the film was indeed "sexist and problematic." The film itself, however,
demonstrates the relative success of Lee's battle against aspects of patriarchy's seductive formulations, a success enabled in large part by the impact of black female
writers on Lee's project. Coming of age artistically during the mid-1980s, when,
for the first time, Afro-American female literary artists were widely perceived to
be offering the thematically and aesthetically most powerful representations of the
race, Lee seeks to move imaginatively in accord with some of the most provocative of their narrative strategies and delineations of intraracial gender relations.
This desire is clear, especially in the film's progress from Lee's masculinist early
vision to its ultimately more nuanced representation of sexuality and sexual violence, wherein his perspectives on the constitution and consequences of rape in
particular seem to have altered exponentially. She's Gotta Have It is testimony to
the transformative potential for a sufficiently receptive male of an open-eyed
"venture into" the imaginative landscapes of counterhegemonic female artists.

In Spike Lee's Gotta Have It, the filmmaker records much of the anxiety and ex-
hilaration that attended his attempts both to secure funding to make the movie
and to produce a film as little influenced as possible by phallocentricism. In his
titular play on biology and perceived need, Lee replaces the third person female
nominative with a self-referential inscription, an act which redirects the objects
of the subject's desire. The "it" that "she," Nola Darling, wants is sex and, as she
says in the epilogue, "control" over "my body, my mind" (361) in part as a response to her lover Jamie Overstreet's forcing her to declare that he controls her
sexual organs. The objects of Lee's desire, on the other hand, include individual
artistic power as well as a black film renaissance larger than himself.[48] But the
journal displays Lee's equally pressing concern about offering a persuasively
counterhegemonic examination of black female sexuality. He says of the film's
imaginative spark:

It's always amazed me how men can go out and bone any and everything between fifteen and eighty and it's OK. They are encouraged to have and enjoy sex, while it's not so for women. If they do what men do they're labeled whore, prostitute, nympho, etc. Why this double standard? Why not explore this? Have a character, a beautiful young black woman who loves sex, and can love more than one man at a time also. So, that's the basic outline-premise. (66)

The anxieties Lee feels in his pursuit of this "basic outline-premise," however, are significant, and they lead him to research aspects of black female experience in a variety of ways. Because of his belief that "it's important that I not exploit women in this film" (79), Lee decides to "talk to as many of my female friends as possible. It can't be bogus. It has to be REAL or I'll lose credibility and get raked over the coals" (67). Lee also expresses a "need to read as much black women's literature as possible—reread *Sula, Bluest Eye, Song of Solomon, Their Eyes Were Watching God, The Color Purple,* some Sonia Sanchez stuff too" (76).

In addition to exploring imaginative figurations of Afro-American women's lives, he seeks to gain access to the gendered other's sexual knowledge and attitudes by creating an "Advanced Sexual Syndrome" questionnaire and circulating it among trusted female acquaintances. The forty-item survey includes the following questions: "Do you think you are sexually adept?" "Is making love different than sex? Why if so?" "Do you feel all men are basically dogs?" "Do you have an aversion to swallowing when a man ejaculates?" "What do you think about a woman that masturbates?" and "Does penis size matter?" (74–75). While Lee records some of his subjects' responses in his journal, he fails to even suggest what value this survey is to his work or to what specific use he puts its findings. His artistic project—portrayal of a starkly unconventional female—appears to be directly at odds with the sophomoric social science project whose results seem more likely to yield a composite, generic character than the unique, rebellious figure that he wishes to portray. Stephen Heath's query whether it is possible "to wonder whether there is not in male feminism, men's relation to feminism, always potentially a pornographic effect" seems prophetic with regard to Lee's research into young Afro-American women's sexual attitudes.[49]

At least in terms of his attempt at disinterested social science, the question of male access to and artistic translation of female "experience" is perhaps in Lee's case more problematic than Lesser claims generally to be the case in provocative male representations. If, indeed, men can imaginatively "venture into women and still remain male," a conditioning aspect of an aesthetically compelling and ideologically progressive "venture" is the ability to bracket, or at least structure productively, that phallic energy and "pornographic effect." If the venture does not require temporary abandonment of the biologically male artistic self, if, as Lesser contends, "to go inside the opposite does not necessarily mean to give up the self—though it may involve risking a temporary loss of some degree of self, or, alternatively, escaping temporarily from oneself," then a crucial aspect of that "loss" and "escape" is a willingness to figure the explicitly sexualized female as much more than mere reward for a stunning exhibition of male power.

Lee's artistic venture into black female imaginative and experiental landscapes, particularly into Zora Neale Hurston's *Their Eyes Were Watching God* (a text whose introductory paragraphs he employs as his movie's epigraph)[50] and Toni Morrison's *Sula,* seems to provide Lee with both impetus and models for embarking upon a temporary escape from phallic maleness. We might base such an assessment of his venture on his own emphasis, throughout his journal, on the influence of black women novelists on his own creation. In the examination of Lee's film that follows, however, I want to move beyond mapping superficial connections, which are relatively easy to find for the critical mind concerned with such detection.[51] Instead, I will interrogate some of what I hold to be the most significant formal and thematic matters Lee's text appears to borrow from Hurston's and Morrison's prompting texts. In this regard, my object is in part an analysis of the trajectory of a intertextual relationship between female precursors and male filmic novice where the inequities of phallic rule are a common, motivating concern.

Speaking of the relationship between films and their literary sources, Keith Cohen argues that "adaptation is a truly artistic feat when the new version carries with it a hidden criticism of its model, or at least renders implicit (through a process we should call 'deconstruction') certain key contradictions implanted or glossed over in the original."[52] If Cohen's formulations are persuasive in describing such intertextualities, it would appear that Lee's film possesses a "deconstructive" rather than a covertly critical relationship to Hurston's text. Many literary critics have attempted to resolve what, following Cohen, we might call the "key contradiction" of Hurston's text: the author's choice to render Janie's life experiences by means of a third-person narrator, when the story's trajectory seems to demand her demonstration of discursive power through a narrative actualization of that power as the controlling storytelling voice in the novel.

Hurston's motivation for such a choice, however, seems to be related explicitly to evidence in the novel of Janie's awareness of the contempt in which she is held by communities of black people—interpreters of her articulated and/or perceived narrative, in other words—who view with palpable rancor her resistance to women's restricted place within androcentric cultural scripts. When she is accused of murdering her rabid husband Tea Cake, she must contend with the "lying thoughts" of other blacks whose belief that she had killed her husband in cold blood was, in her view, "worse than" death.[53] And upon her return to Eatonville after burying Tea Cake, she confronts the "mass cruelty" of townspeople who "sat in judgment" of her and who are now envious of her beauty, socioeconomic status, and other manifestations of her relative freedom; their malice was so profound that she did not believe it was "worth de trouble" to attempt to provide them with a more accurate counternarrative to offset a script that figures her as having been deserted by a youthful, exploitative husband. Despite the self-protective impulses that prevent Janie from telling her story directly to skeptical townspeople, she does share the events of her life with a sympathetic friend, Pheoby, whom she enlists in the role of narrative filter and conduit to relate her story to the Eatonville community. She tells her friend, "Ah don't mean to bother wid tellin' 'em nothin', Pheoby. 'Tain't worth de trouble. You can tell 'em what Ah say if you wants to. Dat's just de same as me 'cause mah tongue is in mah friend's mouf" (6). What follows is an omnisciently rendered detailing of her life story, which, as a narrative device, is meant to approximate Pheoby's projected recitation of Janie's story to a malicious Eatonville audience. Whatever else we can say about Hurston's narrative choice, that choice signifies an apprehension on the author's part about the open-mindedness of her potential readers as least as profound as her character's distrust of her demonstrably hostile townspeople.

Concern about an audience's "judgment" of its female protagonist's refusal to submit to standard androcentric scripts also informs the narrative style of *She's Gotta Have It*. In fact, her resistance serves as justification for the film's introduction of the character of Nola, which interrupts the series of impressive still photos whose subject is urban (primarily black) people at work and at play. Emerging from under the covers of her "loving bed" soon after the epigraphic appearance of the novel's introductory paragraphs, Nola sits up, looks directly into the camera, and says:

> I want you to know the only reason I'm consenting to this is because I wish to clear my name, not that I care what people think but enough is enough. . . .
> And if in the end it helps some other people out that's fine too. I consider myself normal (whatever that means). Some people call me a freak. I hate that word. I don't believe in it or better yet I don't believe in labels. But what are you gonna do? This was the deal. (279)

Janie's skepticism about her audience's judgment occasions a third-person narration through which her story and voice are filtered as a self-protective measure. Nola's equally legitimate distrust of her audience—and her attempt to escape pejorative judgments—inspires her to participate in a fictive documentary filmmaker's project as its framing voice and object of the retrospective figurations of others, particularly those of former male lovers who feel they have been wronged by her as a consequence of her "freak[y]" nature. The visual medium through which Lee works offers little possibility for sustained first-person narration.[54] His storytelling challenge, therefore, is not to seek a means of combining first-person narrative, as some have argued is Hurston's intent and dilemma, but instead to problematize versions of the "REAL" by foregrounding, and playing experimentally with, interpretive differences resulting in large part from gendered self-interest.[55]

In many ways, Lee encourages the audience's sympathetic judgment of Nola, but no more provocatively than in his final choice of occupation for his protagonist. His journal indicates that in order to highlight the gulf between appearance and reality, he intended originally to make her a secretary—an occupation generally viewed as a relatively mundane and largely female service profession that requires conservative behavior in support of male power. Lee explains:

> It's important that audiences have sympathy with Nola. She can't be a FREAK, hence we can't have her walking around in black leather, chains and whips. That's bogus. Nola will be beautiful, normal, if you know what I mean. She's beautiful, but she dresses and looks like a normal woman, this will make her more interesting. In real life it's the normal ones, the secretaries, etc., who are the undercover freaks. We shouldn't be able to look at her and tell SHE'S GOTTA HAVE IT. (69)

While Lee's intent here may have been progressive, his words express undeniably androcentric ideas about women. Despite his nominally "advanced" sexual survey, clearly he has preconceived notions about aspects of female sexuality, however contradictory these notions appear: that female normality connotes sexlessness; that normality is merely a mask that seeks to shield the insatiable "FREAK" from detection by the larger society; that, in essence, women are all either "undercover freaks" or freaks under covers, from those who parade their sexuality by "walking around in black leather, chains and whips" to those seemingly "normal ones" who dress conservatively but who may be wearing Victoria's Secrets lace panties under their starched dresses.

For reasons he does not discuss, Lee radically alters his plans. Instead of being a secretary, Nola is a "layout, paste up artist" who works for magazines and, more important for my purposes here, creates a large mural in and for her domicile. As a layout artist, Nola's profession approximates, in its reliance on an ability to make expressive wholes out of heretofore disparate fragments, the role of the postmodernist creator generally and of the filmmaker specifically. The craft of filmmaking involves, that is to say, the creation of a coherent narrative from scraps extracted from numerous recorded takes and retakes, complex editing decisions, the addition of voiceovers, music, a list of credits, and so on. Even a film such as *She's Gotta Have It,* which reflects what Linda Hutcheon calls "postmodernism's initial concern . . . to de-naturalize some of the dominant features of our way of life"[56] in its problematizing of its audience's faith in a retrievable objective truth by forcing that audience to choose between sometimes competing versions of reality, nevertheless emerges as a unified story as a consequence of an editing process not radically distinct from that employed to construct the formally most conventional film. Despite Lee's troubling notions about gender relations, which he expresses on several occasions in his journal, he portrays Nola as a much more self-possessed and formidable character than he had originally intended. More than any of the male characters, it is she who displays the artistic temperament and the counterhegemonic perspectives that most closely approximate those espoused by Lee.

Nola's status as artist adds an important dimension to the film, especially when considered in light of the views expressed by Hurston, Morrison, and Walker (black women novelists whose work Lee embraces as models) concerning the consequences for females of being denied avenues of self-expression.[57] The title character of *Sula,* for example (a text whose conflation of fire, dreams, and female desires for retribution seems to have influenced *She's Gotta Have It*), lived "an experimental life" dedicated to "exploring her own thoughts and emotions, giving them full reign, feeling no obligation to please anybody unless their pleasure pleased her" (118).[58] Sula is described as an artist without an expressive medium: "Had she paints, or clay, or knew the discipline of the dance, or strings; had she anything to engage her tremendous curiosity and her gift for metaphor, she might have exchanged the restlessness and preoccupation with whim for an activity that provided her with all she yearned for. And like any artist with no art form, she became dangerous" (121). For the black community in which Sula lives, her status as pariah results in large part from her manner of sexual expression. Morrison writes that Sula knew

> they despised her and believed that they framed their hatred as disgust for the easy way she lay with men. Which was true. She went to bed with men as frequently as she could. It was the only place where she could find what she was looking for: misery and the ability to feel deep sorrow. . . . Although she did not regard sex as ugly, . . . she liked to think of it as wicked. But as her experiences multiplied she realized that not only was it not wicked, it was not necessary for her to conjure up the idea of wickedness in order to participate fully. During the lovemaking she found and needed to find the cutting edge. . . . And there was utmost irony and outrage in lying

under someone, in a position of surrender, feeling her own abiding strength and limitless power. (122–123)

Although she shares with Morrison's character a lack of respect for sexual convention, Nola's participation in the sex act itself does not evince a "cutting edge." In fact, we might argue that until what Nola terms her "near-rape" by Jamie, the non-phallocentric meanings of Nola's sexual expression are not really at issue in a manner equivalent to Sula's pursuit of sex. It is intercourse that provides Sula with an avenue through which to gain access to her own "abiding strength and limitless power." *She's Gotta Have It* does not figure sex as an instrument of self-comprehension and self-creation in the ways that Morrison's novel does; in fact, while Lee speaks of her as a "FREAK" with an insatiable sexual appetite, the film offers little to confirm such a view beyond the fact that Nola has three male lovers, which is a reflection more of her attitudes toward monogamy than of her level of sexual desire. And unlike *Sula,* the figuration of whose protagonist's sexuality concentrates on her psychic state, what Lee portrays is a sexual economy wherein intercourse generally is proffered by Nola as a reward for male accomplishment: to Jamie for articulating convincingly loving words as opposed to practiced pickup lines; to Greer for his modeling success (he has been chosen to grace the cover of GQ); and to Mars for his ability to make her laugh uncontrollably.[59]

In part because of her access to other arenas of self-expression, sex itself is less of a self-defining act for Nola than it is for Sula. While Sula brings an intense need for self-exploration and self-expression to the moment of "postcoital privateness in which she met herself, welcomed herself, and joined herself in matchless harmony" (123), Nola seems to regard sex as entertainment and as a mode of reward. Perhaps her work provides her with another means of self-expression and permits Nola to view her lifestyle merely as a manner of resisting patriarchal notions of the proper expression of sexuality; conceived in such a way, her sexuality need not serve the dual purpose of fighting patriarchy and enabling self-interrogation. At any rate, while the pleasure and danger of female sexuality that Ellen Carol DuBois and Linda Gordon speak of in one of this essay's epigraphs are evident in Nola's expression of sexuality, intercourse is for her a way of practicing her beliefs rather than a means of formulating a gynocentric theory or, in fact, a self.[60]

Nola's self-control and artistic skills are manifested in her creation and designation of a womanist space for her lovemaking. Nola's "loving bed," as Lee's screenplay calls it, is the only space where she pursues sexual adventure; in Carol Vance's term, it is her "safe zone."[61] As she informs Jamie, "I can only do it in my own bed" (283). She decorates her "loving bed" with candles in a manner that enshrines her own pursuit of counterhegemonic sexual pleasure. Although Lee's journal and screenplay provide no overt explanation of Nola's unwillingness to engage in intercourse in any place or space other than her own bed, that decision seems to have been affected by her analysis of sexual politics. In a viciously patriarchal society, where a measure of males' problems with intimacy is represented by the film's "dogs" who spout comic pickup lines that become the subject of Nola's and the audience's bemused ridicule, Nola uses her own domestic space as a site of resistance, as a fortress against phallic rule. The bed becomes a symbol of her rebellious heterosexual gynocentric stance, an altar to an alternative womanist cosmology. Nola's loft, then, serves within the film as a "safe zone" wherein we witness the achievement of what Vance and others identify as a feminist dream: a space within which the dangers of female sexuality are minimized and its pleasures can be pursued in relative safety. If, as Jamie speculates, Nola's inability to have intercourse in any other location suggests that her counterhegemonic exploration of her sexuality is supported by her bed's "magical powers," her refusal reflects her dedication to gynocentric views.

In an examination of disputes, in Lacanian and other feminist psychoanalytical circles, about the meanings of the phallus and the distinction between it and the penis as sources of female oppression, Jane Gallop argues that by

> insisting on the penis, I was looking for some masculine body, some other body, some bodily object of female heterosexual desire, trying to find not just the institution of heterosexism but also the experience of heterosexuality. I cannot disintricate the penis from phallic rule but neither is it totally synonymous with the transcendent phallus. At this point in history I don't think they can be separated, but to insist on bodily masculinity is to work to undo the heterosexist ideology which decrees the body female, to be dominated not by a male body (too disorderly to rule) but by an idealized, transcendent phallus. I want to render that idealization impossible.[62]

What Gallop seeks is a manner of struggling against transcendent phallic rule while preserving or creating the possibility for feminists of satisfying female heterosexual desire. She acknowledges "the impossibility, at this moment in our history, to think of a masculine that is not phallic, a masculine that can couple with a feminine."[63] But her attempt to distinguish the phallus as hegemonic principle from male bodies theoretically capable of withstanding the urgings of that principle signifies, at least in part, a guilt-free effort to figure the penis as acceptable site of feminist (and, more generally, heterosexual female) desire and pleasure. To play on the title of Vance's collection on female sexuality, Gallop wants heterosexual pleasure with a minimum of phallic danger.[64] The inability of feminists to maintain that separation between phallic principle and potentially resistant male embodiment is not a function of deep, abiding distrust so much as it is a sign of men's inability generally to conceive of and to practice a masculinity uncontaminated by desires for phallic rule over female bodies, among other contested, feminized areas. Nevertheless, this search must continue if heterosexual feminists wish to share "loving beds" with males.

Nola's creation of a "loving bed" and her refusal to have intercourse anywhere else seem to be astute responses to this troubling dilemma. If public space—that is, virtually all of the world except for her domicile—is dominated by phallic rule, then creating a nonpatriarchal safe zone serves as her means of making possible both a degree of psychic autonomy and the pursuit of sexual pleasure with a variety of embodied males. And while Nola confronts alternate possibilities in the form of a lesbian Opal Gilstrap and attempts at masturbatory self-satisfaction, she seems to reject them as surrogate or even supplemental means to sexual and psychic fulfillment because, like Gallop, she is concerned with non-phallocentric heterosexual satisfaction.

A brief look at Hurston's figuration in *Their Eyes Were Watching God* of a separation of public and private domestic space might help to clarify elements of what I view as Lee's subtle employment of Nola's loft as gynocentric safe zone. In Hurston's novel, Janie responds to her husband Joe Starks's efforts to belittle her and control her will by employing a mode of self-division that distinguishes between strategic social facade and psychic actuality:

> Time and scenes like that [Joe's insistence on women's intellectual inferiority] put Janie to thinking about the inside state of her marriage. Time came when she fought back with her tongue as best she could, but it didn't do her any good. It just made Joe do more. He wanted her submission and he'd keep on fighting until he felt he had it.
>
> So gradually, she pressed her teeth together and learned to hush. The spirit of the marriage left the bedroom and took to living in the parlor. It was there to shake hands whenever company came to visit, but it never went back inside the bedroom again. So she put something in there to represent the spirit like a Virgin Mary image in a church. The bed was no longer a daisy-field for her and Joe to play in. It was a place where she went and laid down when she was sleepy and tired. (67)

Janie's resistance to her husband's attempts to gain "her submission" includes ending their heretofore mutually pleasurable sex life. In the more public areas of domestic space, she plays parlor games, putting a positive face on a marital situation which has become increasingly intolerable for her, but in the privacy of their bedroom she refuses to serve as a receptacle for her husband's lust. Because Janie is treated with barely the respect Joe accords the spittoons he purchases as a sign of his class status, her sexual attraction to him and vision of her marital bed as a "daisy-field" disappear. She later learns, as does Nola, that when the efforts of the male will to power to gain female "submission" by means of psychological manipulation are thwarted, that will often expresses itself through terroristic acts of violence.

An interrogation of the implications of Nola's art and its connection to black female novelists' figurations is central to my reading of She's Gotta Have It, because it offers an otherwise unavailable avenue of explaining her rationale for resisting phallic rule by creating in her loft a self-protective gynocentric space. The importance of such a creation cannot be overlooked, I believe, if we are to comprehend aspects of the lessons Lee appears to have learned from black women novelists. It might be argued, for example, that Janie's home comes to represent just such a space upon her return to Eatonville, but hers is a space financed by the entrepreneurial maneuverings of an unrepentant oppressor, her second husband, Joe, and enlivened by the memory of a charming third husband, whose exalted stature in Janie's eyes depends in part on her ability to forget aspects of the truth about his mistreatment of her. Conversely, Nola's domestic space, whose most prominent features are its "loving bed" and constantly in-process mural, is largely self-created in the sense that she imposes upon it her own views of a counterhegemonic sexual order.

However, Nola's artistic vision and pursuit of the experience of heterosexuality unencumbered by debilitating phallic rule are forced to compete with notions held by Jamie, Mars, and Greer of a blissful monogamy. One major difficulty with Nola's alternate sexual cosmology, in fact, results not from her unwillingness to compromise her vision, but at least in part from her inability to articulate that vision patiently to others who, despite their dedication to patriarchal views, nonetheless might profit from comprehending its motivations and consequences. She seems ill-equipped, in other words, to make clear her need to practice an alternative version of heterosexuality. This silence may be merely a function of Lee's own imaginative limitations or of his sense of the difficulty of articulating, in a movie aimed at a mass black audience, a vernacularly resonant equivalent of the sort of high academic analysis Gallop offers of the theoretical separation between phallus and penis. For whatever reason, Nola seems incapable of clearly articulating her ideological positions. When, for instance, Jamie, assuming that her rejection of a monogamous lifestyle is a function of an existential crisis, asks her, "What are you searching for"—what, in effect, her "freakishness" is a substitute for—she responds, with what the screenplay's direction calls a "la-di-da attitude," "Whatever" (343).

Jamie's is a traditional view of heterosexuality which cannot long entertain perspectives or modes of being threatening to its sense of moral and spiritual correctness.[65] When he issues his ultimatum to Nola that she choose either to begin a monogamous relationship with him or lose him completely, he informs her, "I'm not like you. I can't spread myself between two or three people" (337). And in fact, when we first meet Jamie, he tells us,

> I believe there is only one person, only one in this world that is meant to be your soul mate, your lifelong companion. And the irony is, rarely do these two people hook up. You just wander about aimlessly. But if you're lucky and you do meet this person, you can't blow it. . . .
> Nola was the one. (280)

Nola is unable or unwilling to share with him or others her rationale for her lifestyle, to articulate, that is to say, her sense of the pervasiveness and hence the dangers of phallic rule. And perhaps as a consequence of her inability to express herself and her contempt for traditional heterosexuality, she has no patience for the invasion of androcentric perspective into her own "magical" domestic space. Therefore, she is surprised that what Greer sarcastically terms Nola's "brilliant idea" to invite all three lovers to Thanksgiving dinner turns out to be, in a word, ill-advised. The success of Nola's counterhegemonic stance depends, in the long run, on her ability to convince others of its necessity and merits, particularly if she wishes to have long-term, emotionally intimate relationships with men who are invariably schooled in patriarchy. However, she appears unwilling or unable to engage in any extended acts of either education or persuasion. Hence, Nola's resistance to monogamy is figured by Greer as a symptom of sexual addiction and by Jamie as a sign of an indeterminate search. Because she cannot say what besides psychic maladjustment or existential restlessness motivates her behavior, Nola seems purely selfish to her lovers rather than driven by an ideological imperative.

Nola is adept at resisting the efforts of both Mars and Greer to persuade her to stop seeing other men. She tells Greer, who has invited her on a Caribbean vacation as a prelude to their development of a monogamous relationship, "I don't think I can stand two weeks with you alone, to tell you the truth" (339), and she tells Mars after he insists that he loves her, "You're in love with my lovemaking. Don't mess it up" (317). She is, however, generally less self-assured in her responses to Jamie's requests for a sexual and emotional exclusivity. She admits to being upset when Jamie informs her that he has begun to see another woman, and she considers entering into a monogamous relationship with him. Later, when she informs Jamie that she will abandon her untraditional sexual practice "soon," Jamie retorts, "I've been hearing that from day one" (344), which suggests that they have often talked about establishing such a relationship.

The lovers reach an impasse, ultimately, because of their conflicting and intractable views: he is unable to remain "open-minded" enough to continue dating her without feeling that he is "being played for a sucker" (336), and she is unwilling to abandon the self-protective security of her gynocentric heterosexual practice to participate in a mode of being designed always to benefit men and disadvantage women. That confrontation seems to result in part from the fact that Nola places too much faith in her "magical" gynocentric space to clarify the unuttered.

A particularly provocative passage from Jacques Lacan's "The Meaning of the Phallus" serves to illuminate aspects of Nola's and Jamie's dilemma. According to Lacan, "for each partner in the relation, the subject and the Other, it is not enough to be the subjects of need, nor objects of love, but they must stand as the cause of desire." He goes on to say, "This truth is at the heart of all the mishaps of sexual life."[66] Lacan suggests here that the "mishaps" of intimacy result from a fear—or, rather, an awareness—that sexual desire might arise in the other from causes independent of external prompting or, at the very least, from external prompting that is not the "partner." If Lacan is correct, then elements of a range of human behavior, from a jealous response to a partner's interested gaze at a desirable other, to an institutionalizing of monogamy, to a rapist's belief that his transgressive thrustings can indeed be satisfying to his victim all might be seen to reflect an urge to be not merely desire's instrument or receptacle, but its "cause," its sole prompting.

Nola's counterhegemonic resolve begins to break down as a consequence of a fear not only of losing Jamie as a sexual partner and friend but of being replaced by another woman as "the cause of desire," a fear, in other words, of having blown the status of soul mate. This breakdown, this corruption of a gynocentric safe zone, permits the strategies of phallic rule to gain dominion in an arena heretofore protected from its taint by counterhegemonic "magical powers." Whereas earlier Nola's refusal to compromise a belief system led Jamie initially to consider her "brutally honest" (293), she persuades him to visit her after their breakup on a pretense not wholly unlike Mike Tyson's vague words of enticement to Desiree Washington; Nola says, "I want to see you. It's very important" (347). When Jamie arrives, having effectively ended his relationship with his new lover in the process, Nola informs him that the "important" matter is her sexual desire: "I need you" (348). (I believe this is the only case where Nola solicits sex rather than offering herself as reward for male achievement.) And in response to his malice-tinged, "Once a freak always a freak," she insists that he recognize her capacity to transform herself: "That was before. I can change" (348).

In acknowledging a willingness to abandon her gynocentric worldview in order to guarantee Jamie's presence in her life, Nola disperses the "magical powers" which had guarded her feminist space from the intrusions of phallic rule. It would appear that her expressed desire to change shifts the balance of power in their relationship in his favor, but her willingness to compromise fails to appease an increasingly frustrated Jamie, who, knowing full well that he is not "the cause of desire," or not its sole cause, performs a transgressive sexual act that Nola refers to subsequently as a "near-rape." Having lost his illusions about winning the hand of his "soul mate" and, hence, a romanticism that seems to be the source of Nola's preference of him over an insecure Mars and an egomaniacal Greer, Jamie becomes like the "dogs" whose staged pursuit of women is largely an exercise in masculine power. Jamie is no longer either the "one guy [who] was different" or "safe" (288, 289), as Nola had identified him previously, but becomes instead the most dangerous type of "dog": one who feels compelled, like a rabid Tea Cake, to protect his turf and who believes he is fully justified in using any available tactic to achieve that end, including, in this case, employing his penis as a means of extending phallic rule.

During the act of sexual violence—in which Jamie enters his bent-over "soul mate" from behind, thereby literalizing his newly achieved status as dog—Nola's heretofore carefully patrolled gynocentric space becomes indistinguishable from any other place subject to phallic rule where, as Catharine MacKinnon argues, "sexuality is the dynamic of control by which male dominance—in forms that range from intimate to institutional, from a look to a rape—eroticizes and thus defines man and woman, gender identity and sexual pleasure" (137). If Nola's "safe zone" had enabled the possibilities of the experience of heterosexuality, it has now become a site of "male dominance." Given "the dynamic of control" to which MacKinnon alludes, given the inability of many feminists to envision males unencumbered by desires for the phallic rule of which Gallop speaks, the abandonment of the female self to the demands of a traditional heterosexuality is, as Nola seems to sense, highly dangerous both emotionally and physically.

In its exploration of aspects of this gendered "dynamics of control," Lee's film further demonstrates its thematic affinities with black female novels, particularly Morrison's *Sula*. Like *She's Gotta Have It, Sula* explores the consequence for a generally satisfying relationship of a heretofore unconventional woman's decision to embrace traditional societal norms that are devised to be debilitating to women. Once Sula, like other women in the Bottom community, "began to discover what possession was" in her relationship with Ajax, she adopts a mind-set both she and Ajax had previously condemned. On hearing of her lover's hassles with white policemen—and after her assumption of the community's ideals of commendable female behavior has led her to clean her home, wash her sheets, and decorate herself with a carefully arranged green ribbon and "the deadly odor of freshly applied cologne"—she tells a fiercely independent Ajax, "Come on. Lean on me" (134, 133). After witnessing Sula's surprising transformation, Ajax "dragged her under him and made lover to her with the steadiness and intensity of a man about to leave for Dayton" (134). The embrace of conventionality on the part of both Nola and Sula, then, precipitates or is accompanied by significant changes in their lovers' heterosexual practices.

Another connection between Sula and Nola is the nature of their texts' conflation of art, sex, and male acts of "fucking" as opposed to "lovemaking." In

Morrison's text, Sula creates an immaculate domestic space and presents herself as what MacKinnon speaks of as "a beautiful thing" (130), thus aligning herself with socially privileged conventions of acceptable avenues of women's self-expression. However, in its conformity to gendered scripts in which Ajax has no interest, Sula's choice dooms her efforts to failure if her goal is, indeed, "possession." In Lee's film, the aesthetic is employed in an even more provocative manner. We see hanging behind Jamie during the near-rape a diminutive reproduction of Nola's mural; it is no longer a sprawling work-in-progress that dominates a wall of the loft, but a tamed down, contained—domesticated—version. The piece features Malcom X and Zora Neale Hurston (I cannot make out with any certainty the other figures) and, given the original work's inclusion of newspaper clippings that center on Bernard Goetz and much-discussed black victims of interracial violence—including Nelson Mandela, Eleanor Bumpors, and Edmund Perry, a prep school graduate who was killed reportedly during a violent attack on a white undercover policeman—one can surmise that Nola is concerned with white acts of violence against blacks.

To argue that Nola's racial art inspires or explicitly represents gendered resistance is, on the surface at least, problematic. But if the subject of Nola's art is racial inequity, the key figure on the mural—the figure which Jamie's body does not hide during the transgressive act—is a visibly pained black everyman/woman with outstretched arms and hands, which, like those shouts of an everlasting "nay" that conclude both *School Daze* and *Jungle Fever,* implore onlookers to do their part to ensure the end of offending behavior. While clearly referencing the interracial travails of blacks, that position serves as a comment on the act in question, especially given both the visibility of this figure during the rape and Lee's decision to focus his camera on it after Jamie's departure. Viewed as unconcealed commentator on transgression, Nola's everyman/woman—and her art generally—subtly connects racially and sexually motivated violence. Lee might be said to be attempting to come to grips here with the intrinsic connections between racism and sexism sketched by Audre Lorde:

> Black male consciousness must be raised to the realization that sexism and woman-hating are critically dysfunctional to his liberation as a Black man because they arise out of the same constellation that engenders racism and homophobia. Until that consciousness is developed, Black men will view sexism and the destruction of Black women as tangential to Black liberation rather than as central to that struggle. So long as this occurs, we will never be able to embark upon that dialogue between Black women and Black men that is so essential to our survival as a people.[67]

Irrefutably, Lee's film has contributed to that necessary dialogue.

Nola's mural. Reprinted with permission from Forty Acres and a Mule Filmworks, Inc.

However, in scaling down the manifestation of Nola's aesthetic gifts, in domesticating the wild work-in-progress, Lee suggests that the protagonist's counterhegemonic views no longer represent the energizing forces that inform and protect her domicile. In its greatly diminished scale, Nola's art is similar to Sula's domestic beautification in that it connotes the possibility of containing the heretofore disruptive and resistant female within phallocentric scripts.[68]

In phallocentric scripts and spaces—and Nola's domicile becomes just such a space as a function of her expressed willingness to compromise her values and Jamie's treatment of it as such—sex is frequently utilized as a means of asserting masculine control. In response to Nola's request, "Make love to me," Jamie says, "You don't want me to make love to you. You want me to fuck you." There are at least two ways in which his interpretation of her desire is significant. First, his words and actions suggest that lovemaking is impossible for the phallic male incapable of otherwise imposing his will upon the desired female object. Equally important, Jamie transfers his own desires to use his penis as an instrument of phallic rule onto Nola, indicating a belief that his act of brutality is, in fact, merely his way of fulfilling her unarticulated wish to become a victim of sexual violence. According to MacKinnon, who speaks persuasively about the fact that "to woman is attributed both the cause of man's initiative and the denial of his satisfaction"

Nola's Everyman/woman. Reprinted with permission from
Forty Acres and a Mule Filmworks, Inc.

(175), "To be sexually objectified means having a social meaning imposed on your being that defines you as to be sexually used, according to your desired uses, and then using you that way. Doing this is sex in the male system" (140). Because Nola has been transformed in his estimation from soul mate to sexual object, Jamie performs upon her body—putatively in response to Nola's desire to be "fucked" — what is perhaps the most physically devastating act against women sanctioned within the "male system." Although his victim, who throughout the film is hesitant to discuss the inequities of phallic rule, cannot call it rape, its nearness to rape is such that the audience can so designate Jamie's act of brutality.

In her reading of Jamie's act, Michele Wallace argues: "Although it is Jamie who finally rapes Nola into submission when she refuses to marry him [sic], Lee's journal clearly suggests that he views Jamie as the best man among her lovers. . . . He doesn't know how Nola should react to Jamie's rape. Should she enjoy it? He settles for having Jamie reluctantly admit that *he* enjoyed it. Perhaps most important, Lee never calls it a rape (102). Unlike Wallace, who sees Lee's indecision about the location of pleasure in sexual violence as a sign of his unresolved phallocentrism, I believe Lee's record of struggle with this scene is perhaps the most salient indication of his ultimately successful battle against the interpretive structures of phallic rule. In the first instance in which he makes mention of his proposed scene of sexual violence and its consequences, Lee says: "It is there [after her "near-rape"] that she decides it's Jamie she truly loves and she's ready for one man but that she's gonna be celibate for an indefinite period of time. Now you know I'm playing dynamite with this subject matter. IT'S IMPORTANT THAT THE CHARACTER OF NOLA DARLING NOT BE EXPLOITED" (86–87). Perhaps it is testimony to Lee's knowledge of the workings of patriarchy that he reminds himself to be attentive to the need to protect Nola from exploitation in a screenplay that he himself composes. Certainly that vigilance is necessary, as in this very passage Lee allows himself to indulge the androcentric fantasy that one good "fuck" could awaken Nola to both male charms and the benefits of monogamy. As phallocentric rape fantasies go, this one is astonishingly commonplace.[69]

Later in his journal, he writes:

> I came up with a great idea for the final bone scene. . . . Now when Jamie is boning Nola the rougher he gets the more she likes it, she's saying stuff like "HARDER, HARDER," she's coming close to orgasm. Also he's saying stuff like "Is this as good as Mars?"—FLASHCUT TO MARS getting it. "Is this as good as Greer?"—FLASHCUT TO GREER getting it. "What about Opal?"—FLASHCUT TO OPAL getting it. Then when Jamie sees Nola is beginning to actually get into this, she's actually enjoying this, this bothers him. Here he is trying to dog her and she likes it. So Jamie stops just about when she is gonna come. When he pulls out, she looks at him, unbelievable. "Why did you stop? Why did you stop? I was almost there. I like it when you're rough with me." (133)

Lee's "great idea" to have Nola to enjoy her victimization, to "get off" on rough love—to "com[e] . . . close to orgasm" as a consequence of this mixture of "boning" and verbal derision—continues this line of phallocentric thinking. Here, Nola regrets the termination of brutality and finds it "unbelievable" not that Jamie could engage in such behavior, but that he would cease that behavior before she experienced her fullest sexual pleasure.

In the journal's screenplay and in the actual film, Opal is eliminated from this scene's list of threats to Jamie's possession. The screenplay, however, maintains the idea that Nola enjoys her victimization. After Nola tells Jamie, "You're hurting me," he asks her, "Whose pussy is this?" Tortured by this act of penile/phallic domination, she responds, "It's yours," but then, as the screenplay's directions state, "Jamie notices that Nola is beginning to get into this [verbal and physical assault] and stops." By way of explanation, he says, "Here I am trying to dog you the best I can and you are enjoying it. But what bothers *me* is that I was getting off too" (350). The published script suggests the possibility of mutual erotic enjoyment of the exercise of penile/phallic power, and that what "bothers" Jamie is not that Nola could enjoy being violated but that he could find the role of male oppressor pleasurable.

In the film, however, for reasons Lee leaves unexplained, the "near-rape" is not presented as a source of mutual (although for Jamie, guilty) pleasure, and leads him alone to experience the transgressive act as sexually fulfilling. After he has withdrawn his penis from a sobbing Nola—he refuses to lie in the "loving bed" and to be influenced potentially by the remnants of its counterhegemonic "magic powers"—he walks to the door and says to her, "Here I am trying to dog you the best I can, and what bothers me is that I enjoyed it." The precise source of Jamie's pleasure is not specified; it may be a strictly physical pleasure resulting from his selfish thrusting within vaginal space and/or psychic pleasure as a consequence of using his penis in an uninhibited exercise of phallic rule. At any rate, Nola's reaction is much changed from screenplay to film. Instead of a (romanticized) phallocentric sadomasochistic episode with comic overtones, as presented in the screenplay, and in spite of the filmmaker's and his female character's reticence to so name the act, what we witness on the screen, what Lee films, is in fact an act of rape.[70]

Wallace argues that Lee's high regard for Jamie is evidence of his capitulation to phallic rule, his inability to recognize the devastating consequences for women of sexual brutality and a view that women can be raped into submission. It would appear, however, that Lee's film acknowledges the physically devastating impact of androcentric brutality by scripting Nola's decision to keep her promise to an increasingly dictatorial Jamie and having her search him out in a manner consistent with the behavior of victims of acquaintance rape who try to convince themselves either that they had not been raped or that they might hereafter exert a degree of control over their victimization.[71] Rather than seeing *She's Gotta Have It* along the lines of Wallace's plausible reading of it as a film whose "mistrust of female sexuality is disturbingly obvious," I believe that the film and journal provide even more evidence of Lee's growing "mistrust" of phallic rule. If, as Wallace argues, "In many ways, especially in the scene where Lee's puckered lips traverse her flesh, Nola seems less a character than a dark continent to be explored and conquered" (103), that reading is made possible not only by the critic's resistance of the androcentric demands of Lee's film, but is enabled in part by the filmmaker's design. *She's Gotta Have It,* in other words, encourages such an interpretation.

As I suggested earlier, one of the most significant points of connection between *She's Gotta Have It* and *Their Eyes Were Watching God* is their complex problematizing of narrative voice. In addition to Hurston's formal and thematic exploration of narrative control, her novel is replete with instances where others—especially male—fail to comprehend Janie and attempt to impose upon her as incontestable truth their readings of the world and of her.[72] Lee's film takes from Hurston the issue of imposed (and competing) interpretations, particularly in his use of a documentary narrative strategy that permits Nola's lovers to tell aspects of her story and assess their meaning. In essence, the audience is provided not only with Nola's own name-clearing account of her life, but with the self-serving and sometimes contradictory narratives of rejected male lovers ultimately incapable of exerting phallic dominion over her, and unsuccessful in their efforts to become, in Lacan's phrase, "the cause of desire."[73] As Nola insists, her participation in this project hinges on its capacity to legitimize her and her chosen lifestyle. The narrative, despite Nola's failure to exert a controlling influence over it, does just that: We witness Greer's insufferable self-satisfaction; Mars's profound insecurities about his height and sexual performance, and his use of humor to shield himself from confronting those feelings; and, most important, Jamie's capitulation to the urgings of phallic rule. Their own narrative recollections implicate these self-described wronged male lovers more effectively than Nola's pejorative comments could because, as their own narrative acts, they are these men's best (and, in the final analysis, worst) defense against rejection by the audience of the film.

If Nola fails to rise above the status of dark continent, as Wallace suggests, that may well be a function of Lee's inadequacies as a scripter of female subjectivity, might be, that is to say, evidence of the failures of his attempts to learn from female writers to depict women in a manner he might call "REAL." But given the structure of the film, it seems to me more plausible to say that it *represents* his male characters' inability to conceive of Nola as more than mysterious other. Lee thus structures into his film a way of identifying the perceptual problems of androcentric renderings of females in a society in which we are generally unable to distinguish between the phallus as hegemonic symbolic order and the penis as an instrument of both pleasure and danger. If Hurston does not present Janie in the role of narrator in *Their Eyes Were Watching God* because she realizes that her story will not be received by either an intratextual or reading audience that sympathizes with counterhegemonic responses to racial and gendered dominance, then Lee lets his male characters speaks in order to demonstrate the intractable nature of androcentrism. Further, if Lee fails to represent Nola as other than site of potential phallic conquest, that failure is not his alone but, as his narrative strategies serve to underscore, a socially produced male interpretive trait. *She's Gotta Have It* seeks neither to escape that social truth nor to insist on Lee's ability to transcend phallic rule, but it does manifest his knowledge of and ability to represent—and, I believe, to critique—such matters. In addition, the film exemplifies the pressing need to create and maintain gynocentric spaces and perspectives in which and with which we can combat the hegemonic order. In that regard, at least, Lee demonstrates how much he has learned, from black women's literature and elsewhere, about the power of patriarchy.

I write without gender focus. . . . It happens that what provokes my imagination as a writer has to do with the culture of black people. I regard the whole world as my canvas and I write out of that sensibility of what I find provocative and the sensibility of being a woman. But I don't write women's literature as such. I think it would confine me. I am valuable as a writer because I am a woman, because women, it seems to me, have some special knowledge about certain things. [It comes from] the ways in which they view the world, and from women's imagination. Once it is unruly and let loose, it can bring things to the surface that men—trained to be men in a certain way—have difficulty getting access to.

Toni Morrison, "An Interview with Toni Morrison"

5

"Unruly and Let Loose": Myth, Ideology, and Gender in *Song of Solomon*

Where the issues this study focuses on are concerned, *Song of Solomon* is the most challenging text Toni Morrison has yet produced. The interpretive challenges presented by the novel have as their primary source the nature of the author's appropriation of the myth around which she structures what has been called a tale of Afro-American "genealogical archaeology." As Dorothy Lee asserts in her discussion of the epic qualities of Morrison's text, the author "draws on specific Afro-American legends of Africans who could fly and who used this marvelous ability to escape from slavery in America; that is, literally to transcend bondage."[1] However, Morrison does not simply draw on this myth; rather, what she offers, in the narrative of Solomon's mythic flight, is a radically transformed version of the legend, which suggests the immense, and in many respects injurious, changes that have occurred over the course of the history of blacks in America. Indeed, a careful analysis of the subtle, appropriative nature of Morrison's mythic figurations (including what is apparently a traditional heroic male act of archaeology—its protagonist Milkman Dead's "archetypal search for self and for transcendence") reveals her complex inscription of ideology, or, more accurate, *ideologies:* the afrocentric and feminist politics that inform *Song of Solomon.*[2]

Comments offered by Morrison in "Rootedness: The Ancestor as Foundation" appear to corroborate the general critical emphasis on the epic qualities of *Song of Solomon.* In a discussion of what she views as the Afro-American novel's destiny to replace the celebrated forms of Black expressivity (blues, jazz, spirituals, and folktales) as a primary locus for preserving and transmitting Afro-American cultural wisdom, Morrison argues that "the novel is needed by African-Americans now in a way that it was not needed before—and it is following along the lines of the function of novels everywhere. We don't live in places where we can hear those stories anymore; parents don't sit around and tell their children those *classical, mythological, archetypal stories* that we heard years ago. But *new information* has got to get out, and there are several ways to do it. One is the novel."[3] Despite its apparent support of an unproblematized reading of her third novel as black male odyssey par excellence, Morrison's statement strongly suggests a dual—and, in some respects, potentially conflicting—function for the novel, particularly for a purposefully "classical, mythological, archetypal" text such as *Song of Solomon.* These two functions are to preserve the traditional Afro-American folktales, folk wisdom, and general cultural beliefs; and to adapt to contemporary times and needs such traditional beliefs by infusing them with "new information" and transmitting the resulting amalgam to succeeding generations. While both the conservative and transformative functions are ideologically charged—they are informed by the desire to convey to Afro-American readers "how to behave in this new world" (340)—it is quite easy to see that certain profound conflicts might arise between the old (the archetypal tales) and the "new."[4]

In fact, the criticism devoted to Morrison's use of myth and epic in *Song of Solomon* has failed to respond adequately to the author's inscription of the "new." For Morrison's version of the myth of the flying African is in several crucial respects strategically altered in the form of an updated version of the traditional narrative, which is, as Lee argues, "revitalized by a new grounding in the concrete particularities of a specific time and place."[5] That new grounding is represented by Solomon's apparent lack of an accompanying sense of social responsibility. The nameless black slaves in versions of the flying African myth such as Julius Lester's "People Who Could Fly," invested with the transcendent power of the word by a young witch doctor, literally rise en masse in response to the plight of blacks weakened as a consequence of working in heat that made "the very air seem . . . to be on fire." This witch doctor, who "carried with him the secrets and powers of the generations of Africa," employs these black powers to lead a stirring mass exodus from deep South fields.[6] When the witch doctor is himself struck by an overseer who recognizes his role in aiding the infirm to "surrender to the air,"[7] he instructs "Everyone" to escape: "He uttered the strange word, and all of the Africans dropped their hoes, stretched out their arms, and flew away, back to their home, back to Africa."[8]

What is striking about this traditional version of the myth, particularly in comparison to its updating in *Song of Solomon,* is the communally beneficial nature of the witch doctor's employment of the liberating black word.[9] In Lester's version of the myth, tribal wisdom is employed to make possible a group transcendence of the debilitating conditions of American oppression. The young African witch doctor, who possesses the power of flight, employs his knowledge at the appropriate moment—when the representative of white power punishes the weakened and defenseless, and seeks to destroy the bearer of African cultural wisdom—to effect a communal escape from the site of mistreatment and oppression.

Morrison's appropriation of the myth, while it preserves a clear connection to mythology representing black flight's possibilities, divests the narrative of its essential communal impulses. In *Song of Solomon,* the empowered Afro-American's flight, celebrated in a blues song whose decoding catapults Milkman into self-conscious maturity, is a solitary one; in other words, his discovery of the means of transcendence—the liberating black word—is not shared with the tribe. He leaves his loved ones, including his infant son Jake, whom he tries unsuccessfully to carry with him, with the task of attempting to learn for themselves the secrets of transcendence. The failure of Solomon's efforts to take Jake with him, in fact, serves to emphasize the ultimately individualistic nature of the mythic figure's flight.[10] And while the narrative suggests that the offspring of the legendary Solomon do not perceive themselves as adversely affected by his act—they, in fact, construct praise songs in recognition of his accomplishments—his mate Ryna, who bears his twenty-one children, is so aggrieved at her loss that she goes mad. (Her grief, like Solomon's transcendent act, assumes legendary proportions in the history of Milkman's people.)

The conflict between the archetypal and the "new" in *Song of Solomon,* then, is of particular significance where gender is concerned because, as is generally the case in Western mythic systems, including the genre of the epic, Morrison's updated version suggests that masculinity has become a virtual prerequisite for participating in transcendent action. In this respect, Morrison's appropriation differs significantly from Lester's version of the traditional myth, where flight is delineated not as an individual but as a communal act, an act not limited to the biologically male.

An analysis which suggests, either implicitly or explicitly, that the novel's inscription of an ideology of race is privileged over its figurations of a politics of gender cannot capture the complexities of Morrison's mythic narrative. For, despite her ambiguous claim, recorded in this chapter's epigraph, that she writes "without gender focus," her attraction to the "unruly" features of "women's imagination," which "can bring things to the surface that men—trained to be men in a certain way—have difficulty getting access to," inspires her demonstration of certain masculinist features of mythic narrative specifically and of cultural practice generally.[11] The text of *Song of Solomon* serves as a wonderfully appropriate site for a black feminist criticism—for a discourse attuned to intersections between afrocentric and feminist ideologies.

Such an analysis needs to be preceded, however, by a discussion of the relationship between myth and ideology that might inform our comprehension of their intersections in Morrison, and by a brief exploration of the largely andro-centric epic tradition whose masculinist biases the "unruly" black female author critically revises.

The folklorist Alan Dundes has suggested that "myth is a sacred narrative explain-ing how the world and man came to be in their present form."[12] But if myth, as he argues, possesses the function of clarifying origins, its articulation also explains how man and woman can cope, in a culturally approved fashion, with difficulties wrought in the present by natural and supernatural forces. The mythic/epic hero's merits and the quality of his achievements are measured in terms of what George deForest Lord calls "the success of the hero in search of himself and his success in restoring or preserving his culture."[13] Consequently, myth's function is to contribute to the maintenance of the norms and values of the culture out of which "sacred narrative" emerges.

Richard Slotkin helpfully illuminates the ideological underpinnings of myth. He defines it as a "body of traditional stories that have . . . been used to summarize the course of our collective history and to assign ideological mean-ings to that history." Slotkin analyzes the essentially ideological function of myth in the following way:

> The terms "myth" and "ideology" describe essential attributes of every human culture. Ideology is an abstraction of the system of beliefs, values, and institutional relationships that characterize a particular culture or soci-ety; mythology is the body of traditional narratives that exemplifies and his-toricizes ideology. Myths are stories, drawn from history, that have acquired through usage over many generations a symbolizing function central to the culture of the society that produces them. Through the processes of tradi-tionalization historical narratives are conventionalized and abstracted, and their range of reference is extended so that they become structural meta-phors containing all the essential elements of a culture's world view. . . . Myths suggest that by understanding and imaginatively reenacting the conflict resolutions of the past, we can interpret and control the unresolved conflicts of the present.[14]

Myths, then, are implicitly ideological in conveying and advocating their culture's belief systems in symbolic forms that are both historically significant and immediately relevant. To use Morrison's phrase, they inform their culture's inhabitants "how to behave" in a time-tested, culturally approved manner.

Slotkin's sense of myth's implicitly ideological function of "defining and defending [the society's] pattern of values" accords with Morrison's own formu-lations concerning mythic narratives in "Rootedness."[15] Arguing that fiction "must be political" (344) in order to be of value to society, Morrison insists that novels have always "provided social rules and explained behavior, identified outlaws, identified the people, habits, and customs that one should approve of" (340). Apparently, her interest in myth derives, at least in part, from an awareness of its usefulness in the transmission of ideology and in the preservation of cultural wisdom, values, and worldviews.

Morrison's position as black and female, however, problematizes her relation to myth because of the fact that traditional myths, like most other cultural forms preserved from an androcentric past, tend to inscribe as part of their truth a subordinate and inferior status for women. While a close examination of Morrison's corpus discourages a reading of her work as radically feminist, clearly the author's novels are infused with a consistently female-centered perspective. Such an ideological stance leads Morrison to confront the sometimes virulently phallocentric nature of traditional Western myths, including Afro-American ones.[16] Indeed, Gerry Brenner's essay on *Song of Solomon* asserts that Morrison ironically applies, and forcefully rejects, the (masculinist) monomythic principles delineated by Otto Rank.[17] Brenner's astute perceptions concerning Morrison's comprehension of the sexism implicit in the epic suggest the appropriateness of an analysis of the ways in which the novelist's woman-centered ideology complicates her use of (afrocentric) myth.

Such an analysis is facilitated by the formulations of feminist critic Rachel Du Plessis, particularly her discussion of contemporary women writers' manipulation of traditional myth. Du Plessis, who has argued that twentieth-century women's literature is characterized by manifestly ideological efforts to create narrative strategies "that express the critical dissent from dominant [androcentric] narrative,"[18] says of the female confrontation of traditional mythological forms:

> When a woman writer chooses myth as her subject, she is faced with material that is indifferent or, more often, actively hostile to historical considerations of gender, claiming as it does universal, humanistic, natural, or even archetypal status. To face myth as a woman writer is, putting things at their most extreme, to stand at the impact point of a strong system of interpretation masked as representation, and to rehearse one's own colonization or "iconization" through the materials one's culture considers powerful and primary. (106)

Joseph Campbell's discussion in *The Hero with a Thousand Faces* of women's roles within the male monomyth confirms Du Plessis's assertions that sacred narrative excludes the female as subject:

> Woman, in the picture language of mythology, represents the totality of what can be known. The hero is the one who comes to know. . . . Woman

is the guide to the sublime acme of sensuous adventure. By deficient eyes she is reduced to inferior states; by the evil eye of ignorance she is spellbound to banality and ugliness. But she is redeemed by the eye of understanding. The hero who can take her as she is, without undue commotion but with the kindness and assurance she requires, is potentially the king, the incarnate god, of her created world.[19]

According to Campbell, the informing principles of myth inscribe woman as supplement and object, as a lesser being "redeemed" by the heroic male "eye of understanding," as one who requires male "kindness and assurance" to escape pejorative evaluations of her character and being.

Clearly, Campbell's influential formulations demonstrate the virtual impossibility of an uncritical contemporary female author's employment of traditional myth. For, in his discussion and apparent advocacy, for instance, of the Adamic myth of women's origins inside man, Campbell validates the phallocentric belief that women's role is to complete—to make whole—the heretofore psychologically fragmented and defeminized male hero. The mythic (and historical) role of the female as supplement, then, reflects androcentric ideology in ways suggesting the utter difficulty and manifest dangers for female writers of employing traditional myths in uncritical ways. To do so is, in Du Plessis's words, "to rehearse one's own colonization or iconization.' "

Du Plessis argues that white female writers who feel altogether excluded from and subjugated by traditional Western sacred narratives view these myths' radical subversion as a means of "delegitimating the specific narrative and cultural orders of [the past]" (34). For such writers, among whom Du Plessis counts Adrienne Rich, Sylvia Plath, and Margaret Atwood, the goal of myth's appropriation is both to critique the phallocentric nature of traditional myth and to create the possibilities for female-centered myths with women as hero and subject.

For an afrocentric female writer like Morrison, however, who sees great value in Afro-American sacred narrative, despite its phallocentricism, the employment of traditional myth is problematic because of the necessity of affirming the ideological perspectives of these narratives where they involve the nature of black survival, while at the same time critiquing their male centeredness. The author must produce narratives which clearly demonstrate her advocacy of elements of afrocentric ideology, while simultaneously condemning myth's general failure to inscribe the possibilities of a full female participation as subject in the story of black American self-actualization and cultural preservation.[20]

Its success in navigating between these ideological terrains suggests that *Song of Solomon* neither falls outside of the womanist and afrocentric concerns of Morrison's other 1970s novels, nor does it, as Susan Willis has asserted in a

provocative analysis of Morrison's corpus, serve to "reinvent the notion of patrimony that emerges even as [Milkman] puts together his genealogy."²¹ Viewing
Song of Solomon in terms of its informing ideologies facilitates the reader's discern-
ment of the ways in which the novel offers a disruption of the androcentric
sequence both of Western sacred narrative in general, and specifically, of (appropriated) Afro-American myth.

Morrison's appropriation of the monomyth is, indeed, quite subtle, a subtlety
suggested by the relative lack of extended critical comment about her choice of
a male protagonist. Despite the clearly female-centered nature of her earlier
novels, *The Bluest Eye* and *Sula,* critics generally have been remarkably untroubled by Morrison's creation of an apparently androcentric narrative. Such an
untroubled response is manifested even in Genevieve Fabre's essay on the novel,
despite the fact that this essay begins by situating Morrison in a continuum of
black female writers who attempt "to achieve literacy . . . [and] freedom," and
argues that "Black women writers call attention to the distinctiveness of their
experiences and vision" by composing works "deliberately disruptive and
disturbing in their bold investigations [that] are part of a struggle against all
forms of authority."²² Although the essay demonstrates an acute understanding of Morrison's afrocentric and feminist concerns, Fabre proceeds to offer a
reading of *Song of Solomon* that concentrates almost exclusively on Milkman's
"genealogical archaeology" and virtually ignores the problematics of gender as
a major consideration. Fabre's curious reticence about gender in her analysis of
Morrison's novel, however, does encourage a crucial question: How does what
she calls Morrison's "dramatization of an archetypal journey across ancestral
territory" really reflect, where it pertains to the insights Fabre offers in her
introductory contextualizing of the novelist's ideological aims, "the essential
significance of [black female] *difference?*"²³

An answer to this question is not quickly forthcoming, for in addition to
what critics have generally read as Morrison's inscription of a privileged maleness
in *Song of Solomon,* several of her own comments seem intended to discourage
analyses of her work whose orientation is primarily feminist. In "Rootedness,"
for example, she says, in response to a question concerning "the necessity to develop a specific Black feminist model of critical inquiry", "I think there is more
danger in it than fruit, because any model of criticism or evaluation that excludes
males from it is as hampered as any model of criticism of Black literature that
excludes women from it" (344). Perhaps even more inhibiting to a limited feminist reading of *Song of Solomon* are comments she offers to explain the roots of
Hagar's ultimately debilitating problems, despite her possession of a wondrously
self-actualized mentor: her grandmother Pilate. Morrison says of Hagar:

The difficulty that Hagar . . . has is how far removed she is from the experience of her ancestor. Pilate had a dozen years of close, nurturing relationships with two males—her father and her brother. And that intimacy and
support was in her and made her fierce and loving because she had that
experience. Her daughter Reba had less of that and related to men in a very
shallow way. Her daughter [Hagar] had even less of an association with men
as a child, so that the progression is really a diminishing of their abilities
because of the absence of men in a nourishing way in their lives. Pilate is the
apogee of all that: of the best of that which is female and the best of that
which is male, and that balance is disturbed if it is not nurtured, and if it is
not counted on and if it is not reproduced. That is the disability we must be
on guard against for the future—the female who reproduces the female
who reproduces the female. (344)

Morrison rejects the radical feminist idea or ideal of exclusively female communities as the best means of maximizing possibilities of black female psychic and
emotional health. Indeed, the question of gender-specific exclusion is profoundly
important to Morrison's formulations here, for it serves as her motivation both for
assertions about the potential dangers of a narrowly focused black feminist criticism and, in her reading of incidents in *Song of Solomon,* for the ultimate demise of
Hagar. Clearly, for Morrison, black female psychic health cannot be achieved
without the cooperative participation of both females and males in its creation
and nurturance. Indeed, male participation helps to provide the novice female
with a sense of "balance" between "the best of that which is female and the best of
that which is male" without which gendered and tribal health is, for Morrison,
quite unlikely.

Such comments might be read as confirmation of Willis's assertion above
that *Song of Solomon* tends to "reinvent the notion of patrimony." However, its
complex inscription of afrocentric and feminist ideologies can be more fruitfully
read in terms of Du Plessis's formulations with respect to contemporary women
writers' efforts to disrupt traditional androcentric narrative sequences and strategies. According to Du Plessis, contemporary women writers' work is committed
to "rupturing language and tradition sufficiently to invite a female slant, emphasis, or approach," and to "delegitimating specific narrative and cultural orders
of [the past]" (32). I want to argue here that Morrison's appropriation of the
monomyth and of Afro-American sacred narrative are motivated by such
rupturing, delegitimating impulses.

Later I will further explore the sense of narrative rupture and breakage implicit in Morrison's appropriations of the male monomyth. That exploration will
focus on two crucial aspects of the novel: (1) Morrison's literal breaking of the

monomythic sequence by her interruption of the narrative of Milkman's male heroic quest with the specifically antithetical story of Hagar's tragic demise; and (2) the particular implications of the narrative of Solomon's flight.

In order to discuss fully Morrison's manipulation of the privileged text to mythic (male) transcendence, I must begin with a brief delineation of the particulars of Milkman's journey. Milkman's quest is undertaken initially to provide him access to the gold he believes Pilate has left behind as a means of securing a lasting economic and emotional self-sufficiency. In other words, his quest is inspired by an urge to avoid emotional commitment and familial responsibility:

> He just wanted to beat a path away from his parents' past, which was also their present and which was threatening to become his present as well. He hated the acridness in his mother's and father's relationship, the conviction of righteousness they each held on to with both hands. And his efforts to ignore it, transcend it, seemed to work only when he spent his days looking for whatever was light-hearted and without grave consequences. He avoided commitment and strong feelings, and shied away from decisions. He wanted to know as little as possible, to feel only enough to warrant the curiosity of other people—but not their all-consuming devotion. Hagar had given him this last and more drama than he could ever want again. (180–81)

Milkman's journey begins, then, as an effort to gain freedom from obligation to others by taking possession of a familial treasure. Instead of gold, however, what he finds, after a series of episodes conforming to traditional monomythic paradigms for the male hero called to adventure, is a mature sense of his familial obligations, an informed knowledge of familial (and tribal) history, and a profound comprehension of tribal wisdom.[24] His newly achieved knowledge of self and culture is manifested dramatically during the course of an initiatory trial by fire in Shalimar, in which black male elders invite the bourgeois urbanite on a long, arduous hunting trek and then leave the novice hunter behind to fend for himself. Forced to use his wits to navigate a forest filled with wild animals, Milkman considers the treatment he has received since his arrival, and, more important, the ways he has treated others. Asking himself, "What kind of savages were these people?" and believing momentarily that "he had done nothing to deserve their contempt (279), a significantly more introspective Milkman recognizes the necessity of abandoning such immature perspectives:

> It sounded old. Deserve. Old and tired and beaten to death. Deserve. Now it seemed to him that he was always saying or thinking that he didn't deserve

some bad luck, or some bad treatment from others. He'd told Guitar that he didn't even "deserve" his family's dependence, hatred, or whatever. That he didn't even "deserve" to hear all the misery and mutual accusations his parents unloaded on him. Nor did he "deserve" Hagar's vengeance. But why shouldn't his parents tell him their personal problems? If not him, then who? And if a stranger could try to kill him, surely Hagar, who knew him and whom he'd thrown away like a wad of chewing gum after the flavor was gone—she had a right to try to kill him too. (279–80)

His achievement of a radically reconceptualized view of self and family, and of his responsibilities thereto, occurs when, near the end of his ancestral quest, he is overcome by a feeling of homesickness as he listens to a group of Shalimar children singing "that old blues song Pilate sang all the time: 'O Sugarman don't leave me here'" (303). This homesickness is accompanied by, and is, indeed, a function of, a more mature and complete awareness of the factors that motivated his family's behavior. He comprehends, for example, that his mother's eccentricities—including the fact that she nursed him well past an age that such a practice was necessary for his nourishment—are in part the result of "sexual deprivation", a deprivation that "would affect her, hurt her in precisely the way it would affect and hurt him" (303). Subsequently, he wonders, "What might she have been like had her husband loved her?" (304). Further, he begins to understand the source of his father's perversely acquisitive nature. "As the son of Macon Dead the first, [his father] paid homage to his own father's life and death by loving what that father had loved: property, good solid property, the bountifulness of life. He loved these things to excess. Owning, building, acquiring—that was his life, his future, his present, and all the history he knew. That he distorted life, bent it, for the sake of gain, was a measure of his loss at his father's death" (304).

In addition to comprehending the ridiculousness of hating his parents and sisters, and being overcome with a thick "skin of shame" For "having stolen from Pilate" (304), he turns his thoughts to Hagar, the person whose life his selfishness has most seriously affected. Wondering why he had not exercised more sensitivity in ending their relationship, he sees that his egotistical masculinist treatment of Hagar had extended even to his response to her hysterical attempts to end his life:

> He had used her—her love, her craziness—and most of all he had used her skulking, bitter vengeance. It made him a star, a celebrity in the Blood Bank; it told men and other women that he was one bad dude, that he had the power to drive a woman out of her mind, to destroy her, and not because she hated him, or because he had done some unforgivable thing to

her, but because he had fucked her and she was driven wild by the absence
of his magnificent joint. (305).

A thoughtful and less self-protective appraisal of his personal history, motivated by the trials and tribulations that constitute his heroic ordeal and that
include his rejection of an injuriously materialistic perspective, forces Milkman
to comprehend the serious errors of his self-centered ways. Like the traditional
monomythic hero, he achieves a sense of his identity that is firmly rooted in his
relationship to his family and community. for he has learned, in short, that he can
achieve a sense of self only when he is able to embrace his unavoidable responsibilities to family and humanity, when he can recognize and relish a sense of
membership with his people. Liberated from the shallow and selfish perspectives
that had previously characterized him, Milkman has ended his division from self
and tribe and become whole, has achieved a "coming together . . . into a total
self" (70).

Ultimately, Milkman, whose gender permits Morrison to construct the narrative of his ancestral quest in general compliance with the parameters of the classical monomyth, is able to perform the culture-preserving service necessary for
the maintenance of his community. In accordance with the requirements for the
successful monomythic hero, he returns to his Michigan community to share
what he has decoded of the sacred narrative's cryptic lyrics with a family hopelessly divided by decades of mistrust and perverse mistreatment of one another.
Milkman's odyssey confirms the accuracy of his father's previous conflation of
selfhood and knowledge. Earlier, when Milkman intervenes in a psychologically
and physically violent dispute between his mother and father by striking Macon
Dead II, his father says to him: "You a big man now, but big ain't nearly enough.
You have to be a whole man. And if you want to be a whole man, you have to deal
with the whole truth" (70). Having investigated, in a seemingly thorough manner, his ancestral heritage, Milkman learns a good deal of "the whole truth,"
which provides him access to what Joseph Campbell calls "the unquenched
source through which society is reborn."[25] An achieved sense of wholeness
and access to the "unquenched source"—in particular, the history of the Dead
clan; more generally, Afro-American culture, and its timeless truths—allows
Milkman to embark on the monomythic hero's second task, "to return then to
[his 'disintegrating society'] transfigured, and teach the lesson he has learned of
life renewed."[26]

Those lessons, however informative and powerful, cannot alter the most
chilling consequence of his former "disintegrat[ed] psyche": his mistreatment of
Hagar, and her ultimate death.[27] Concurrent with Milkman's achievement of indispensable awareness of self and culture is Hagar's painful quest to achieve bour-

geois American society's standards of female beauty. Indeed, Milkman's and Hagar's gendered situations in a patriarchal capitalist system ultimately delimit their journeys' very nature and success.

Chapter 13 of *Song of Solomon*, which records the circumstances surrounding Hagar's death, offers a literal—and strategic—breaking of the male monomythic sequence. The structure of Morrison's novel encourages a contrast between Milkman's (male) monomythic quest for self and community, and his cousin Hagar's deathward march toward what Susan Willis has identified as reification. (89) This juxtaposition is, in fact, quite striking. For example, the journeys of both characters are embarked upon as a consequence of their attitudes about bourgeois capitalist values. Milkman, whom Morrison is able to write into the traditional (male) epic quest plot, seeks to escape his environment not because its bourgeois values are oppressive but because they demand a psychic involvement and sense of empathy for which he is clearly unprepared. On the other hand, Hagar's journey to reification and, ultimately, physical death, has its source in her adoption of a patriarchal society's almost timeless figuration of woman as object, in her futile attempt to achieve the bourgeois society's notions of female beauty. Having apparently inherited from her female forebear Ryna the capacity for immeasurable grief as a consequence of male abandonment, Hagar concludes, after gazing in a mirror at her own image, that Milkman's failure to love her is a function of her unglamorous, un-Cosmopolitan appearance.

Hagar's female status denies her entry as actor and subject to paradigmatic epic means of transcendence. Consequently, she is denied access to the transformative possibilities of a regenerative necessary distance from a corruptive mainstream American bourgeois value system. Because the mythic black narrative of communal transcendence is no longer extant—and has, in fact, been replaced by an individualistic and androcentric (familial) text—Hagar has no means of achieving a nurturing knowledge of self and culture that would make it possible for her to reject the debilitating tenets of what George deForest Lord calls "a destroyed city, a ruined culture."[28] Hence, she can see possibilities for self-improvement only in the terms that a "ruined" bourgeois American society suggests are proper for her sex. In other words, in a society where female self-actualization is, by and large, impossible outside of the context of an interactive relationship with a man, Hagar's concentration on Milkman's unwillingness to love her is, however injurious, utterly logical. While Milkman comes to a marvelously useful comprehension of history, myth, and nature, Hagar's status as bound, in both the spatial and the narrative senses of the phrase, to oppressive domestic plots—a virtual requirement for the abandoned female lover in the Western epic—precipitates in a dissociation of sensibility and an acceptance of the bourgeois society's views of women. This acceptance is reflected particularly in her wholehearted adoption of its ideas of female beauty.

It is specifically in terms of the image of female mirror-gazing that Morrison figures the conclusion of Hagar's grief-inspired aphasia and her discovery of what she believes is a means by which to rekindle Milkman's interest. When an almost catatonic Hagar sees herself in a compact mirror Pilate holds before her, she is convinced that she has found the source of Milkman's antipathy—her appearance:

> "No wonder," she said at last. "Look at that. No wonder. No wonder. . . .
> "Look at how I look. I look awful. No wonder he didn't want me. I look terrible." Her voice was calm and reasonable, as though the last few days hadn't been lived through at all. "I need to get up from here and fix myself up. No *wonder!*" Hagar threw back the bedcover and stood up. "Ohhh. I smell too. Mama, heat me some water. I need a bath. . . . Oh Lord, my head. Look at that." She peered into the compact mirror again. "I look like a ground hog. Where's the comb?" (312)

Hagar sets out enthusiastically to achieve the bourgeois society's ideal of beauty. Believing "I need everything" to transform her black difference—what she refers to as her "ground hog" appearance—into the bourgeois society's glamorous feminine ideal, she spends an entire business day shopping for "everything a woman could wear from the skin out." She purchases, among other things, "a Playtex garter belt, I. Miller No Color hose, Fruit of the Loom panties, . . . two nylon slips", an expansive Evan-Picone outfit, and cosmetics (314). Hers is a shameless act of commodity consumption, a desperate attempt to make herself into an incontestable example of American feminine beauty in order to be worthy of Milkman's love. Her instruments of transformation are soaked and soiled, however, in a downpour of rain, and her efforts to employ these ripped clothes and rain-soaked cosmetics to remake herself prove far from successful. Hagar understands this when she sees Pilate's and Reba's reaction to her appearance. "It was in their eyes that she saw what she had not seen before in the mirror: the wet ripped hose, the soiled white dress, the sticky, lumpy face powder, the streaked rouge, and the wild wet shouls of hair. All this she saw in their eyes, and the sight filled her own with water warmer and much older than the rain" (318).

Hagar comes to the bitter realization that he efforts to achieve American society's ideal of female beauty are utterly fruitless. Her brief, painful attempt to compensate for lacking the physical qualities of which she knows Milkman approves of—"silky, [penny-colored] hair," "lemon-colored skin," "gray-blue eyes," and a "thin nose" (319–20)—ends, not with transcendent knowledge of the world as does the male protagonist's epic journey, but rather with an awareness that her (ruined) society will never provide her opportunities for the types of transformations necessary to win the love of the man with whom she feels she belongs. Exhausted, and feeling the full hopelessness of her dilemma, she tells Pilate: "He's never going to like my hair" (320).

Morrison interrupts Milkman's monomythic quest, or, in Du Plessis's phrase, breaks the (sacred) narrative sequence, in order to expose phallocentric myth's failure to inscribe usefully transcendent possibilities for the female. This interruption serves to problematize a strictly celebratory afrocentric analysis of Milkman's achievements. Such an analysis fails to permit focus on the clear presence of (female) pain that permeates *Song of Solomon*'s final chapters. Male culpability in the instigation of such pain is evident, for example, in Milkman's revelations about the motivations for his treatment of Hagar. He comes to understand that he "had used her—her love, her craziness—and most of all . . . her skulking, bitter vengeance" (304) to achieve heroic—or what the narrative refers to as "star"—status.[29]

Analyses of Morrison's novel must be attentive both to the transcendent joy of knowledge-informed male flight and to the immeasurable pain of desertion felt by females like Hagar and Ryna, whose agony at the loss of Solomon "like to killed the woman" (326) and was so profound in its intensity that "she screamed and screamed, lost her mind completely" (327). Future readings must, in other words, acknowledge that the blues lyrics and the novel encode *both* an afrocentric appreciation of the power of transcendence and a convincing critique of the fact that, in the updated version of the myth, such power is essentially denied to Afro-American women. Morrison's appropriation of the myth approximates the narrative structures of phallocentric Western myths to the extent that males are figured as actors, while females are aggrieved, deserted, and—because of the masculinist perspectives of both culture and narrative form—permanently grounded objects. As Kimberly Benston argues, "Read as a transparency of a more subversive feminist manifesto, . . . Morrison's analysis is, on the one hand, a covert interrogation of the propriety of that male quest—its costs and exclusions—and, on the other hand, of its implicitly enabling denial of female presence and voice."[30] The ideological complexity of Morrison's representation of her woman-centered and afrocentric politics is suggested in the lyrics' inscription of transcendence and abandonment: "Solomon done fly, Solomon done gone" (307).

Morrison's delineation in her novel of feminist concerns is perhaps most clearly evident in the (predominantly) female voices of dissent that operate as a censorious chorus in the last chapters of *Song of Solomon*. Shalimar females such as Susan Byrd and Sweet are, by and large, remarkably unimpressed by Solomon and by his transcendent act. Susan Byrd, in fact, openly criticizes him for his desertion of Ryna and his offspring. While Byrd recounts to Milkman the provocative aspects of Solomon's mythic flight—she tells Milkman, "according to the story, he . . . flew, like a bird. Just stood up in the fields one day, ran up some hill, spun around a couple of times, and was lifted up in the air. Went right on back to wherever it was he came from" (326)—her narrative focuses primarily on the pain felt by others as a consequence of his desertion. Indeed, it is Susan Byrd who informs Milkman of the derivation of the name Ryna's Gulch: "Sometimes you can hear this funny sound by [the gulch] that the wind makes. People say it's the wife. Solomon's wife, crying. Her name was Ryna" (326–27). In addition to censorious assertions such as "he disappeared and left everybody" (326), she comments further on the ramifications of his leave-taking flight: "They say she screamed and screamed, lost her mind completely. You don't hear about women like that anymore, but there used to be more—the kind of woman who couldn't live without a particular man. And when the man left, they lost their minds, or died or something. Love, I guess. But I always thought it was trying to take care of children by themselves, you know what I mean?" (327). While we might rightly question here the reliability of Susan Byrd's "speculations" (327)—for instance, the Song of Solomon is no mere, negligible "old folks' lie"; further, Hagar's response to Milkman's desertion is of a kind with Ryna's, and her grief clearly has nothing to do with the difficulty of single parenthood—certainly the reader can trust her recollections of the particulars of the mythic narrative. That the reader should trust her view of the magnitude of the deserted female's pain is confirmed by the reactions of Sweet and ultimately of Milkman to male acts of abandonment and transcendence.

Milkman's archaeological act fills him with an "incredible high" (330) under whose influence he relates to his Shalimar lover Sweet the fact that he is a descendant of Solomon. Having taken possession of his familial history—he asserts proudly of the ring shout that accompanies the recitation of the song of Solomon, "It's my game now" (331)—he says of his forebear: "The son of a bitch could fly! You hear me, Sweet? that motherfucker could fly! Could fly! He didn't need no airplane. Didn't need no fuckin tee double you ay. He could fly his own self!" (332) Unimpressed by the knowledge of Milkman's royal heritage—after all, as Susan Byrd tells him, "everybody around here claims kin to him" (326)—Sweet tries to force her lover to consider the consequences of Jake's transcendent act by asking, "Who'd he leave behind?" (332). Still mesmerized by his status as descendant of such a magical figure, Milkman giddily responds: "Everybody! He left everybody down on the ground and he sailed on off like a black eagle" (332). It is only when he is forced to confront the consequences of his desertion of Hagar that he is capable of sensitivity to the socially irresponsible nature of his ancestor's actions, and, further, of his own.

Such confrontation occurs when, on his return to Michigan, Milkman is exposed to male flight's significant, sometimes deadly, consequences. Recovering consciousness in Pilate's cellar from a blow by his justifiably angered aunt, Milkman comes to understand the tragic ironies of a phallocentric social (and narrative) structure that refuses female access to the culture's sources of knowledge and power. The narrative informs us of Milkman's revelations: "He had left her. While he dreamt of flying, Hagar was dying" (336). Milkman, who, despite his infinite leap in knowledge, clearly still has much to learn, then recalls Sweet's question about the victims of Solomon's departure, a question which he had not seriously pondered previously. He begins to see a clear connection between his act and that of his mythic forebear, the full impact of whose flight he can now understand:

> Sweet's silvery voice came back to him: "Who'd he leave behind?" He left Ryna behind and twenty children. Twenty-one, since he dropped the one he tried to take with him. And Ryna had thrown herself all over the ground, lost her mind, and was still crying in a ditch. Who looked after those twenty children? Jesus Christ, he left twenty-one children! . . . Shalimar left his, but it was the children who sang about it and kept the story of his leaving alive. (336)

It is only at this point, when he learns of the painful consequences of the celebrated male act of flight, that Milkman's comprehension of his familial heritage and the song of Solomon can be said to move toward satisfying completion. Such understanding requires coming to terms with his familial song's complex, sometimes unflattering meaning, and acknowledging both its prideful flight and the lack of a sense of social responsibility in the mythic hero Solomon's leavetaking.

Song of Solomon, then, is a record both of transcendent (male) flight and of the immeasurable pain that results for the female who, because she has no access to knowledge, cannot participate in this flight. In breaking the monomythic sequence, Morrison provides the possibilities for a resistant feminist reading that suggests the consequences of male epic journeys: the death-in-life, or actual death, of the female whose only permissible role is that of an aggrieved, abandoned lover.

Thus, an analysis that foregrounds not only Milkman's archaeological quest but also Hagar's disintegration—in other words, an afrocentric feminist reading of *Song of Solomon*—allows for an interpretation that most closely suggests the complexity of Morrison's appropriation of the epic form and the Afro-American folktale. Such an analysis is necessary, in fact, if we are to comprehend the black and feminist poetics that inform not only *Song of Solomon* but the author's entire corpus. Rather than reinventing patrimony, Morrison's novel affirms the timeless relevance of the folktale's cultural truths, while exposing contemporary perversions of the myth's insistence on the importance of transcendent flight as implicitly phallocentric in their inscription of a perpetually inferior—non-"heroic"—status for the female.

Morrison's male epic does not represent a break with the female-centered concerns of works such as *The Bluest Eye* and *Sula,* but is a bold extension of these concerns in a confrontation with the tenets of Western literature's most "sacred narrative" form. Like Guitar, who insists that he has earned the right to censorious analyses of the actions of Afro-Americans, Morrison asks, in effect, "Can't I criticize what I love?" While she dearly wishes to preserve the wonder and wisdom of black culture, Morrison perceives the need to invest the preserved forms of culture with "new information." If cultures generally are not static but are in the process of continual and dynamic development, clearly Afro-American culture, if it is to be valuable in the present as a means of explaining a rapidly changing world in which women are increasingly important and influential public actors, cannot continue to produce perspectives which lead to the further creation of narratives that trivialize or marginalize the female. Such recognition does not mean a replacement of afrocentric ideology with feminism but the creation of spaces that will allow for their necessary and potentially fruitful interaction. In that sense, *Song of Solomon,* besides reflecting the perspectives of Afro-American culture, seeks to contribute in significant ways to its transformation.

A co-incidence of contingencies among individual subjects who interact as members of some community will operate for them as noncontingency and be interpreted by them accordingly.

Barbara Herrnstein Smith, *Contingencies of Value*

We must remember that ideology also functions overtly, censoring and editing in the name of moral, economic, and political righteousness.

Donald F. Larsson, "Novel into Film"

How can a whole people share a single subjectivity?

Vincent Crapanzano, "Hermes' Dilemma"

6

"The Crookeds with the Straights": On *Fences,*
Race, and the Politics of Adaptation

In asserting in " 'I Want a Black Director' " that race largely determines the nature of a director's interpretive and, ultimately, filmic response to black-authored texts, playwright August Wilson calls attention to the potential impact of ideological and cultural difference on filmic adaptations of literary sources. His insistence to executives of Paramount Pictures, the studio which in 1987 purchased the film rights to the Pulitzer Prize–winning *Fences,* that a black person be found to direct the film version of this play startled many observers inside and outside of the Hollywood community because it represents "the kind of thorny racial issue that Hollywood, with its long-standing concern for the bottom line, is typically reluctant to address."[1] Among the forces of resistance with which Wilson's beliefs must contend are the views of film and literature scholars, which, almost without exception, are unsympathetic to claims that movie adaptations need necessarily position themselves as pictorial or even thematic realizations of their sources. Although film criticism has become generally much more attentive to the impact of ideology on narrative, theories of adaptation have not moved radically away from the position first espoused in 1957 by George Bluestone, who, in his seminal study *Novels into Film,* argues that the filmist need be only minimally concerned with reproducing significant aspects of the prompting textual event. For Bluestone, those who expect more from films operate in terms of naive notions of the relationship between films and their literary sources. The filmed adaptation, he argues, "becomes a different *thing* in the same sense that a historical painting becomes a different thing from the historical event it illustrates":

> In the last analysis, each is autonomous, and each is characterized by unique and specific properties.
> What happens, therefore, when the filmist undertakes the adaptation

of a novel, given the inevitable mutation, is that he does not convert the novel at all. What he adapts is a kind of paraphrase of the novel—the novel viewed as raw material.[2]

Following Bluestone's example, contemporary studies of film adaptation have focused generally on the formal and aesthetic similarities and differences between these diverse modes of storytelling, assuming that calls for investigation of the motivations for specific alterations reflect, in the words of Neil Sinyard, either "ignorance" about film's responsibilities to prompting texts or "a tone of academic superiority and condescension towards the newer art form."[3] Thus, despite contemporary criticism's focus on the ways in which ideologies are reproduced and reinforced in filmic and other representations, theorists of adaptation continue to insist that to examine in a potentially critical way the trajectory of film's appropriation of the "raw material" even of works that may be said to represent challenges to hegemonic points of view is to participate in a retrograde and hopelessly naive interpretive endeavor. As a consequence, discussions like Wilson's (or, for that matter, the hotly contested debates about Steven Spielberg's adaptation of Alice Walker's black feminist novel, *The Color Purple*)[4] enter the national consciousness without the sound theoretical interventionist possibilities that leftist academics are prepared to contribute to, say, debates about Clarence Thomas's fitness for appointment to the Supreme Court; such debates centered on complex—but, for many of us, quite familiar—issues such as sexual politics, racial identity, the consequences of ideological predisposition, and, perhaps most perplexing for the diverse groups for whom Thomas's nomination hearings were watershed events, autobiographical narrative's limitations as an indisputable truth-telling device.

In part, the silence about difference and filmic adaptation—a process that Bluestone and virtually every scholar who has written on the subject equate with critical interpretations—might reflect our general unease with the full exegetical implications of foregrounding critical positionality. Contemporary theory's loss of faith in objectivity has turned the unavoidability of misreading into a commonplace, the inevitable consequence of the defining properties and limitations of language, ideology, and the human psyche. That skepticism, however, has invaded our rhetoric about interpretations much more deeply than it has our analytical practices, which continue generally to be governed by a desire to uncover if not the single true reading, then at the very least a truer reading than those of our ideological adversaries. To accept and operate wholeheartedly in terms of a sense of subjectivity's dominion over the critical project (without, for example, a reliance on an intimate knowledge of a particularly narrow literary tradition or the protection of a strategically articulated sense of affinity with some empowering ideology) is not necessarily to open the doors to a type of radical relativism, but it does force us to question the accuracy and veracity of our own interpretive conclusions. If literary texts are, indeed, no more than interpretations's "raw material," which, within certain limits, the filmist generally can employ as he or she sees fit, then despite our best efforts, we may be no more effectively engaged with the texts we critique than are our ideological adversaries.[5] And while the following discussion will not pretend to resolve this interpretive dilemma, it does strive to examine the motivations for Wilson's demands within the context of systems of meaning making that see manifestations of ideology and definitions of race as powerful, though contestable, constructs.

In "'I Want a Black Director,'" Wilson says of "a well-known, highly respected white director [identified by James Greenberg as Barry Levinson,[6]] who wanted very much to direct the film" version of *Fences*: "I accept that he is a very fine film director. But he is not black. He is not a product of black American culture—a culture that was honed out of the black experience and fired in the kiln of slavery and survival—and he does not share the sensibilities of black Americans" (15). Wilson's perspectives do not represent in the strictest sense of the term what Donald Larsson calls, in his reading of critical theory's utility in analyses of the politics of adaptation, a "new ideology."[7] Indeed, they demonstrate the continuing impact of a belief that the cultural manifestations of race or its performative dimensions remain ideally the province, the possession, if you will, of the group that has produced them. Notwithstanding the technical and discursive distinctions between music and film production, Wilson's argument is analogous to the notion that whites cannot offer emotively authentic renderings of the blues and, to cite a more contemporary manifestation of this perception at work, the belief expressed on T-shirts worn by some black youths, proclaiming the exclusive and exclusionary nature of knowledge with the words, "It's a black thing. You just wouldn't understand." Wilson articulates his views on the matter in the following way:

> As Americans of various races, we share a broad cultural ground, a commonality of society that links its diverse elements into a cohesive whole that can be defined as "American."
>
> We share certain mythologies. A history. We share political and economic systems and a rapidly developing, if suspect, ethos. Within these commonalities are specifics. Specific ideas and attitudes that are not shared on the common cultural ground. These remain the property and possession of the people who develop them, and on that "field of manners and rituals of intercourse" (to use James Baldwin's eloquent phrase) lives are played out. (15)

Challenges to the notion that race determines a predispositional fixity are currently widespread enough that we possess a shared term by which to call and thereby contain that notion: racial essentialism. In an attempt to protect himself from charges that his views are indeed essentialist, Wilson insists that he is referring not to biological but to cultural "qualifications"; he states that he "declined a white director not on the basis of race but on the basis of culture. . . . The job requires someone who shares the specifics of the culture of black Americans." According to Wilson, "no matter how astute a student or how well-meaning their intentions," nonblacks will always remain outsiders with limited access to the specific meanings of that culture's ethos.

Wilson's articulation of his sense of directorial qualifications might be said both to confirm and to challenge what has become for many an indisputable truism: that race is a trope, a necessary fiction used by both hegemonic and anti-hegemonic forces in our complex battles for power. We might be able to observe further some of the most provocative dimensions of Wilson's comment in relation to this truism if we consider it in the context of the insights offered by Michael Omi and Howard Winant. Omi and Winant employ the term "racial formation" in an effort to displace views that race is either "something fixed, concrete and objective" or "mere illusion, which an ideal social order would eliminate." According to Omi and Winant, race is *"an unstable and 'decentered' complex of social meanings constantly being transformed by political struggle*. . . . The crucial task . . . is to suggest how the widely disparate circumstances of individual and group racial identities, and of the racial institutions and social practices with which these identities are intertwined, are formed and transformed over time. This takes place . . . through *political contestation over racial meanings.*"[8] Rather than being either condemned to fixity or assigned a significant status merely because of an imperfect practice of democracy, race for Omi and Winant is best understood as a meaningful entity whose precise definitions are continually under dispute even in the very institutions and social practices whose self-appointed task is to represent and clarify its meanings. This definition of race, while supporting Wilson's analysis in that it emphasizes the centrality of learned modes of interacting with and interpreting the world, insists that we examine Wilson's and any other statements that seek to describe and ascribe definitive racial characteristics as explicitly or implicitly formative constructs.

Omi and Winant's formulations correspond with the explicitly poststructuralist interrogations of the meanings of culture offered by James Clifford in his introduction to the collection, *Writing Culture,* where he outlines his reasons for believing that we need to be more judicious in defining that term. Insisting that we be attentive to the operation of ideology in constructions of cultural meaning that present "partial truths" about a people as indisputable defining characteristics, Clifford argues that culture is not "a unified corpus of symbols and meanings that can be definitively interpreted. Culture is contested, temporal, and emergent. Representation and explanation—both by insiders and outsiders—is implicated in this emergence."⁹ Clifford is concerned primarily with articulating his sense of the potentialities and the limitations of the Western ethnographic enterprise in poststructuralist interpretive contexts. But because Clifford also implicates cultural "insiders" as ideologically motivated contributors to a belief in perspectival unanimity and fixity, he urges us to test these views in the context of intracultural acts of meaning making such as that which Wilson provides in "'I Want a Black Director.'" For while Clifford calls for a more judicious investigation of the other's cultural difference(s) by those white scholars who profit from ethnography's disciplinary authority, he insists also that his readers recognize the persuasiveness of poststructuralist perspectives in the examination of our own cultural milieu, for even at home "there is no whole picture that can be 'filled in,' since the perception and filling of a gap lead to the awareness of other gaps."¹⁰

Keeping in mind notions of race and culture provided by Omi and Winant and by Clifford, I will interrogate below what appear to me to be both the persuasive elements and the conceptual gaps in Wilson's efforts to undermine pejorative notions of black people by proposing a definition of Afro-American culture as an essentially unitary, fixed, and historically static entity.

Wilson asserts that even at the level of language production and usage in American culture, ideology is in evidence, as is best exemplified by the fact that whiteness is defined as free from blemish, moral stain or impurity, and blackness as outrageously wicked; expressing menace; sullen, hostile; unqualified. But if the chromatic terms we employ as shorthand to connote race are, indeed, obviously contaminated with the taint of caucacentric cultural bias, with the stain of ideology, so, too, is the discourse Wilson produces to describe and protect blackness. For while aspects of black American identity can indeed be brought under Wilson's designation of the race as "an African people," the group as a whole reflects the widest possible range of conscious and unconscious connection to Africa as originary source. Certainly it is not the case that all of the sometimes competing institutions and institutionally empowered individuals who speak for or in the name of black Americans are in agreement about the constitutive qualities of black religion, manners of social intercourse, style, language and/or esthetics—or, more to the point, about the significance of these modes of action and being for Africa's late twentieth-century descendants on American shores—despite the fact that Wilson acts as though, with some notable exceptions, "we . . . African people" generally agree on these modes of difference. While it is apparent that he has in mind primarily the forces of white hegemony, whose historical control over the dissemination of black cultural production has served to reinforce pejorative interpretations of black character, he also takes to task those Afro-Americans who as a rule question "the skills of black lawyers, doctors, dentists, accountant and mechanics," thereby evincing their internalization of white hegemony's negative representation of blackness.

Ultimately, Wilson is concerned not simply with the persistence and conceptual brilliance of these cultural forms but with claiming ownership over them, with promoting his belief that they "remain the property and possession of the people who develop them." Regardless of whether we feel that certain manners of religious practice or modes of expression are more authentic or intrinsically more black than others, we must acknowledge that his notion that Afro-Americans "own" cultural forms belies both anthropology's sense of the manner in which culture is practiced in the world and, more important, the ways in which cultures interact in ethnically and racially diverse nations such as America. Despite my profound differences with aspects of Werner Sollors's project, clearly he is correct in asserting that people of varied ethnic and racial cultural origins borrow from one another continually in a multicultural America.[11] Because our advanced capitalist society makes forms of culture available to all with the resources to purchase or otherwise interact with them, black culture's contemporary dissemination cannot be said to occur only in relatively homogeneous spheres like black neighborhoods, urban or rural or, for that matter, in Pentecostal, Baptist, or African Methodist churches. Aspects of these modes of cultural production are, in fact, bought and sold in a manner not wholly distinguishable from soap, mouthwash, and designer basketball sneakers.[12] Indisputably, some part of a contemporary Afro-American's education in blackness is influenced by these modes of cultural dissemination in a manner similar to an interested suburban white youth's interaction with such material, regardless of whether that Afro-American inhabits a predominantly black or a racially heterogeneous environment. In part because aspects of black culture have for decades been the topic of sophisticated academic and mass cultural inquiry—often in the work of white scholars—it seems to me impossible to argue convincingly that whites cannot learn enough to internalize or reproduce features of the culture's complex ethos. Additionally, we must acknowledge here the difficulty for Afro-Americans who move outside of an exclusively black nexus to be imbued with or necessarily employ significant features of that ethos in interracial situations such as their neighborhoods and workplaces, including the academy. And if the nonblack "remains an outsider" to black culture, so, too, in a sense, does the Afro-American, if we accept the notion espoused by Clifford and others that culture is being continuously (re)produced and, therefore, is continually being altered.

Spokespersons for specific forms of black ideology throughout the twentieth century have invested significant amounts of intellectual energy in formulating and reproducing perceptions of black culture as a fixed entity with identifiable connections to a monolithic African sensibility. Whatever resistance is encouraged by formulations such as Clifford's to notions of a transhistorical, transnational blackness, the question of "property and possession"—what Wilson speaks of later in the essay as "control"—represents simultaneously much firmer and much more shaky ground for his insistence on finding a black director for his award-winning drama. Wilson speaks of his efforts as a logical response to the racist climate in which Afro-American art is created:

> Despite such a linguistic environment, the culture of black Americans has emerged and defined itself in strong and effective vehicles that have become the flag-bearers for self-determination and self-identity.
>
> In the face of such, those who are opposed to the ideas of a "foreign" culture permeating the ideal of an American culture founded on the icons of Europe seek to dilute and control it by setting themselves up as the assayers of its value and the custodians of its offspring.
>
> Therein lies the crux of the matter as it relates to Paramount and the film "Fences"—whether we as blacks are going to have control over our own culture and its products. (15)

Wilson seeks, then, to contribute to the efforts of Afro-Americans to demonstrate an intellectual, technical, and entrepreneurial acumen by providing avenues whereby the "strong and effective vehicles" members of the race have created to probe the consequences of black presence in the West can be disseminated without the diluting, distorting intervention of caucacentric protectionism. As ideological strategy, as a gesture whose intent is to intervene on centuries of white control over the representation—and the meanings—of blackness, Wilson's formulations are clearly defensible, for no one should deny him the right to use the cultural material he has produced to serve the admirable political ends to which he is committed.

As self-conscious ideologue, then, it behooves Wilson to employ his significant power in an attempt to actualize his goal, namely, to disseminate relatively undiluted narratives that highlight in aesthetically satisfying ways the presence of "black self-determination and self-identity." But his argument is weakened, in my view, by his efforts to polarize white and black means of access to Euro-American and "'foreign'" (in this case, black) cultural production. The problem is not that his exploration of traditional caucacentric perspectives on black art is unpersuasive, but rather that he suggests, despite the technological advances that have made possible a wider dissemination of black cultural material, that an Afro-American ethos remains inherently less available to a white interpreter than, say, the aesthetics of Euro-American drama are to a black American such as himself. Wilson admits that much Afro-American art results from a process whereby black artists appropriate and transform Euro-American discursive forms by infusing them with "the ideas of a 'foreign' culture."[13] Hence, he would acknowledge the veracity of Henry Louis Gates's claim that in employing the Western dramatic form as a vessel for the expression of a black blues sensibility, he (and other black writers) "creates texts that are double-voiced in the sense that their literary antecedents are both white and black, but also modes of figuration lifted from the black vernacular tradition."[14] More to the point, Wilson insists that an identifiably Afro-American art derives from the abilities of its creators to master the formal "icons of Europe"—including, no doubt, Western dramatic principles—to the extent that such "vernacular" resonances and complex manifestations of black "self-determination" can be recorded despite the English language's status as a tool of caucacentrism. *Fences's* artistic ancestry is at least as much Euro-American as African, for the play's blues sensibilities (themselves an American invention) are figured in a text that displays its creator's obvious mastery of conventional Euro-American theatrical structure, pace, and methodology. Furthermore, its narrative events, particularly its exploration of family dynamics, appear to be intended to recall, in particular, Arthur Miller's classic mid-twentieth-century American drama, *Death of a Salesman*.[15]

Wilson's ruminations thus leave unanswered a crucial question, Why, if black Americans are able to gain a formal mastery over "the icons of Europe," are white Americans incapable of similar mastery of black "style," "language," and "esthetics"? While his suggestion that "as Americans of various races, we share a broad cultural ground" would seem to indicate a belief that Euro-American literary genres represent dimensions of that common ground, their communal nature is merely a function of their wide institutional endorsement and dissemination in and by America's schools, book publishers, theater groups, and other avenues of cultural distribution. What makes this "broad cultural ground" possible, certainly, is not that American ideals and social practices are somehow inherently more accessible to a larger number of the nation's citizens than, say, call-and-response verbal forms or the adoption of a blues ethos as a means of responding to the inevitable pain of living in the world, but because centuries of American propagandists and other perpetuators of the self-evident truths of our nation's constitutive texts have worked tirelessly to convince the population to see its values as natural or, at the very least, superior to all other forms of human interaction and self-governance. Like American citizenry, like, for that matter, the production of dramatic texts deemed Broadway-worthy, participation in an ethos of blackness is a form of learned behavior which, with an even more effective propaganda machine behind it, might become for millions of the nation's nonblack citizens part of that "broad cultural ground" which many share.

Just as, in recent years, the blues as recorded and concert event has been supported almost exclusively by white middle-class audiences, in its Broadway run *Fences*—a play whose central character, Troy Maxson, and general thematics (most succinctly articulated in Maxson's oft-repeated "Take the crookeds with the straights") seem clearly infused with a blues sensibility—"appealed largely to white theatergoers" with the financial resources and inclination to witness its performance on the Great White Way.[16] Furthermore, given the fact that much of what "Americans of various races" have in common—"certain mythologies," "history," "shared political and economic systems"—was created and/or typically presided over by whites, including the dramatic tradition in which Wilson participates so effectively, the playwright's identification of certain "broad . . . elements" as common American ground and, therefore, accessible to all with the willingness to develop the talent to use it, seems to me indisputably strategic, particularly if we consider this view in light of his unwillingness to acknowledge that black cultural products are equally susceptible to white mastery. These are dangerous arguments, if only because they seem to echo those of unself-reflective white racists who, informed by a sense of perpetual Afro-American cultural outsiderness quite similar to Wilson's views on white interaction with black cultural forms, seek to justify their perceptions of exclusive caucasian rights to citizenship and, indeed, location on American shores.

I want to turn now to *Fences* itself, a text we might consider what Wilson calls in "'I Want a Black Director'" one of the "strong and effective vehicles that have become the flag-bearers for [Afro-American] self-determination and self-identity" (15). The play, which explores, among other matters, male intergenerational conflict and the motivations for and repercussions of the protagonist's extramarital affair, is peopled with characters who attempt to erect domestic and social boundaries—literal and figurative fences, if you will—as a means of marking both domestic space itself and its inhabitants as "property and possession" in order to shield them from the corruptive and murderous forces of the outside world while, at the same time, protecting the marking subject from the threat of abandonment. Ultimately, I want to investigate Wilson's examination of the possibilities of erecting protective fences around black familial space in terms of the quite different trajectory of Wilson's efforts to find a black film director in order to protect his creation from potentially contaminating caucacentric forces. While the playwright orchestrates the search for what are ideologically justifiable reasons, its perspectives appear on the surface at least to be at odds with *Fences'* inquiry into the advisability of protectionist imperatives.

An interrogation of boundaries commences in the first act, which offers a series of pointed delineations of the social and personal restrictions placed on racial and gendered interaction which the protagonist, Troy Maxson, seeks to negotiate. *Fences* begins with Troy and Jim Bono entering the former's partially fenced yard on "Friday night, payday, and the one night of the week the two men engage in a ritual of talk and drink" (1). This ritualistic space is filled immediately with discussion of contrasting means of responding to racially motivated socio-economic inequality. In the first instance, Troy describes one such type of negotiation whose rejection serves as a means by which to introduce both Troy's subversive act and Wilson's own afrocentric thematics.

> TROY: I ain't lying. The nigger had a watermelon this big. Talking about
> . . . "What watermelon, Mr. Rand?" I liked to fell out! "What water-
> melon, Mr. Rand?" . . . And it sitting there big as life.
> BONO: What did Mr. Rand say?
> TROY: Ain't said nothing. Figure if the nigger too dumb to know he carry-
> ing a watermelon, he wasn't gonna get much sense out of him. Trying to
> hide that great big old watermelon under his coat. Afraid to let the white
> man see him carry it home. (1–2)

In its reference to watermelons, apparent black simpletons, and white male authority figures involved in a comic interchange about petty larceny, Troy's language recalls—and rejects vehemently as a mode of interracial interchange—a tradition of minstrelsy that, according to Houston Baker, is characterized by "nonsense, misappropriation, or mis-hearing."[17] At one time a popular theatrical behavior which operated as a dramatic formalizing of hegemonically enforced manners of black behavior, minstrelsy was a "device," according to Baker, "designed to remind white consciousness that black men and women are mis-speakers bereft of humanity—carefree devils strumming and humming all day—unless, in a gaslight misidentification, they are violent devils fit for lynching, a final exorcism that will leave whites alone" (21).

Wilson sets the stage, as it were, for a different style of black dramatic representation by offering, in the opening lines, discursive structures which both recall and forcefully repudiate this comically-influenced modality whose social practice had previously constituted a means by which to contain both white and black violent impulses. Thus the initial scene attempts to bracket or set boundaries around traditional notions of black theatrical representation, thereby insisting that what follows will not conform to the nonsense syllables and actions historically characteristic of black participation in the theater of America. After relegating this manner of negotiating difference to the realm of the antiquated—Bono says pointedly, "I'm like you . . . I ain't got no time for them kind of people" (2)—the men then begin to discuss Troy's enactment of other, newer strategies of black behavior whose purpose is to effect social change.

> TROY: I ain't worried about them firing me. They gonna fire me cause I asked a question? That's all I did. I went to Mr. Rand and asked him, "Why?" Why you got the white mens driving and the colored lifting?" Told him, "What's the matter, don't I count? You think only white fellows got sense enough to drive a truck. That ain't no paper job! Hell, anybody can drive a truck. How come you got all whites driving and the colored lifting? He told me "take it to the union." Well, hell, that's what I done! Now they wanna come up with this pack of lies. (2–3)

If minstrel performances such as those of the watermelon-stealing "nigger" (and scores of other Afro-Americans in their interactions with representatives of a white hegemonic structure) might be effectively characterized in terms of the serious play with pejorative racist stereotypes and other extent cultural forms that Baker calls "the mastery of form," then Troy's insurgent act, which insists on white confirmation of its responsibilities to ensuring constitutionally guaranteed Afro-American rights, might well be viewed as an instance of a black "deformation of mastery." For Baker, "deformation is a go(uer)rilla action in the face of acknowledged adversaries" (50). While watermelon theft seeks as its end the temporary satisfaction of black desire, deformation—a formal challenge to the racially hierarchical status quo—attempts to delegitimize permanently the hegemonic structures which have sought historically to contain and control that desire.

Troy and Bono move directly from the subject of negotiating interracial relations to an investigation of heterosexual politics and dynamics. Specifically, they begin discussing "that Alberta gal" and the relative success of the efforts of males in their community—themselves included—in attracting her attention. Again, they speak in terms of respecting (or rejecting) boundaries:

> BONO: . . . I see where you be eyeing her.
> TROY: I eye all the women. I don't miss nothing. Don't never let nobody tell you Troy Maxson don't eye the women.
> BONO: You been doing more than eyeing her. You done bought her a drink or two.
> TROY: Hell yeah, I bought her a drink! What that mean? I bought you one, too. What that mean cause I buy her a drink? I'm just being polite. (3)

What concerns Bono is that his friend, whom he admires, as Wilson's stage directions indicate, for his "honesty, capacity for hard work, and his strength" (1), is not cognizant of the potentially disruptive nature of his interest in Alberta to others' and Troy's own sense of his character and integrity. Indeed, as Bono later suggests, the threat of disruption, of dissolution of a lifestyle that she has come to see as normative, motivates Rose's desire to have a fence built around the Maxson home. As he tells Troy: "Some people build fences to keep people out . . . and other people build fences to keep people in. Rose wants to hold on to you all. She loves you" (61).

Specifically, Bono is worried that Troy's attention to Alberta, which he is aware includes not only the polite purchase of "a drink or two," but also frequent visits to her apartment, suggests that his best friend may overstep the boundaries of acceptable marital behavior, that his actions may compromise his sense of self and his relationship with Rose, whom both men describe as "a good woman" (62). Troy's extramarital desires trouble Bono not merely because of his concern for Troy's well-being, but because, as he tells him later, Troy is his role model:

> When you picked Rose, I was happy for you. That was the first time I knew you had any sense. I said . . . My man Troy knows what he's doing . . . I'm gonna follow this nigger . . . he might take me somewhere. I been following you too. I done learned a whole heap of things about life watching you. I done learned how to tell where the shit lies. How to tell it from the alfalfa. You done learned me a lot of things. You showed me how to not make the same mistakes . . . to take life as it comes along and keep putting one foot in front of the other. (62)

When Troy commences a more public relationship with Alberta, the affair leads to the dissolution of the rituals of friendship with Bono in part because the ground upon which Bono's admiration is based—Troy's clearsightedness, his ability to understand and not be tempted to overstep the boundaries with which his life presents him—has been undercut.

One of *Fences'* most resonant examinations of boundaries appears in Troy's discussion with Lyons about the material and psychological benefits of gainful employment.

> TROY: I done learned my mistake and learned to do what's right by it. You still trying to get something for nothing. Life don't owe you nothing. You owe it to yourself. . . .
> LYONS: You got your way of dealing with the world . . . I got mine. The only thing that matters to me is the music.
> TROY: Yeah, I can see that! It don't matter how you gonna eat . . . where your next dollar is coming from. You telling the truth there.

Lyons: I know I got to eat. But I got to live too. I need something that gonna help me to get out of bed in the morning. Make me feel like I belong in the world. I don't bother nobody. I just stay with my music cause that's the only way I can find to live in the world. Otherwise there's no telling what I might do. (18)

Here we are presented with a contrast between two poles of available male behavior: Troy's hypermasculine sense of self-sacrifice and economic responsibility, and Lyons's self-indulgent search for personal fulfillment. What is particularly striking about this scene is its principals' energetic articulation of positions which, at this moment in the history of their weekly ritual of filial borrowing of money and paternal castigation, they preach much more energetically than they practice. For Lyons is only minimally dedicated to his art—the stage directions which precede his appearance describe him as "more caught up in the rituals and 'idea' of being a musician than in the actual practice of the music" (13)—and Troy has slipped from the lofty position from which he has somewhat self-righteously critiqued others. (Moreover, as we will see, Lyons's discourse of self-fulfillment and irresponsibility is later echoed in his father's description to Rose of the motivations for his infidelity.)

While in Troy's talks with Lyons and, later, Cory, about financial responsibility, he demonstrates some of the more admirable aspects of his character, in his discussion with his younger son about paternal displays of affection he most poignantly displays both his most positive and most negative dimensions. After Troy asserts that his son's continued participation with football depends on a virtually impossible commitment to both housework and store employment, Cory asks whether his father's generally harsh treatment of him is motivated by a lack of paternal affection. Troy responds:

Liked you? Who the hell say I got to like you? What law is there say I got to like you? Wanna stand up in my face and ask a dam fool-ass question like that. Talking about liking somebody. . . . I go out of here every morning . . . bust my butt . . . putting up with them crackers everyday . . . cause I like you? You about the biggest fool I ever saw. . . . It's my job. It's my responsibility! You understand that? A man got to take care of his family. You live in my house . . . sleep your behind on my bedclothes . . . fill you belly up with my food . . . cause you my son. You my flesh and blood. Not 'cause I like you! Cause it's my duty to take care of you. I owe a responsibility to you! . . . Mr. Rand don't give me my money come payday cause he likes me. He gives me cause he owe me. . . . Don't you try and go through life worrying about if somebody like you or not. You best be making sure they doing right by you. You understand what I'm saying, boy? (37–38)

To Troy, Cory's question demonstrates that he is unaware of the boundaries of interpersonal responsibility, of the central role an economics of duty plays in profitable human interactions. While this perspective may encourage appropriate responses to a society characterized by deceit and institutionalized inequality, clearly it fails to help foster an appreciation of the potential tenderness of intimate human relations. Put another way, an economics of duty, learned by Troy from a father most notable for his sense of responsibility to his children and an accompanying ill-temperedness, is equipped to deal most effectively with adversity. "Doing right," in such relations, is not merely providing clean sheets and nourishing foods, but also demonstrating an intense concern about the psychic welfare of those for whom one has assumed responsibility. Troy's discussion of familial duty, then, reflects inherent flaws in his worldview caused, it would appear, by his failure to attend to crucial aspects of intimacy.

I am suggesting, then, that when we meet him Troy's code of living is defective because it leaves no space for a pursuit of self-fulfillment. While this self-protective mechanism of maintaining boundaries serves effectively to check the impulse toward familial abandonment that Troy terms the "walking blues" (51), a condition manifested in the form of "a fellow moving around from place to place . . . woman to woman . . . searching out the New Land" (50), it is limited as a means of responding to the full range of human emotional possibilities.

Apparently, as evidenced in his discussions about his affair with both Bono and Rose, he recognizes that the absence of joy in his own life renders him unable to reconcile his words and actions to the philosophical views by which he had been governed. When Troy states, for example, "I can't shake her loose," Bono insists that he remain true to his oft-stated perspectives on individual culpability and responsibility:

> BONO: You's in control . . . that's what you tell me all the time. You responsible for what you do.
> TROY: I ain't ducking the responsibility of it. As long as it sets right in my heart . . . then I'm okay. Cause that's all I listen to. It'll tell me right from wrong every time. And I ain't talking about doing Rose no bad turn. I love Rose. She done carried me a long ways and I love and respect her for that. (63)

His intentions not to do Rose a "bad turn" and his faith in his heart notwithstanding, his manner of constructing his motives for infidelity makes it clear that the pursuit of self-fulfillment has served effectively to block his limited capacity to attend to his wife's feelings. Troy tells Rose:

It's just . . . She gives me a different idea . . . a different understanding about myself. I can step out of this house and get away from the pressures and problems . . . be a different man. I ain't got to wonder how I'm gonna pay the bills or get the roof fixed. I can just be a part of myself that I ain't never been . . . I can sit up in her house and laugh . . . I can laugh out loud . . . and it feels good. It reaches all the way down to the bottom of my shoes.
(*Pause*)
Rose, I can't give that up. (68–69)

After an interchange most notable for its evidence of the participants' communicative gaps or discursive boundaries (he employs baseball metaphors, a mode of discourse which Rose considers inappropriate, telling him, "We're not talking about baseball! We talking about you going to lay in bed with another woman . . . and then bring it home to me"), Troy seeks to win his wife's sympathy by turning his attention to the difficulty he has encountered in being confronted with evidence of his inadequacy.

TROY: Rose, you're not listening to me. I'm trying the best I can to explain it to you. It's not easy for me to admit that I been standing in the same place for eighteen years.
ROSE: I been standing with you! I been right here with you, Troy. I got a life too. I gave eighteen years of my life to stand in the same spot with you. Don't you think I ever wanted other things? What about my life? What about me? Don't you think it ever crossed my mind to want to know other men. That I wanted to lay up somewhere and forget about my responsibilities? That I wanted someone to make me laugh so I could feel good? You not the only one who's got wants and needs. But I held on to you, Troy. I took all my feelings, my wants and needs, my dreams . . . and I buried them inside you. I planted a seed and watched and prayed over it. I planted myself inside you and waited to bloom. And it didn't take me no eighteen years to find out the soil was hard and rocky and it wasn't never gonna bloom. (70–71)

Rose shifts the discursive ground from a masculinist metaphorics of individually determined psychic and socioeconomic advancement to a nature-centered figuration of the growth of the un(der)developed. In figuring the interior spaces of the self-protective male as potential uterine site of her own development, Rose defies—and, in fact, denies—the limitations of both the biological and Troy's economics of duty. Just as Troy believes that imparting to Cory his philosophy of financial self-support will allow him to discharge his parental responsibilities adequately so, too, does he feel that by sleeping every night with Rose and turning over his weekly pay to her, he is fulfilling his marital duties.

But for Rose, the costs of accommodating herself to this worldview by containing and thereby ignoring her own desires are extremely high, as she tells Cory upon his return home for his father's funeral:

> I married your daddy and settled down to cooking his supper and keeping clean sheets on the bed. When your daddy walked through the house he was so big he filled it up. That was my first mistake. Not to make him leave some room for me. For my part in the matter. But at that time I wanted that. I wanted a house that I could sing in. And that's what your daddy gave me. I didn't know to keep up his strength I had to give up little pieces of mine. I did that. . . . It was my choice. It was my life and I didn't have to live it like that. But that's what life offered me in the way of being a woman and I took it. I grabbed hold of it with both hands. (98)

Rose describes here the consequences of her emphasis on material space, chief among them her failure to pursue other desires so that she could direct her attention to satisfying the wishes of her forceful husband. Given the gender politics of the period and the direct correlation between Rose's self-sacrifice and Troy's fairly stable and positive self-image—as she says, "to keep up his strength I had to give up little pieces of mine"—her immolation apparently was necessary in order to stave off the onset of masculinist "walking blues." To put the matter somewhat differently, the cost of maintaining material space for even a restricted articulation of female song is the loss of verbal strength and the possibility of self-actualization within a domicile dominated by Troy's pragmatic economics of duty. The fences that Troy and Rose place around their marriage, their feelings, and their unarticulated desires for a more fulfilling existence are effective while these characters exclude intense self-investigation from their rituals of living. The price both pay for self-protection—for the protective barriers of "fences"—includes stagnation and their refusal to acknowledge their intense dissatisfaction.

But how do we accommodate Wilson's figurations of the motivations for and consequences of the construction of self-protective fences—not the least of which is psychic inertia—with his protectionist insistence on finding a black director for the film version of his play, an insistence that seems to reflect a cynicism about the trajectory of racial progress over the last half century on the level of the protagonist, Troy? The play itself is infused with a poetics of progress and boundary breaking. For example, all of Troy's articulations of his sense of the fixity of race relations—his insistence that his inability to become a major league baseball player after his incarceration and a young Roberto Clemente's initial failure to become an everyday player for the Pittsburgh Pirates are solely a function of racism; his view of the inevitable fruitlessness of his son's attending college on an athletic scholarship—are effectively challenged either within the context of the play or by our historical knowledge of changes that have taken place in American race relations since the 1950s. Moreover, the epigraph Wilson composed for the play insists on the possibility of improving upon, or transcending, the negative aspects of a cultural legacy:

> When the sins of our fathers visit us
> We do not have to play host.
> We can banish them with forgiveness
> As God, in His Largeness and Laws.

Indeed, it is the importance of banishing the sins of our fathers with forgiveness, while at the same time recognizing the significance of spiritually beneficial paternal gifts, that motivates Rose's concluding words to Cory, whose bitterness is so intense that he threatens not to attend Troy's funeral: "I took on to Raynell [Troy's and Alberta's daughter] like she was all them babies I had wanted and never had. . . . Like I'd been blessed to relive a part of my life. And if the Lord see fit to keep up my strength . . . I'm gonna do her just like your daddy did you . . . I'm gonna give her the best of what's in me" (98). Rose encourages Cory to move beyond the self-protective bitterness that he has employed to shield himself from his painful memory of his father's treatment of him and to strive to comprehend the nature of the psychic inheritance bequeathed him by Troy. Noting her own ability to come to terms with her husband's transgressive behavior, her capacity to "take the crookeds with the straights," Rose urges Cory not to seek to erase the aspects of his character and imaginative repertoire which reflect his father, but instead to combine these characteristics with other conceptually persuasive modes of being in order to develop his own ethics of living. Rather than attempt to deny Troy's influence in forming him, Rose challenges him to honor and improve upon that which was good about her husband.

In addition to its call for psychic generational advancement, Wilson's play reflects an awareness that socioeconomic progress has been a dimension of Afro-American life over the last three decades. When, for example, Troy complains to Mr. Rand and subsequently to the union about a hierarchization of labor in the garbage collection company for which he works, he is promoted to the status of driver, thereby achieving a measure of racial justice of the sort he believes he was denied during a prestigious baseball career when major-league strictures confined him to the Negro Leagues. But Wilson is also cognizant of the cost of those changes, including the onset of socioeconomic stratification of members of the

Afro-American community, as is evidenced by the fact that Troy considers retiring soon after he is promoted because occupying the heretofore exclusively white space as driver is akin to "working by yourself" (83). More important, Wilson seems to recognize that comprehensive transformations in American race relations are necessary before the fact of greater access for a select few to the promises explicit in the recorded ideals of the nation's founding fathers—its constitutional "gifts," as it were—will ameliorate the effects of the sins of these fathers and their offspring, committed on the bodies and minds of black countrymen and women. Whatever we make of Troy's affair with Alberta, clearly his psychic inertia before he starts to date her is in large part a function of a personal history in which he had to confront as a skilled sports laborer the racist boundaries to constitutionally guaranteed opportunity.

Until more comprehensive changes are made in the basic structure of American society—changes that will impact the grammar of motives upon which significant aspects of our shared culture is constructed—seemingly major incidents such as Troy's improved employment status, August Wilson's own success as a dramatist, and Hollywood's recent interest in sophisticated representations of Afro-American life such as *Fences* will constitute merely local, individual victories. Wilson seems cognizant of one of American hegemony's strategies of operation vis-à-vis the oppressed wherein it presents impressive gifts to individual members of disenfranchised groups as a substitute for a wider redistribution of its socioeconomic and cultural assets. Apparently he is less concerned with personal profit from the returns for a film version of his play than in employing the cultural capital he had earned in order to further efforts to ensure the continued alteration of racist American discourse that always already questions Afro-American qualifications.

Despite his insistence at some points in "'I Want a Black Director'" to the contrary, whether or not whites can understand and disseminate the culturally specific aspects of *Fences* is not the central issue in Wilson's formulation of his position. Of preeminent importance to the playwright, I believe, is whether, given the persistence of caucacentric discourse and actions in our nation, Afro-Americans can afford to allow patterns of expressive cultural distribution to continue wherein blacks remain pawns to the whims and racialist will of white entrepreneurial forces interested primarily in economic bottom lines rather than in working to destroy the existing barriers to social, economic, and cultural power for a large portion of the black population. If Wilson's play and his polemic do indeed complement each other in their examination of the dangers of boundaries, that complementarity is reflected in their common skepticism about the benefits of minimal alteration in the nation's practice of racial politics. The sins of the nation's white founding fathers and its sons and daughters—

including the fences they constructed by way of its governing laws, bylaws, and historical practices whose intent seems to be to encourage Afro-American inequality virtually in perpetuity—can be banished only through herculean energy and ideologically informed activity because, however pronounced our desire to forgive and move on, they visit us continually.

Crossing racial lines usually results in punishment.

Isaac Julien, "Black Is, Black Ain't:
Notes on De-Essentializing Black Identities"

I began to study up on skin diseases and found out that the girl was evidently suffering from a nervous disease known as vitiligo. It is a very rare disease. . . . It absolutely removes skin pigment and sometimes it turns a Negro completely white but only after a period of thirty or forty years. It occurred to me that if one could discover some means of artificially inducing and stimulating this nervous disease at will, one might possibly solve the American race problem. My sociology teacher had once said that there were but three ways for the Negro to solve his problem in America . . . "To either get out, get white or get along." Since he wouldn't and couldn't get out and was getting along only differently, it seemed to me that the only thing for him was to get white.

George Schuyler's character, Dr. Junius Crookman, explaining his
inspiration for creating his deracinating machine in *Black No More*

There is a conflict between public and private life, and it's a conflict that I think ought to remain a conflict. Not a problem, just a conflict. Because they are two modes of life that exist to exclude and annihilate each other. It's a conflict that should be maintained now more than ever because the social machinery of this country at this time doesn't permit harmony in a life that has both aspects. . . . There must have been a time when an artist could be genuinely representative of the tribe and in it; when an artist could have a tribal or racial sensibility and an individual expression of it. There were spaces and places in which a single person could enter and behave as an individual within the context of the community.

Toni Morrison, "Rootedness: The Ancestor As Foundation"

Gaze upon your self. Dis-ease grips you as well. We are all mutually bound, sick, trapped. Except you, many of you, persist in the illusion of safe, sage detachment.

Do you honestly think you can so closely, critically examine me without studying or revealing yourself? Or do you really think your progressive, collective "we" is all that's necessary in your performance of reflexivity?

Marlon Riggs, "Unleash the Queen"

7

"A Slave to the Rhythm": Essential(ist) Transmutations; or, The Curious Case of Michael Jackson

In each of the preceding chapters, I have attempted to offer plausible solutions to interpretive problems posed by striking literary, scholarly, and mass cultural moments wherein notions of the complexity and instability of race and gender are placed in conflict with strategic pronouncements that such categories are fundamentally resistant to internal tension and historical change. In this final chapter, which examines the singer Michael Jackson's surgical and cosmetic assaults on American constructions of race and gender, I am seeking not so much the truth of his motivations—no single reading could hope to exhaust the analytical possibilities represented in and by him—as an interpretive stance vis-à-vis his assaults that allows me to intervene productively (if not conclusively) in what Diana Fuss calls the "restrictive, even obfuscating . . . essentialist/constructionist debate."[1] According to Fuss, essentialism is "a belief in the real, true essence of things, the invariable and fixed properties which define the 'whatness' of a given entity" (xi), and constructionism is "the position that differences are constructed, not innate" (xii). Like Fuss, I believe that "the binary articulation of essentialism and difference", or constructionism, like all such binaries, obscures as it reveals, disables as it enables.

Throughout this study, I have been generally much more sympathetic to constructionist perspectives, largely because of my resistance to the types of unitary, programmatic notions of individual subjectivity and group identity that characterize the essentialist project. However, as I hope to show, scrutiny of Jackson's racial and gendered negotiations, which appear to mark him as constructionism's perfect subject, must confront the fact that, at crucial points, Jackson's public appearances and discursive performances manifest conceptual slippage between notions of the natural and the socially constructed, between biological determinism and cultural conditioning. His recourse to notions of an essential(ist) black subjectivity evinces not his inconsistencies so much as the ultimately insoluble nature of this debate as it is presently framed.

Critics concerned with the motivations for and potential social consequences of Jackson's artistic, surgical, and cosmetic work are forced to position themselves vis-à-vis this debate. Taken together, readings of the singer's physical mutations reinforce my lingering doubts as to whether, despite our development of a pointedly unsentimental critical arsenal, it is possible or, for that matter, wise for avowed anti-essentialists concerned with questions of gender and race to embrace constructionist positions wholeheartedly. As I will demonstrate, the dichotomy posited between anti-essentialist views of Jackson's reconstructions as efforts to negotiate inhibiting strictures concerning racial and gendered performance, and essentialist condemnations of him as a racially self-hating, sexually confused, and emotionally repressed manchild ignores what we might regard as his own apparently strategic use of formulations associated with both perspectives in his negotiations of race and gender, of private and public, of the past and the present.

Sympathetic investigators of Jackson include Marjorie Garber, who views Jackson as the "portrait of a man—and an entertainer—who controls how he is read and seen," and Susan Willis, who calls him "the quintessential mass cultural commodity" who provides "so many apparent resolutions of social contradiction" posed by American social constructions of race, gender, and age.[2] According to these readings, Jackson uses the surface of his own body as a text on which he periodically re-articulates his image, situating himself self-consciously at some of the most crucial social divides that confront us as a nation. Another category of responses, some authored by black males, resists attributing to Jackson the status of exemplary postmodernist actor. For example, cultural critic Greg Tate, reviewing Jackson's *Bad* album and lightened skin, indicates his awareness of the constructionist line, asserting, somewhat disingenuously, "there are other ways to read Michael Jackson's blanched skin and disfigured African features than as signs of black self-hatred become self-mutilation." Tate goes on to argue that the singer "has crossed so way far over the line that there ain't no coming back—assuming through surgical transmutation of his face a singular infamy in the annals of tomming."[3] Even more obviously caught in a constructionist conundrum is Kobena Mercer, whose skillful reading of "post-liberated black hair-styling" as counterhegemonic "artform articulating a variety of aesthetic 'solutions' to a range of 'problems' created by ideologies of race and racism," begins with a brief discussion of Jackson.[4] Mercer says of others' responses to the singer's mutations:

Reactions to the striking changes in Jackson's image have sparked off a range of everyday critiques on the cultural politics of "race" and "aesthetics." The apparent transformation of his racial features through the glamorous violence of surgery has been read by some as the bizarre expression of a desire to achieve fame by "becoming white"—a deracializing sell-out, the morbid symptom of a psychologically mutilated black consciousness. Hence, on this occasion [when Jackson's hair caught fire when he was filming a television commercial], Michael's misfortune could be read as "punishment" for the profane artificiality of his image: after all, it was the chemicals that caused his hair to catch fire. (247)

Clearly, Mercer does not himself endorse such "everyday critiques" of Jackson's participation in unnatural acts, which others believe reflect a "subjective enslavement to Eurocentric definitions of beauty" (247).[5] Indeed, he insists that certain types of black self-transformation, specifically the alteration of hair texture, constitute *strategic violations of nature*. For Mercer, "hair functions as a key 'ethnic signifier' because, compared with bodily shape or facial features, it can be changed more easily by cultural practices such as straightening. Caught on the cusp between self and society, nature and culture, the malleability of hair makes it a sensitive area of expression" (250). It is the relative ease with which its texture is manipulated, rather than some essential, ideologically neutral qualities hair possesses, which makes it, in Mercer's estimation, a central site of cultural negotiation. Consequently, Mercer is able to argue that the conk, a hair-straightening style popular among Afro-American men during the 1940s and 1950s, represents, in its self-conscious unnaturalness, a "covert" logic of cultural struggle operating "in and against" hegemonic cultural codes:

> The emphasis on artifice and ambiguity rather than an inversion of equivalence strikes me as a particularly modern way in which cultural utterances may take on the force of "political" statements. Syncretic practices of black stylization, such as the conk, zoot suit or jive-talk, recognize themselves self-consciously as products of a New World culture; that is, they incorporate an awareness of the contradictory conditions of their inter-culturation. (260)

One constitutive aspect of the moment we inhabit is the availability to the masses of both discourses and technologies of self-transformation, which serves to increase desire for and access to avenues of radical change and, therefore, the potential uses of other bodily sites as "'political' statements."[6] Indeed, given Mercer's insistence that "nobody's hair is ever just natural but is always shaped or reshaped by social convention and symbolic intervention," that even the so-called natural black hairstyle, the Afro, is itself "'cultivated' . . . in . . . that it merely provides a raw material for practices, procedures and ritual techniques of cultural writing and social inscription" (252), we might posit that other body parts— including black skin itself—at least theoretically can be employed as sites of a "cultivated" intervention. Specific acts of self-transformation are not by defini- tion, in Mercer's reading, crimes against an ideological blackness. Rather, such "unnatural acts," such inscriptions upon the black body, can be seen as ideologi- cally transgressive because they serve as assaults against caucacentric (and, I would add, afrocentric) assertions of absolute racial difference. Mercer's commentary on Jackson's mutations begs the question, Can *individual* transformations constitute "political statements" or racially inflected acts of "symbolic intervention"?

In an age when academic multitudes have embraced anti-essentialist dis- course, when even the articulation of the phrase "Black is Beautiful" registers for many as an occasion to intervene upon both caucacentric views of the negative connotations of dark skin and afrocentrisms's positivistic investment, might the primary location of racist hysteria and hatred—black skin, or "flesh," to use Hor- tense Spillers's term—be a possible site of transformative "intervention"? If the relative susceptibility of hair to transformative "cultivation" facilitates its utiliza- tion as ideological statement, can the possible malleability of "black" skin in our advanced technoculture challenge hegemonic discourses and practices of racism?

In his televised interview with Oprah Winfrey, Jackson intimated that the suffers from the dermatological condition vitiligo, a disorder characterized "by acquired progressive loss of pigment, resulting from a still unsettled structural and func- tional metabolic defect . . . of the skin" that blocks the skin's ability to produce pigment.[7] As medical researchers note, vitiligo "often leads [its sufferers] to [expe- rience] social embarrassment and psychologic turmoil."[8] Even before this revela- tion, what Afro-British filmmaker Isaac Julien terms, in an essay seeking to point us toward a "de-essentializing [of] Black identities," "the scopic imperatives that mark . . . the contours of Michael Jackson' ghostlike black face" might have been said to indicate, rather than racial co-optation, an individual effort to contain the attendant "psychological turmoil" by critiquing others' delimiting notions of black racial essence.[9] While elements of dominant afrocentric ideology influence, for example, Tate's reading of the changes in Jackson's face, we might do well to recognize that even at the point where, in Tate's view, Jackson's individual artistic efforts were most intensely appreciated by Afro-Americans during the capitalist miracle that accompanied the release of *Thriller,* he had already begun to undergo cosmetic work whose ultimate effect was to erase his own natural blackmaleness.

The ghosts evident in Jackson's surgically transformed face are not simply ancestral traces[10] but also the much-photographed, negroid-featured lead singer of the fabled Jackson Five to which the adult singer is always visually, if not stylistically, compared.[11] However Jackson looks now, however far his appearance changes from what might have been, in the absence of skin disease and cosmetic intervention, his natural visage and "flesh," he remains, because of the widely distributed pictorial history of his dark past, indelibly black. So when he proclaimed to Winfrey—herself the victim of racial ridicule at one point because of her choice to wear green contact lenses—"I'm a black American. . . . I'm proud to be a black American. I'm proud of my race," he acknowledged both the transmutability of the flesh and the inescapability of categorical blackness.[12]

Public cognition of Jackson's dark past, the ocular proof of African ancestry manifested in the photographs and memories of a precocious, brown-skinned musical dynamo, is a matter over which he has no control. Despite his claims to racial pride, however, despite the sympathy engendered by his assertion that he suffers from what is often a psychically crippling disease, Jackson's "scopic" assumption of nonblackness must be seen as neither inevitable nor as ideologically innocent. In fact, we might say that his disease has liberated him from being bound to a black physicality and has provided him with the opportunity to choose whether to cover (or, as it were, uncover) whiteness or blackness. The tragic elements of his disorder notwithstanding, Jackson seems to have achieved a constructionist's dream wherein specific elements of his human surface—in this case, racial markings—have become matters of cosmetic choice rather than virtually unalterable states of being. As a condemnatory *Newsweek* article astutely observes in response to the singer's apparent liberation from fixed racial positions, "Most vitiligo sufferers darken their light patches with makeup to even the tone. Jackson's makeup solution takes the other tack: less ebony, more ivory."[13]

Jackson's "makeup solution" to cover the darkness remaining on his diseased flesh would appear to belie his vehement assertion of racial price, were it not for the fact that in America "black" covers a huge spectrum of shades and pigmentation. In *Who is Black?* F. James Davis argues that "one need not look black in order to be black, following the one-drop rule."[14] The one-drop rule, which had its genesis in American slavery, was a strategy for increasing the white southern aristocracy's store of inexpensive labor in the face of white men's miscegenational activities, which Europeanized much of the slave class's gene pool. According to Davis, that rule has more recently been appropriated by Afro-Americans in an effort to multiply their membership: "The overwhelming reality is that most blacks in the United States have taken the one-drop rule for granted for a very long time, feel that they have an important stake in maintaining it, socialize their children to accept it, and rally to its defense when it is challenged" (139). If blackness is not necessarily determined by how one looks (Davis demonstrates that frequently "appearance and actual genetic makeup were irrelevant, strange as that may sound to the rest of the world" [126]) but by what may be a visually untraceable one drop of blood or genetic material, then it is a category whose referents are not always easily discernible. In other words, by its very (American) definition, blackness can be masked effectively behind an apparently white physicality.

In a passage quoted earlier, Tate grants that "there are other ways to read Michael Jackson's blanched skin and disfigured African features than as signs of black self-hatred become self-mutilation" (96). While one such interpretive angle might be that the singer's cosmetic changes represent his effort to move himself, at least in appearance, from an obviously black to a white positionality, both the natural Jackson and his unnatural current self fall within the range of physical shadings associated in America with blackness. If, physically, Jackson has become, as it were, an ex-colored man, he is, unlike James Weldon Johnson's nameless protagonist, a quintessentially public figure whose past is no "great secret" and who, rather than having sold his "birthright for a mess of pottage," continues to use musical and dance talents and tropes whose source is, indisputably, black culture.[15]

And though I have referred to Johnson's paradigmatic text of racial passing, *The Autobiography of an Ex-Colored Man,* in examining Jackson's position, I want to emphasize here my sense of the essential differences between passing and what I term *transraciality.* A mode of negotiating American racial boundaries which, like transraciality, can be said potentially to highlight race's constructedness, passing requires that its participants be born with physical characteristics associated with the racial other. By contrast, transraciality as a mode of masquerade necessitates the radical revision of one's natural markings and the adoption of aspects of the human surface (especially skin, hair, and facial features) generally associated with the racial other. Both states offer opportunities for the transgressive subject to experience positive and negative aspects of an altered racial designation and social position. But while passing serves as a form through which we can interrogate some of the implications of America's one-drop rule of racial designation despite many blacks' acceptance of its fictive truths, transraciality, as social practice and artistic concern, potentially offers an even more effective means of uncovering the constructedness of the rules of racial being. For while the ability to pass demonstrates that one's ancestors had already moved sexually—voluntarily or not—across racial lines, transraciality represents an individually determined, surgically-and/or cosmetically-assisted traversal of boundaries that putatively separate radically distinct social groups.

Texts like *The Autobiography of an Ex-Colored Man* and Nella Larsen's aptly titled *Passing* explore the dilemmas faced by racial hybrids whose ancestry is scopically European rather than African and who, despite the one-drop rule's insistence upon their categorical blackness, are capable of moving across the lines created to reinforce American rules of racial order. These texts, which narrativize variations on the formula "tragic mulatto," effectively employ notions of the differences between being and seeing, between (racial) essence and appearance, positing, each in its own gender-specific manner, that passing for white ultimately is unsatisfying because of the psychic impossibility of ignoring black biological imperatives and cultural connections. On the other hand, texts of transraciality, such as memoirs, novels, and films by John Howard Griffin, Grace Halsell, George Schuyler, Eddie Murphy, and Melvin van Peebles, generally delineate a relative neophyte's education in the effects of legislative and more informal (but no less rigidly enforced) dicta concerning the social meanings of racial difference to which that figure has gained access specifically as a result of his or her transformation.[16] The plots of such narratives can conclude with an endorsement of black militancy, as in van Peebles's and Murphy's work; or in the articulation of better-informed pleas for racial understanding that characterize Griffin's and Halsell's texts; or in the resolution of the interracial romance plot as in *Soul Man;* or, for that matter, in a superlative intermingling of many such elements in *Black No More.* But whatever form their narrative resolutions take, texts of transraciality generally posit that the specific dimensions of the racial other's cultural life are otherwise unknowable and inaccessible. Unlike narratives of passing, which are concerned fundamentally with exposing the ease with which racial barriers can be transgressed, texts of transraciality generally insist on the impenetrability, the mysteriousness, of the racial other's cultural rituals and social practices.

If the distinction I've made between forms of racial transgression seems plausible, then we must recognize that fleshly reembodiment—the assumption of traits of difference of the racial other—cuts directly to the heart of essentialist formulations of racial difference. If, potentially, transraciality is an interpretively rich intervention upon rigid rules of racial order, perhaps it is time to begin to deal with the fact that radical transformation has become, for those with the capital to access new technologies, an irrefutable "sign of the times," to cite lyrics by Jackson's perhaps most talented musical contemporary.[17] If this is so, then threats to essentialist notions of racial difference may arise more frequently not only as a result of the cultural crisscrossings I discuss in my Introduction, but specifically in the form of transracial acts wherein dissatisfied racial subjects strive to transcend their boundedness to a state of racial being whose meanings are in a myriad of ways overdetermined. In seeing transraciality as not merely a near-suicidal white liberal response or a science-fiction fantasy but as a distinct cultural and scopic possibility in our time, we might be able both the discover some of the meanings signified by the transracial as cultural metaphor and to move toward more illuminating assessments of the challenges represented by Jackson's reconfigurations.

Generally, texts of transraciality suggest that the ultimate outcome of the assumption of the other's traits of physical difference is neither abandonment of origin nor wholehearted adoption of either group's ideology, but is the creation of another category, another state of racial being. In *Vested Interests,* an investigation of sexual and gendered boundary crossings, Marjorie Garber refers to the state created by transvestite activity as "the 'third,'" which represents, in her view, "a mode of articulation, a way of describing a space of possibility" (15). For Garber, the binary male/female provides little room for creative, counterhegemonic self-expression, and the transvestite (one who assumes the cloaked surface of the sexual other), occupying a pointedly unspecified "third" term that challenges either/or thinking about gendered performance, is strategically situated to undermine aspects of the cultural hegemony of that restriction.

Of course, racial designations number much more than two, though American discourse only rarely acknowledges categories beyond black and white in its formulations of race's meanings. Like the transvestite, the transracial subject provides what Garber speaks of as the grounds of a profound "category crisis." She explains what she means by the term:

> By "category crisis," I mean a failure of definitional distinction, a borderline that becomes permeable, that permits border crossings from one (apparently distinct) category to another: black/white, Jew/Christian, noble/bourgeois, master/servant, master/slave. The binarism male/female, one apparent ground of distinction (in contemporary eyes, at least) between "this" and "that," "him" and "me," is itself put in question or under erasure in transvestism, and a transvestite figure, or a transvestite mode, will always function as a sign of overdeterminism—a mechanism of displacement from one blurred boundary to another. (16)

As evidence of categorical permeability, transraciality represents a potentially astute response to perspectives on race that continue to reflect the still-powerful one-drop rule's economic or class origins rather than scientific or even "scopic" imperatives. In an American context, to be categorically betwixt and between, to choose to defy rigid, essentialist rules of racial being, is to serve, in Garber's terms, as a "mechanism of displacement," disrupting what both the one-drop rule and the very possibility of impersonating racial others demonstrate to be boundary-policing social constructs. Texts of transraciality seek to clarify the arbitrariness of racist notions of essential difference, the ideological contamination of racial categories themselves.

The dilemma posed by Michael Jackson's case is, perhaps, even more poignant than those found in such texts. Earlier I suggested that whatever physical changes he makes, those changes can never be considered essentially transforma-tive because of the inescapability of Jackson's black roots. There are a number of explanations available for his numerous transmutations: a sign of black-self hatred; an attempt to erase evidence of his abusive father's features from his face; a signal of his addiction to plastic surgery; and evidence of his efforts to approximate the appearance of (choose one) Diana Ross, Brooke Shields, Elizabeth Taylor, or Sophia Loren. Whichever of these explanations we choose individually to em-brace, it is clear that Jackson, as Susan Willis argues, employs transmutation as a mode of bold self-expression:

> For Jackson . . . each new identity is the result of surgical technology. Rather than a progressively developing and maturing public figure who erupts into the social fabric newly made up to make a new statement, Jack-son produces each new Jackson as a simulacrum of himself whose moment of appearance signals the immediate denial of the previous Michael Jackson. Rather than making a social statement, Jackson states himself as a commod-ity. . . . The original Michael Jackson, the small boy who sang with the Jackson Five, also becomes a commodified identity with respect to the sub-sequent Michael Jacksons. . . . The Michael Jackson of the Jackson Five becomes "retroactively" a simulacrum once the chain of Jackson simulacra comes into being. (187–88)

Doubtless, the notion that, in his transmogrifications, Jackson constitutes a postmodernist chain of being is interpretively attractive for some, especially con-sidering that in his transmutation from a black to a white surface he might be seen as seeking to improve his hierarchical position as Western citizen in terms of that long-antiquated racialist construct. According to this argument, he clearly recognizes the currency of what Stuart Hall terms an "ethnic scale," the codifica-tion of particularities of physiological and cultural being that historically have helped to determine individual black citizens' social status.[18]

Advertisements promoting his interview with Oprah Winfrey reflect Jackson's willingness to employ transraciality as ratings ploy. In an ad that appeared in the February 8, 1993, edition of *People* magazine, Jackson, lighted so that his facial profile appears as a silhouette that emphasizes his straightened hair, aquiline nose, and thin lips, stands beside a smiling, dazzlingly coiffed Winfrey whose left hand surreptitiously points toward—and may be posed to uncover—the singer's shad-owed face. This advertisement (along with a photo in *TV Guide* wherein Jackson stands looking down, the camera's access to his face blocked by a hat and his pose) creates an air of mystery about Jackson's transmutations whose purpose, no doubt, is to entice viewers to watch the interview.

But the shaded profile signifies in other ways as well, calling attention to the singer's altered state as well as to the possibility of controlling darkness and light and, thus, the terms of the viewer's access to Jackson's scopic difference. Despite the cosmetic changes he attempted to downplay during his interview, Jackson's (black) shadow is clearly intended both to mask and to call attention to that difference. Is he, as Tate would suggest, merely a shadow of his former racialized self? Is he striving to negotiate what Toni Morrison identifies as "the conflict between public and private life" by figuring a mode of self-representation that both reveals and resists self-disclosure, both covers over and uncovers significant aspects of himself? Or—and this is the reading that most compels my interpretive fancy— does his stance serve as a critique of other's critiques of his putatively deracializing transformations by suggesting, in this manipulation of the viewer's access to his visage, that the human body has come to represent an extremely malleable surface and that others' efforts to read his altered state as a manifestation of an absence of racial pride are themselves operating in terms of limited notions of blackness? Privileging scopic blackness as the ideal in Afro-American aesthetics, essentialists who police the boundaries of race underplay the visual range represented by those who are unified under the term *blackness,* and argue that those who alter aspects of their surfaces necessarily evince a desire to "conform to the Nordic ideal" (Tate 95). In ways that strike me as potentially profound, Jackson's image might be said to constitute a fundamentally artistic effort—and here I will use Tate's own compelling critique of the limitations of black theoretical discourse against him—to "open . . . up the entire 'text of blackness' for [postmodernist, technocultural] fun and games" (200).

If we can open up interpretive space to allow for a possible reading of Jackson's transmutations as astute anti-essentialist comment rather than merely as evidence of self-hatred, we might more effectively problematize the protectionist impulses manifest in our investments in race both generally, as a sign of irreducible difference, and specifically, as they relate to the transracial singer. Jackson's song, "Black or White," may assist those efforts.[19] The *Dangerous* compact disc packaging includes song lyrics, and those of "Black or White" occupy a page adorned by a zebra, an animal whose black-and-white markings possess a figurative relationship to vitiligo's transformative effects upon dark-skinned sufferers. In addition, the zebra is used in this case to symbolize a racial subject whose behavior is deemed representative of neither black nor white difference but of an identifiable commingling of these polarized cultural styles.

If the zebra can signify both skin disease and what some hold to be the social disease of American cultural hybridity, the lyrics themselves explore instances wherein the song's exasperated persona, who acknowledges, "I am tired of this stuff," confronts figures who espouse rigid rules of racial behavior. After condemning others' narrow-minded views of interracial dating and journalists who "print my message/in the saturday sun" and nevertheless are unschooled in the specifics of racial "equality," Jackson's persona engages in a bit of macho bravado. Specifically, the song records his contempt for intimidating family members and the Ku Klux Klan, two traditional forms of institutional protection against transgressive sexuality: "I ain't scared of your brother/I ain't scared of no sheets/I ain't scared of nobody/Girl when the going gets mean." Then, at the end of a rap lyric that implores the listener to see race as merely "where your blood comes from," "Black or White" moves to a conclusion which challenges notions that Jackson's transmutations are designed to allow him to occupy a white subject position: "I'm not going to spend/My life being a color." To move beyond views that race constitutes the grounds of ultimate difference, especially when we are aware of the protectionist energies that have been expended policing (however ineffectively by certain measures) the sexual and social boundaries between whites and blacks, is to contest both caucacentric and afrocentric assertions of a fundamentally unbridgeable gulf between these polarized states of being.

In comments that support aspects of (or at least my reading of) Jackson's acts, Stuart Hall urges us to recognize the conceptual flaws inherent in essentialist notions of race:

> The essentializing moment is weak because it naturalizes and dehistoricizes difference, mistaking what is historical and cultural for what is natural, biological, and genetic. The moment the signifier "black" is torn from its historical, cultural, and political embedding and lodged in a biologically constituted racial category, we valorize, by inversion, the very ground of the racism we are trying to deconstruct. In addition, . . . we fix that signifier outside of history, outside of change, outside of political intervention. And once it is fixed, we are tempted to use "black" as sufficient in itself to guarantee the progressive character of the politics we fight under the banner—as if we don't have any other politics to argue about except whether something's black or not. We are tempted to display that signifier as a device which can purify the impure, bring the straying brothers and sisters who don't know what they ought to be doing into line, and police the boundaries—which are of course political, symbolic, and positional boundaries—as if they were genetic.[20]

In the context of the present discussion, Hall's comments are illuminating, especially his emphasis on the utilization of the "cultural signifier" blackness as a "device which can purify the impure, . . . straying brothers and sisters." In promoting a constructionist reading of blackness, Hall insists that we attend more energetically to that concept's historical and cultural production. The reduction of the signifier "black" to an undifferentiated, ideologically static "color," to reference Jackson's lyrics, replicates to some degree caucacentric efforts to position a putatively primitive Africa and her descendants outside history and thus resist the notion that black people actually adapt to historical change. Jackson's acts can be said to intervene upon the reduction of blackness to the status of fixity and ideological overdeterminacy, though his lyrics, "it's tough for them/To get by," demonstrate an awareness of the difficulties they pose for those—black or white—invested in blackness as what Hall describes as a mechanism of social control. Jackson's figuratively resonant zebra, like its conceptual counterpart, hybridity, recognizes the amalgam of cultural styles that generally constitutes human subjectivity in this age of widespread intranational and global migration.

In an autobiographical examination of her own dilemmas as a light-complexioned Afro-American, the philosopher and artist Adrian Piper, who insists that "we are almost all in fact racial hybrids," asserts, "I've learned that there is no 'right' way of managing the issue of my racial identity, no way that will not offend or alienate someone, because my designated racial identity itself exposes the very concept of racial classification as the offensive and irrational instrument of racism it is."[21] How to manage racial identity is the issue that most concerns me here, not the articulation of ubiquitous strategies of black being. If we fail to interrogate essentialist constructions of blackness, we submit to a racial irrationality that heretofore marked blacks as less than human and continues to exert its influence upon what many of us hold as the most fundamental personal areas of our lives as Americans: our formulations of subjectivity and community. If, for example, we continue to accept uncritically the one-drop rule of racial determinacy, do we not, however unwittingly, implicitly confirm caucacentric notions of whiteness as purity and of even a touch of blackness as profound taintedness? Dramatic gestures such as Jackson's transmutations offer occasions for a reconsideration—and, perhaps, at least an individual reconstruction—of the meaning of blackness passed down to us that we would perhaps do well not to pass on.

However attuned this chapter has been to racially inflected aspects of Jackson's manipulations and seeming motivations, it has failed to consider seriously his performance of gender. Certainly, we might argue that Jackson's surface evinces not only transracial but, as Marjorie Garber insists, transvestite marks, especially if we embrace her notion of black male participation in transvestism as "synecdochic quotation":

> By "transvestism" I mean here to designate not only full gender-masquerade, . . . but also the synecdochic quotation of transvestism, as in

the wearing of earrings or gold necklaces by black men, like Mr. T., coded as he-men and heterosexual objects of desire. For such quotations deliberately flaunt what had been previously seen as demeaning. They turn inside-out the valuation of cross-dressing, male-to-female and female-to-male, producing it not as an imposed and enslaving act of castration or ungendering, but rather as a language of reassignment, empowerment, and critique. (275)

Garber's attempts at definitional expansion are not fully convincing, in part because, according to her definition, any minor incursion into the vested interests of the gendered other—say, a male's wearing of a pink tie—can be viewed as transvestism, and in part because she recognizes here only the West's evaluative criteria for appropriate gendered behavior. Some notion of intercultural nexus between Western and black American constructions of West African practices, for example, might effectively explain the categorical tensions manifest in Mr. T.'s comic hybrid costume. Certainly, however, it is difficult not to see Jackson—whose speaking voice, fascination with appearance, straightened hair and seemingly permanently affixed lipstick and mascara, all fall within the confines of a Western categorical femininity—as involved in some form of gender-blending and -bending. However, I believe it is most profitable in this regard to concentrate not on Jackson's appearance per se but rather on his gendered performance generally, which is, at the very least, complexly inconsistent. Jackson's various performances can be read not strictly as signs of what Judith Butler has termed the "gender trouble" that afflicts Western culture, but as evidence of the trouble with employing constructionist paradigms alone to evaluate the singer's negotiations.

According to Garber, who sees transvestism as a provocative response to protectionist caucacentric formulations of black male sexuality, these formulations are fundamentally "paradoxical":

> Paradoxically, the black American male has been constructed by majority culture as both sexually threatening *and* feminized, as both super-potent and impotent. The easy "equation" between castration and feminization, offensive alike to men and to women—as if the violent mutilation of the black male body somehow made it equivalent in power and social status to that of a woman—is an all-too-clear demonstration of the ways in which categories like "gender" and "race" have been made to intersect and cross over one another in the service of political rhetoric and cultural domination. (271)

Garber identifies dimensions of the protectionist racialist constructions of black male sexuality, but to my mind unpersuasively conflates categorical contingency with simultaneity. Hegemonic ascriptions to black males of such qualities as "super-potent and impotence" are, by and large, situationally determined and function (at the present moment at least) as distinctly sexual and economic signifiers respectively. While racist fantasies of hypersexuality are products of fears of Afro-American male engagement in sexual traffic across racial lines, notions of black male impotence specifically connote a putative black male lack largely in the area of nonsexual male performance (such as personal autonomy, earnings potential, and familial protection, in the broadest sense of that phrase). Such designations are not necessarily paradoxical at all, in fact, but evidence that black men historically have been figured in interracial and economic settings as both "threatening and feminized," as both more and less than a white man. It is precisely the contingency of these seemingly paradoxical roles, the imposition of caucacentric definitions of black masculinity as—at varied moments—feminized and hypersexual, that helps explain what I have termed Jackson's gendered inconsistencies.

Jackson's combination of effeminate speaking voice, long, processed hair, makeup, and surgically feminized features contribute to his transvestite appearance. In the "real world"—as opposed to the place of the stage, the realm in which, Jackson has acknowledged, he feels most comfortable, most self-assured, most himself—he appears to be the unthreatening, de-sexualized eunuch of racist white-male fantasies. But on stage, his most public arena of work, Jackson strives to exude sexuality in his dancing, in his vocal stylings, and, certainly, in his crotch-grabbing. To conflate Jackson's offstage and onstage gendered performances, to see them as "paradoxical," is, I think, to misread an important aspect of the singer's self-presentation. Critics seem generally to make just that mistake, confusing his "private" and "public" personas and, in the process, overlooking an essential aspect of Jackson's performative appeal.

From his earliest recorded moments as a public entertainer, Jackson was perhaps best characterized as a supremely talented imitator of James Brown's and Jackie Wilson's energetic, funky dance dexterity, Little Stevie Wonder's joyful vocal play, and Smokey Robinson's falsetto sweetness and determination. The young Jackson's "act," his engagement of black male entertainers' lexicon of sexual moves, seemed unnaturally, prematurely enlightened. As a consequence, he was able, as Greg Tate puts it, to "arouse the virginal desires" of female fans much his senior. Tate goes on to discuss his performative maturity:

> At age 10, Jackson's footwork and vocal machismo seemed to scream volumes about the role of genetics in the cult of soul and the black sexuality of myth. The older folk might laugh when he sang shake it, shake it baby, ooh, ooh or teacher's gonna show you, all about loving. Yet part of the tyke's appeal was being able to simulate being lost in the hot sauce way before he

was supposed to know what the hot sauce even smelt like. No denying he *sounded* like he knew the real deal. (96)

Here, Tate grapples with contradictions inherent in performative notions of blackness, which he identifies specifically as "the cult of soul and the black sexuality of myth." After toying with the idea that Jackson's precocious "black" talent "seemed" genetically predetermined, he acknowledges that, at least with respect to the disjunction between his youth and apparent performative knowledge, Jackson's act was not inspired by the "blood" at all but was, rather, an artful simulation. But if we embrace constructionist views of subjectivity as the product of an amalgam of social practices, all of the categories implicated in Tate's passage—age, gender, race, and sexuality—are essentially simulacra, are, that is to say, to some degree enactments of various available scripts of social performativity. By Tate's own account, despite the fact that the critic ultimately (and perhaps understandably) takes refuge in a discourse of racial treason, Jackson's talent from the very beginning was for being other than he seemed, was, at its core, self-consciously imitative and mimetic. Because simulation was such a central feature of his art, we might speculate that he learned early in his life that, in virtually every aspect, human identity was essentially performative rather than, as it were, a performance of essence.

Thus, when Ann Powers argues that Jackson's contemporary performances are not sufficiently sexual, she touches upon but misses the fuller implications of his split subjectivity. According to Powers, "his music has always communicated sexuality, but he has failed to confidently incorporate sex into his persona. . . . [His songs that explore aspects of human sexuality] take sex to the point of surrender but don't cross the line. They are a virgin's dream of danger, in which sensuality is always tied to frustration and anxiety."[22] Clearly, Jackson's off-stage persona seems a by no means confident enactment of male phallic principles. But his stage persona—melismatic note-bending, pelvis thrusting, shirt ripping, crotch grabbing, and general "hot sauce" lostness—appears as masculinized and sexualized as a "family" entertainer could be. And given Jackson's (overused) video records of young females fainting in apparent response to his stage eroticism, it seems difficult to sustain an argument that his has not been a demonstratively effective incorporation of sexuality, however cognizant we are of the artifice of spectator response to staged stimuli.[23]

One of the most persuasive theoretical critiques of essentialist notions of gender has been offered by Judith Butler. She argues that we must begin to come to grips with the fact that gender is merely an inscription of discursive imperatives, is, that is to say, an elaborate, socially conditioned "fabrication": "If the inner truth of gender is a fabrication and if a true gender is a fantasy instituted and inscribed on the surface of bodies, then it seems that genders can be neither true nor false but are only produced as the truth effects of a discourse of primary and stable identity."[24] To recognize gender as a fabrication is not, of course, to doubt its existence but to locate it squarely in the realm of cultural production. To the extent that gender is produced, to the degree that cultural rather than biological imperatives govern its enactment "on the surface of bodies"—the separation of gender from biological sex represents a first stage in the negotiation of what are often inhibiting behavioral norms. As is the case with Hall, who advocates a paradigmatic rejection of notions of a fixed, historically unresponsive "inner truth" of blackness, Butler urges us to address the manifest consequences of "a discourse of primary and stable [gender] identity."

Generally, Jackson's negotiations of categories of difference can be said to reflect a keen recognition of race and gender as cultural "fabrications." Indeed, Jackson's representation of himself as split gendered subject, his private effeminacy and his public efforts to embody a phallic male sexuality, explains, for me, his signal importance for constructionist formulations. These binary gendered performances, like Jackson's self-conscious assumption of racial hybridity and his resistance to being reduced to "a [single] color," demonstrate a desire, in Garber's formulation, to occupy an unspecifiable, categorically disruptive "third" term between binary positions that cannot be fixed, one whose meanings are always in flux. Gender, like race, appears always a matter of self-conscious negotiation in Jackson's enactment of it.

But I do not believe that we can figure Jackson as unproblematic cultural site upon which constructionists can build their disruptive churches. For, at crucial moments when, in the estimation of others, his distinct gender performances appear to clash with one another, Jackson uses ideological and/or essentialist pronouncements that manifest little, if any, poststructuralist enlightenment. I have already noted one such moment when, in response to inquiries concerning the connections between his racial transmutations and his psychic, emotional, and ideological blackness, Jackson asserts that he possesses a very healthy amount of racial price. Similarly, when confronted by criticism of his public, performative crotch-grabbing, Jackson asserts a belief in a black aesthetic unconscious. According to Jackson, the gesture is not planned at all but is motivated "subliminally" and is a manifestation of the fact that during his phallic, masculinized performance he is "a slave to the rhythm."[25]

This historically pregnant phrase, like Clarence Thomas's similarly self-defensive assertion that he was the victim during Senate Judiciary Committee hearings of a "high-tech lynching," seeks to reinscribe the meanings of racially and sexually charged signifiers. Thomas's phrase implies that racialist imperatives continue to motivate white males, threatened by a further disruption of caucacentric power, who employ technocultural mechanisms (most notably, television) to make a public spectacle both of an always already sexualized black male and of their efforts to neutralize him.[26]

Jackson's defensive discourse, on the other hand, has other resonances. Slavery, in Jackson's phrase, has been transformed into a privately motivated compulsion, not in the sense of an internalization of caucacentric perspectives on blackness that could result in the development of what commentators on Jackson's transraciality might term "an inferiority complex," but as a response to irrepressible African drums that historically have been assumed to beat, literally or figuratively, in every drop of black blood. Despite his cosmetic and surgical choices, then, Jackson is, according to his own essentialist pronouncement, "a slave" not to white hegemony but to natal tribal imperatives whose locus, in this new world setting, is his presumably still black (or ex-colored?) phallus.

The black phallus, of course, was the focus—indeed, very often, the site—of much of lynching's ritualistic concern and energy, as the intent of this social practice was to deny to black men their own lives, the threatening body part which could be used to assist the creation of new Afro-American generations, and access to a constitutionally guaranteed masculine power.[27] As counterhegemonic gesture—and it seems to be impossible to read it in any other manner, even if my own construction of its meanings seems imprecise or implausible—Jackson's crotch-grabbing and its attendant discourse can be seen as both essentialist and obviously socially constructed. Even if, as I believe, Jackson's gesture is not compelled instinctually, but is staged, the spectacle seems intended effectively to problematize formulations of his asexuality produced by our interactions with his private persona.[28] Further, this gesture signifies resoundingly upon historical formulations of black masculinity that, through the ritualistic hanging, castrating, and burning of black male bodies, suggested white hypersensitivity to the perceived dangers of the black phallus. The best Afro-American man imaginable to racist white men and women was a dead, castrated, and therefore, according to androcentric notions, feminized man.

Jackson's pronouncements, then, if examined through a historical prism of interracial violence, provide a means by which to view the quandary in which historically oppressed subjects are placed when they attempt to resolve debates about essentialist and constructionist epistemologies or choose the latter as the governing structure of their philosophical perspectives and ideological behavior. Given our necessary negotiation of a limited range of social practices around which essentialist formulations have already calcified, even the most enlightened constructionist gesture is susceptible to strategic essentialist reading. With Jackson's explorations of transracial and transvestite postures in mind, which I have attempted to demonstrate are profoundly disruptive instances of "category crisis," we might consider the fact that, whatever we wish to be the case, we are always situated between our own and other's fabrications, between historically and ideologically conditioned notions of racialized and gendered performance and essence. Rather than bemoan this fact, or pretend that our situations are otherwise, we might recognize that, for the foreseeable future at least, we occupy what we might call—following Garber—a categorical "third" world in which notions of essence and social practice are contiguous and intersecting.

We must employ whichever hybrid combination of interpretive technologies we can access or create that will help us to illuminate precisely the many ways in which difference continues to matter at the end of twentieth century. Though we may disagree profoundly with Jackson's utopian formulations of difference's essential irrelevance in matters of the heart—his view that "it don't matter if you're black or white"—the singer's negotiations might be employed as an important step in our efforts if not to heal the world, to begin to resolve epistemological tensions which, as this study demonstrates, often result in full-fledged intra- and interterritorial battles.

Introduction: Reading across the Lines

1. Tracy Chapman, "Across the Lines" (*Tracy Chapman*, Electra Asylum Records 60774–1).

2. To use 1970s black song titles which presuppose or explore notions of a black racial essence: pleas to African-American citizens to "be real black for [a racial] me" necessarily evoke inquiries into whether the scrutinized behavior is, in a phrase, "black enough for you." The phrases are from the songs "Be Real Black for Me" by Roberta Flack and Donny Hathaway (*Roberta Flack and Donny Hathaway,* Atlantic Records 7216–2); and "Am I Black Enough for You?" recorded by Billy Paul (*360 Degrees of Billy Paul*, Philadelphia International Records ZT31793).

3. For extensive discussions of Clarence Thomas, see *Race-ing Justice, En-gendering Power: Essays on Anita Hill, Clarence Thomas, and the Construction of Social Reality,* ed. Toni Morrison (New York: Pantheon, 1992); and *Court of Appeal: The Black Community Speaks Out on the Racial and Sexual Politics of Thomas vs. Hill,* ed. Robert Chrisman and Robert Allen (New York: Ballantine, 1992). For Joyce A. Joyce's comments about black engagement of poststructuralist perspectives, comments I examine in some detail in chapter 1, see "The Black Canon: Reconstructing Black American Literary Criticism: and "'Who the Cap Fit': Unconsciousness and Unconscionableness in the Criticism of Houston A. Baker, Jr., and Henry Louis Gates, Jr.," *New Literary History* 18 (1987): 335–44, 371–84.

4. In her illuminating preface, Miller offers the following explanation of the possibilities and the dangers of her self-reflexive work: "The gamble involves repersonalizing my work *in* feminism in order to mark for myself the distinction between (which is not the same thing as a disaffection from) me and feminism, me and its occasions—even at the cost of some embarrassment—in order, as we enter the nineties, to inaugurate the writing of my fifties" (xvi). See Nancy K. Miller, *Getting Personal: Feminist Occasions and Other Autobiographical Acts* (New York: Routledge, 1992).

5. Hortense J. Spillers, "Mama's Baby, Papa's Maybe: An American Grammar Book," *diacritics* (summer 1987), 65.

6. Edward Said, *Beginnings: Intention and Method* (New York: Basic, 1975), 373.

7. See Zora Neale Hurston, *Mules and Men* (1935; reprint, New York: Perennial, 1990), 1; and Henry Louis Gates, Jr., *Figures in Black: Words, Signs, and the "Racial" Self* (New York: Oxford University Press, 1987), 236. Both Hurston and Gates speak of the need to step back from black cultural materials in order to comprehend their meanings sufficiently. While I know that distance is a necessary exegetical condition generally, I am trying to investigate the critical consequences of positioning one's self at what are not always comfortable junctures between and within racial and gendered discourses that have not traditionally been seen as complementary.

8. For illuminating discussions of race and gender respectively as modes of performance, see Houston A. Baker, Jr., *Modernism and the Harlem Renaissance* (Chicago: Univer-

sity of Chicago Press, 1987); and Judith Butler, *Gender Trouble: Feminism and the Subversion of Identity* (New York: Routledge, 1990).

9. James Greenberg, "Did Hollywood Sit on 'Fences' over Hiring a Black Director?" *New York Times* 27 January 1991, sec. 2, p. 18; Playthell Benjamin, "Bearing the Cross," *Emerge* 2 (November 1991), 32; Gates, "Generation X: A conversation with Spike Lee and Henry Louis Gates," *Transition* 56 (1992): 176–90; Bernard Weintraub, "Spike Lee's request," *Ann Arbor News,* 30 October 1992, sec. C1.

10. See Cornel West, "The Dilemma of the Black Intellectual," *Cultural Critique* 1 (1985): 109–24, and "Minority Discourse and the Pitfalls of Canon-Formation," *Yale Journal of Criticism* 1 (1987), 193–201.

11. West, "The New Cultural Politics of Difference," in *Out There: Marginalization and Contemporary Cultures,* ed. Russell Ferguson, Martha Gever, Trinh T. Minh-ha, and West (New York: The New Museum of Contemporary Art and Cambridge: MIT Press, 1990), 26. Subsequent references to this essay appear in the text in parentheses.

12. Lisa Kennedy, "The Body in General," *Black Popular Culture,* ed. Gina Dent, (Seattle: Bay Press, 1992), 107.

13. Henry Giroux, *Border Crossings: Cultural Workers and the Politics of Education* (New York: Routledge, 1992), 28. Subsequent references to this study appear in the text in parentheses.

14. Very early in my career, I was asked to respond to essays by some of the most prominent black feminist critics. While I am not necessarily proud of these often contentious responses, they did provide me with the valuable opportunity to examine the nature of my stake in the black feminist enterprise. See my response to Barbara Christian's "The Race for Theory," in *Gender and Theory: Dialogues on Feminist Criticism,* ed. Linda Kauffman (New York: Blackwell, 1989), 238–46; Response to Deborah McDowell, "Boundaries: Or Distant Relations and Close Kin," in *Afro-American Literary Study in the 1990s,* ed. Houston A. Baker, Jr. and Patricia Redmond (Chicago: University of Chicago Press, 1989), 73–77; and Response to Hortense Spillers, "Black, White, and in Color, or Learning How to Paint: Toward an Intramural Protocol of Reading," presented at the "Sites of Colonialism" retreat, Center for the Study of Black Literature and Culture, University of Pennsylvania, 15 March 1990.

15. Christian, "The Race for Theory," in *Gender and Theory,* 229.

16. John Howard Griffin, *Black Like Me* (New York: Signet, 1961).

17. August Wilson, "'I Want a Black Director,'" *New York Times* 26 September 1990, sec. 1, p. 15. For a discussion of an "increasing white influence on hip-hop culture," see Jonathan Tilove, "Plain White Rappers," *Ann Arbor News,* 28 November 1992, D1.

18. Jerry Watts, Response to Henry Louis Gates, Jr., "Good-bye, Columbus? Notes on the Culture of Criticism," *American Literary History* 3 (1991): 742.

19. Vera Kutzinski, "American Literary History As Spatial Practice," *American Literary History* 4 (1992): 555.

20. Paul Armstrong, *Conflicting Readings: Variety and Validity in Interpretation* (Chapel Hill: University of North Carolina Press, 1990), 21.

21. Armstrong, however, seems virtually to ignore essential features of the contemporary interpretive process, including the fact that critics seldom fully embrace any single "method . . . of understanding." Certainly, the recomposition of a text may be as much the product of conflicts between "methods of understanding" with which the critic works— between deconstruction and feminism, or afrocentrism and feminism, or postmodern-

ism and psychoanalytical theory—as a sign of a literary text's inherent disruptive potential. However, the fact that he sees critical practice as a more methodologically pure activity than it actually is does not prevent Armstrong from offering insights valuable to a theorizing about questions of interpretation at the borders.

22. Armstrong, *Conflicting Readings*, 22.

23. Paule Marshall, *Praisesong for the Widow* (New York: Dutton, 1983).

Chapter One: Race, Gender, and the Politics of Reading

1. Henry Louis Gates, Jr., "Criticism in the Jungle," in *Black Literature and Literary Theory*, ed. Gates (New York: Methuen, 1984), 9–10. Subsequent references to this introduction appear in the text in parentheses.

2. For example, his revisionist certainty of his generation's unprecedented interpretive opportunities notwithstanding, there is, as Gates is well aware, a rather long history of insightful examinations of Afro-American texts which have had a major impact on the analyses of even the essays collected in *Black Literature and Literary Theory*. Further, scholars of any number of non-mainstream American literary "traditions"—Chicano/a, Asian, Native, gay, lesbian, and so on—could challenge Gates's claim that few other traditions suffered more critical neglect than the one that "the critic of black literature" has begun to focus on in a theoretically sophisticated manner.

3. See Joe Weixlmann, review of *Black Literature and Literary Theory*, *Contemporary Literature* 27 (1986): 48–62.

4. Gayatri Spivak, "The Politics of Interpretations," in *The Politics of Interpretation*, ed. W. J. T. Mitchell (Chicago: University of Chicago Press, 1983), 347.

5. Like all designations, *afrocentric* is a term not without problems and imprecision, but I use it because, despite its resonances in our culture, no other more adequately suits my terminological needs. My project is methodologically, ideologically, and philosophically worlds apart from afrocentricity of the Molefi Asante variety as articulated in *Afrocentricity* (Trenton: African World Press, 1989), where Asante calls for the "renunciation of . . . western influences" (7) and strives to "teach our children how to behave like the kings and queens they are meant to be" (47). No doubt Asantian afrocentrists would condemn my view that it is virtually impossible for blacks in any area of the globe to attempt to renounce "western influences," labeling it "madness" and "the direct consequence of selfhatred, obligatory attitudes, false assumptions about society, and stupidity" (47). The terminological connections between our work notwithstanding, it is my firm belief that no one even minimally cognizant of Asante's perspectives could possibly confuse or conflate our quite different uses of "afrocentric."

6. Addison Gayle, Jr., "Cultural Strangulation: Black Literature and White Aesthetics," *The Black Aesthetic*, ed. Gayle (New York: Anchor), 1971, 45.

7. Robert Scholes, "Reading As a Man," in *Men in Feminism*, ed. Alice Jardine and Paul Smith (New York: Methuen, 1987), 206.

8. Houston A. Baker, Jr., *Blues, Ideology, and Afro-American Literature: A Vernacular Theory* (Chicago: University of Chicago Press, 1984), 200. Subsequent references to this study, cited as *Blues*, appear in the text in parentheses.

9. Frederick Douglass, *Narrative of the Life of Frederick Douglass* (1845; reprint, New York: Signet, 1968), 49.

10. "America" and "Black Nationhood" are capitalized here in accord with Houston Baker's efforts in *Blues* "to distinguish between an *idea* and what Edmundo

O'Gorman describes . . . as a 'lump of cosmic matter.'" As Baker suggests, "the sign AMERICA [and, I would add, the sign BLACK NATIONHOOD] is a willful act which substitutes for a state description" (66).

11. Gates, "Writing 'Race' and the Difference It Makes," in *"Race," Writing, and Difference,* ed. Gates. (Chicago: University of Chicago Press, 1986), 12. Subsequent references to this introduction, referred to as "Writing 'Race,'" appear in the text in parentheses.

12. Addison Gayle, Jr., *Black Expression,* ed. Gayle (New York: Weybright and Talley, 1969), xiv–xv.

13. Joyce A. Joyce, "The Black Canon: Reconstructing Black American Literature Criticism," 343.

14. Joyce, "The Black Canon," 339. For their response to this investigation of the black poststructural project, see Gates, "'What's Love Got to Do with It?': Critical Theory, Integrity, and the Black Idiom," *New Literary History* 18 (1987): 345–62; and Baker, "In Dubious Battle," *New Literary History* 18 (1987): 363–69.

15. Joyce, "'Who the Cap Fit,'" 373.

16. See Gates, "Criticism in the Jungle," 2–10.

17. Elaine Showalter, "Feminist Criticism in the Wilderness," in *The New Feminist Criticism,* ed. Showalter (New York: Pantheon, 1985), 246. Subsequent references to this essay, cited as "Wilderness," appear in the text in parentheses.

18. Joyce, "'Who the Cap Fit,'" 382.

19. I am referring to George Kent's superb study, *Blackness and the Adventure of Western Culture* (Chicago: Third World Press, 1972).

20. Stanley Fish, *Is There a Text in This Class?* (Cambridge: Harvard University Press, 1980), 14.

21. Elaine Showalter, "Critical Cross-Dressing: Male Feminists and the Woman of the Year," in *Men in Feminism,* 133.

22. Fish, *Is There a Text in This Class?* 272.

23. Examples of racist and/or sexist reading that Barbara Smith and McDowell cite include Sara Blackburn's suggestion that "Toni Morrison is far too talented to remain only a marvelous recorder of the black side of provincial American life" and that, by turning her attention away from the black masses, she "might easily transcend that early and unintentionally limiting classification 'black woman writer'" (Smith, "Toward a Black Feminist Criticism," in *The New Feminist Criticism,* 171); and the "conspicuous . . . absence" of Afro-American women from Robert Stepto's study *From behind the Veil,* which "purports to be a 'history . . . of the historical consciousness of an Afro-American art form—namely, the Afro-American written narrative'" (McDowell, "New Directions for Black Feminist Criticism," in *The New Feminist Criticism,* 187).

24. Harold Bloom, *Zora Neale Hurston,* ed. Bloom (Philadelphia: Chelsea House, 1986), 1, 4.

25. See Showalter, "Wilderness," 262–64. For Showalter's provocative discussion of her own and Gates's appropriation of and acts of signifying upon Geoffrey Hartman's *Criticism in the Wilderness,* see "A Criticism of Our Own: Autonomy and Assimilation in Afro-American and Feminist Literary Theory," in *The Future of Literary Theory,* ed. Ralph Cohen (New York: Routledge, 1989), 354, 362–63.

26. Judith Butler, "Gender Trouble, Feminist Theory, and Psychoanalytic Discourse," in *Feminism/Postmodernism,* ed. Linda J. Nicholson (New York: Routledge, 1990), 337.

27. Showalter, "Piecing and Writing," in *The Poetics of Gender,* ed. Nancy K. Miller (New York: Columbia University Press, 1986), 222.

28. Scholes, "Reading As a Man," 207.

29. Ibid., 217–18.

30. For all their inspiring and justifiable critique of acts of exclusion and misrepresentation performed by whites and black males on black women's literature, early black feminist critical essays suffer from the types of essentialist biases that plague the work of traditional afrocentric and white feminist critics. For both Barbara Smith and McDowell, for example, just being black and female creates the necessary conditions to lead to acts of black feminist criticism. Smith, who declares that whites and black men are "of course ill-equipped to deal [simultaneously] with the subtleties of [sexual and] racial politics," argues that a black feminist critic "would think and write out of her own identity and not try to graft the ideas or methodology of white/male literary thought upon the precious materials of Black women's art" (Smith, "Toward a Black Feminist Criticism," 170, 175). Similarly, McDowell, in attempting to define black feminist criticism, asserts that "the term can . . . apply to any criticism written by a Black woman regardless of her subject or perspective," regardless, in other words, of whether the work is clearly informed by "a feminist or political perspective" (McDowell, "New Directions for Black Feminist Criticism," 1991). This collision of "black female" and "black feminist," of biological and ideological positions, is problematic, I believe, in quite fundamental ways.

31. Stephen Henderson, *Understanding the New Black Poetry* (New York: Morrow, 1973), 62.

32. Henderson, *Understanding the New Black Poetry,* 65.

33. See Gates, *Figures in Black,* especially 32–36.

34. Clifford Geertz, "'From the Native's Point of View': On the Nature of Anthropological Understanding," *Local Knowledge* (New York: Basic Books, 1983), 70. For Geertz's influential analysis of culture, see "Thick Description: Towards an Interpretive Theory of Culture," *The Interpretation of Cultures* (New York: Basic Books, 1973).

35. Baker, *The Journey Back* (Chicago: University of Chicago Press, 1980), xvi–xvii.

36. In *The Journey Back,* Baker says of the possibility of competent white readings of black texts: "If black creativity is the result of a context—of webs of meaning—different in kind and degree from those conceived within the narrow attitudinal categories of white America, it seems possible that the semantic force of black creativity might escape the white critic altogether" (154).

37. Showalter, "Critical Cross-Dressing," 126–27.

38. Ibid., 129.

39. Annette Kolodny, "Dancing through the Minefield: Some Observations on the Theory, Practice, and Politics of a Feminist Literary Criticism," in *The New Feminist Criticism,* 155.

40. Kolodny, "Dancing through the Minefield," 155–56.

41. Showalter, "Critical Cross-Dressing," 119.

42. Showalter's discussion of Terry Eagleton in "Critical Cross-Dressing" offers a case in point. While she spends pages dissecting the "phallic feminism" of his study *The Rape of Clarissa,* she devotes only a brief paragraph to an acknowledgement of his almost miraculous transformation into a competent male feminist critic. For Showalter, Eagleton's illuminating *Literary Theory* (Minneapolis: University of Minnesota Press, 1983), "where he is no longer scolding feminist criticism," suggests that "feminist ideas have penetrated

Eagleton's reading everywhere [and] . . . along with Marxist aesthetics, they inform his entire account of the development of contemporary critical discourse" (130). This apparently significant accomplishment is backgrounded, however, because of Showalter's dedication to describing what she views as male interpretive inadequacy.

43. Mary Jacobus, *Reading Woman* (New York: Columbia University Press, 1986), 12. Subsequent references to this study appear in the text in parentheses.

44. Jane Marcus, "Still Practice, A/Wrested Alphabet," in *Feminist Issues in Literary Scholarship,* ed. Shari Benstock, (Bloomington: Indiana University Press, 1987), 89.

45. Nina Baym, "The Madwoman and Her Languages," in *Feminist Issues in Literary Scholarship,* 52.

46. Baym, "The Madwoman and Her Languages," 46.

47. The essay Showalter refers to is Jonathan Culler, "Reading As a Woman," *On Deconstruction* (Ithaca: Cornell University Press, 1982), 43–64.

48. Fredric Jameson, "The Symbolic Inference; or, Kenneth Burke and Ideological Analysis," *Critical Inquiry* 4 (1978): 510.

49. Adrienne Rich, "When We Dead Awaken: Writing As Re-vision," *College English* 34 (1972): 18.

Chapter Two: A Black Man's Place in Black Feminist Criticism

1. Joseph Boone's and Gerald MacLean's essays in *Gender and Theory* assume that the foregrounding of gendered subjectivity is essential to the production of a male feminist critical practice. Consequently, in an effort to articulate his perspectives on the possibilities of a male feminist discourse, Boone shares with us professional secrets—he writes of his disagreement with the male-authored essays in Alice Jardine and Paul Smith's *Men and Feminism,* and of being excluded, because of his gender, from a Harvard feminist group discussion of Elaine Showalter's "Critical Cross-Dressing." And MacLean's essay discloses painfully personal information about his difficult relationship with his mother, his unsatisfying experience with psychoanalysis, and an incident of marital violence.

2. Joseph Boone, "Of Me(n) and Feminism: Who(se) is the Sex That Writes?" in *Gender and Theory,* 158–80. Here and below, I quote from p. 159. For my purposes, Boone's remarks are suggestive despite their use of language that might seem to mark them as a heterosexualization of men's participation in feminism ("open up a space," "discover a position"). I believe that Boone's passage implies less about any desire for domination on his part than it does about the pervasiveness in our language of terms which have acquired sexual connotations and, consequently, demonstrates the virtual unavoidability of using a discourse of penetration to describe interactions between males and females. But it also appears to reflect a sense of frustration motivated by Boone's knowledge that while feminism has had a tremendous impact on his thinking about the world he inhabits, many feminists do not see a place in their discourse for him or other like-minded males. In order to make such a place for himself, violation and transgression seem to Boone to be unavoidable.

3. Alice Jardine, "Men in Feminism: Odor di Uomo or Compagnons de Route?" in *Men in Feminism,* 58.

4. Andrew Ross, "No Question of Silence," in *Men in Feminism,* 86.

5. See Georges Poulet, "Criticism and the Experience of Interiority," in *Reader-Response Criticism: From Formalism to Post-Structuralism,* ed. Jane P. Tompkins (Baltimore: Johns Hopkins University Press, 1980), 41–49.

6. Houston A. Baker, Jr., *Afro-American Poetics*, 8.

7. Elizabeth Weed, "A Man's Place," in *Men in Feminism*, 75.

8. Michael Awkward, *Inspiriting Influences: Tradition, Revision, and Afro-American Women's Novels* (New York: Columbia University Press, 1989).

9. About his relationship to feminism, Nelson writes: "Feminism is part of my social and intellectual life, has been so for many years, and so, to the extent that writing is ever 'natural,' it is natural that I write about feminism" (153). Nelson's "Men, Feminism: The Materiality of Discourse" (*Men in Feminism*, 153–72) is, in my estimation, a model for self-referential male feminist inquiries that assume—or, at the very least, seek to demonstrate—a useful place for males in the discourse of feminism.

10. Jardine and Smith, *Men in Feminism*, vii–viii.

11. See Craig Owens, "Outlaws: Gay Men in Feminism," in *Men in Feminism*, 219–32. It is hard to believe that Jardine and Smith's difficulty reflected a lack of interest among Afro-Americans in exploring the relationship of men to black feminism. A number of texts give evidence of interest in "the problem": the 1979 *Black Scholar* special issue devoted to investigating black feminism as manifested primarily in Ntozoke Shagne's *for colored girls* and Michele Wallace's *Black Macho and the Myth of the Superwoman;* Mel Watkins, "Sexism, Racism, and Black Women Writers," *New York Times Book Review,* June 15, 1986, p. 1; Darryl Pinckney, "Black Victims, Black Villains: *New York Review of Books* 34 (January 29, 1987): 17–20); and essays by Valerie Smith and Deborah McDowell from which I draw below.

Jardine and Smith's difficulties might have stemmed from the facts that most of the men who had spoken publicly on the subject were open about their hostility to black feminism, and most of them did not speak the language of contemporary theory, a high academic idiom which demonstrates that the contributors to *Men in Feminism* are, despite significant differences among them, members of the same speech community.

12. Stephen Heath, "Male Feminism," *Men in Feminism*, 1.

13. Ibid., 9.

14. Barbara Smith, "Toward a Black Feminist Criticism," 173, 172; Michele Wallace, "Who Dat Say Dat When I Say Dat? Zora Neale Hurston Then and Now," *Village Voice Literary Supplement,* April 1988, p. 18.

15. Sherley Anne Williams, "Some Implications of Womanist Theory," *Callaloo* 9 (1986): 304.

16. Valerie Smith, "Gender and Afro-Americanist Literary Theory and Criticism," in *Speaking of Gender,* 68.

17. Jardine, "Men in Feminism," *Men in Feminism*, 60.

18. Williams, "Some Implications," 307.

19. Deborah McDowell, "Reading Family Matters," in *Changing Our Own Words: Essays on Criticism, Theory, and the Writing by Black Women,* ed. Cheryl Wall (New Brunswick: Rutgers University Press, 1989), 84.

20. Toril Moi, "Men against Patriarchy," in *Gender and Theory,* 181–88.

21. McDowell's views notwithstanding, constructions of black male and black female subjectivity are too obviously interrelated in black women's narratives for feminist criticism to profit in the long run from ignoring—or urging that others ignore—the important function that delineations of black male subjectivity play in these narratives' thematics. Certainly the threat of antifeminist male critical bias is not cause to erase or minimize the significance of black male characters in these writers' work.

22. Spillers, "Mama's Baby, Papa's Maybe: An American Grammar Book," 80.

23. In this sense, Spillers's perspectives complement those of Sherley Anne Williams, for the latter demands, in effect, that we consider the extent to which black male repression of the "female" results from an attempt to follow the letter of the white Father's law.

24. Paul Smith, "Men in Feminism: Men and Feminist Theory," *Men in Feminism*, 33.

25. Moi, "Men against Patriarchy," 184.

26. Toni Morrison, *Sula* (New York: Plume, 1973), 71. Subsequent references to this novel appear in the text in parentheses.

27. At least one other reading of Eva's murder of her son is possible: as protection against the threat of incest. In a section of her explanation to Hannah—very little of which is contained in my textual citation of *Sula*—Eva discusses a dream she has had concerning Plum:

> I'd be laying here at night and he be downstairs in that room, but when I closed my eyes I'd see him . . . six feet tall smilin' and crawlin' up the stairs quietlike so I wouldn't hear and opening the door soft so I wouldn't hear and he'd be creepin' to the bed trying to spread my legs trying to get back up in my womb. He was a man, girl, a big old growed-up man. I didn't have that much room. I kept on dreaming it. Dreaming it and I knowed it was true. One night it wouldn't be no dream. It'd be true and I would have done it, would have let him if I'd've had the room but a big man can't be a baby all wrapped up inside his mamma no more; he suffocate. (72–73)

Morrison reverses to some extent the traditional dynamics of the most prevalent form of intergenerational incest. Instead of the male parent creeping to the bed and spreading the legs of his defenseless female child, in Eva's dream her man-child Plum is the active agent of violation. Eva's emphasis on Plum's immensity and her own uterus's size makes connections to incestuous creeping and spreading possible. It is not difficult to imagine, given Plum's constantly drugged state, that frustrations caused by an inability to re-insert his whole body into his mother's womb during what Eva views as an inevitable encounter might lead to a forced insertion of a part that "naturally" fits, his penis. At any rate, a reading of this scene that notes its use of language consistent with parent-child incest serves to ground what appear to be otherwise senseless fears on Eva's part concerning both the possible effects of Plum's desire for reentry into her uterine space and her own inability to deny her son access to that space ("I would have done it, would have let him").

28. Spillers, "Black, White, and in Color, or Learning How to Paint: Toward an Intramural Protocol of Reading."

Chapter Three: Negotiations of Power

1. Hoyt Fuller, "Introduction: Towards a Black Aesthetic," *The Black Aesthetic*, ed. Addison Gayle, Jr. (Garden City, NY: Doubleday, 1971), 7.

2. The phrase is from Morrison's Tanner lecture, "Unspeakable Things Unspoken: The Afro-American Presence in American Literature," *Michigan Quarterly Review* 28 (winter 1989): 1–34. For collections that investigate male feminism, see *Speaking of Gender*, ed. Elaine Showalter; *Men in Feminism*, ed. Alice Jardine and Paul Smith; *Gender and Theory* and *Feminism and Institutions*, both edited by Linda Kauffman; and *Engendering Men: The Question of Male Feminist Criticism*, ed. Joseph A. Boone and Michael Cadden (New York: Routledge,

1990). The only contemporary Afro-American literary critic to my knowledge who engages the topic of interpretation and racial "others"—perhaps because of his Black Aesthetic origins—is Houston Baker. His positions have altered from a belief that "the semantic force of black creativity might escape the white critic altogether" (*The Journey Back,* 154) to a view, encouraged by the nonracist critical practice of such scholars as Lawrence Levine and Robert Hemenway, that "through their own investigations of the 'forms of things unknown' in recent years, some white critics have been able to enter a black critical circle" (*Blues,* 84). Seven years later, Baker concludes that the white critic "who honestly engages his or her own autobiographical implication in a brutal past is as likely as an Afro-American to provide such [compelling and informed] nuances" (*Workings of the Spirit: The Poetics of Afro-American Women's Writing* [Chicago: University of Chicago Press, 1991], 48).

3. Sue-Ellen Case, "Women of Colour and Theatre," *Feminism and Theatre* (New York: Methuen, 1988), 95.

4. Charles H. Rowell, "An Interview with Larry Neal," *Callaloo* 8 (1985): 23. Subsequent references to this interview appear in the text in parentheses.

5. David Littlejohn, *Black on White: A Critical Survey of Writing by American Negroes* (New York: Grossman, 1966); Catharine Stimpson, "Black Culture/White Teacher," *Where the Meanings Are: Feminism and Cultural Spaces* (New York: Routledge, 1988), 1–10. Specific references to these studies appear in the text in parentheses.

6. Michel Foucault, "The Subject and Power," in Hubert Dreyfus and Paul Rabinow, *Michel Foucault: Beyond Structuralism and Hermeneutics* (Chicago: University of Chicago Press, 1982), 226.

7. Indeed, Littlejohn argues that reading will lead to a "coexperience" between blacks and whites, although I wonder, given the ahistoricity and the effective bracketing of black oppression evident in Littlejohn's perspectives—his book, mind you, was published during the height of national civil rights agitation, whose history-transforming nature seems not at all to temper or inform his remarks—how "coexperience" can be said to transform his ideal, nonracist white reader.

8. I use the adjective "hesitant" for two reasons. First, Littlejohn comes close to admitting that an editorial decision led to his inclusion of a discussion of texts before 1940 (he regards this period as "the dark ages" for Afro-American literature, admitting that "with the possible exception of Langston Hughes, I would feel compelled to include the work of no Negro writer before 1940 in a fair critical survey of American literature" (21). Second, he admits—apparently with the same lack of self-consciousness that allows him to acknowledge without a hint of a sense of his own inadequacy for the task of writing a study of Afro-American literature that "I had not heard of [Paul Laurence Dunbar] until last year" (67)—that "I have read, or tried to read, about half" of the "over a hundred novels" published between 1940 and 1965 (101).

9. Robert Hemenway, *Zora Neale Hurston: A Literary Biography* (Urbana: University of Illinois Press, 1977).

10. Arnold Rampersad, "Biography, Autobiography, and Afro-American Culture, *Yale Review* 73 (Autumn 1983): 2.

11. Hemenway, *Zora Neale Hurston,* xx.

12. Stephen Henderson, "The Question of Form and Judgement in Contemporary Black American Poetry, 1962–77," in *A Dark and Sudden Beauty: Two Essays in American Poetry by George Kent and Stephen Henderson,* ed. Houston A. Baker, Jr., (Philadelphia: Afro-American Studies Program of the University of Pennsylvania, 1977), 24.

13. bell hooks, *Talking Black* (Boston: South End Press, 1988), 46.

14. Houston A. Baker, Jr., *Blues*, 84.

15. Morrison, "Unspeakable Things Unspoken," 33.

16. Donald Wesling, "Writing as Power in the Slave Narrative of the Early Republic," *Michigan Quarterly Review* 26 (summer 1987), 459. Subsequent references to this essay appear in the text in parentheses.

17. Wesling discusses the slave narrative tradition in relation to the canon of white thought. He explores, for instance, the very different figurations of slavery of white authors such as Stowe, Melville, and Twain, and the fact that, unlike the mainstream American autobiographical impulse which privileges "a bringing to consciousness of the nature of one's own existence, transforming the mere fact of existence into a realized quality and a possible meaning," in slave narratives the autobiographical I is "insistently bound up with the fate of the race and nation" (466).

18. Space permits only brief mention of Wesling's view of the use of standard English in slave narratives. Clearly, though, if deconstruction is correct in asserting that "no original moment exists that would ground truth," then Wesling's suggestion that black English is the "authentic" language of blackness in which a "true" representation of blackness ought to be rendered is itself fundamentally flawed.

19. Frederick Douglass, *Narrative of the Life of Frederick Douglass* (1845; reprint, New York: Signet, 1968), 81.

20. The essay Wesling refers to is Sacvan Bercovitch, "The Problem of Ideology in American Literary History," *Critical Inquiry* 12 (summer 1986): 631–53. A condensed version of Baker's analysis appears in *Ideology and Classic American Literature,* ed. Bercovitch and Myra Jehlen (New York: Cambridge University Press, 1986).

21. Bercovitch, "The Problem of Ideology," 648.

22. Werner Sollors, "A Critique of Pure Pluralism," in *Reconstructing American Literary History,* ed. Sacvan Bercovitch (Cambridge: Harvard University Press, 1986), 251. Subsequent references to this essay appear in the text in parentheses.

23. Bercovitch argues that rather than striving—as Sollors advocates—for the type of consolidation of "a powerful literary-historical consensus," it will be "our task to make the best of what (for lack of a better term) may be called a period of 'dissensus'" (633). We can make the best of dissensus, not by seeking to minimize or erase differences among ideologically diverse contemporary Americanist scholars but by working "to turn the current barbarism of critical debate into a dialogue about common questions. In our ability to keep the dialogue open, while specifying and exploring the questions we share, lies the prospect of our achieving an integrated narrative of American literary history" (653). Though both Sollors and Bercovitch share a common goal—"an integrated narrative of American literary history"—Bercovitch seems aware that such a goal, which he believes may not come to pass until "the next generation," necessitates a generosity of spirit regarding the ideological differences of others.

24. Bercovitch, "The Problem of Ideology," 633.

25. The impact of Sollors's "movement" is manifested, although admittedly in a much less rancorous tone, in the first issue of *American Literary History.* Kenneth Warren, who is black, argues that the three Afro-American literary studies he focuses on in his review essay—Gates's *Figures in Black,* Bernard Bell's *The Afro-American Novel and its Tradition,* and Melvin Dixon's *Ride Out the Wilderness: Geography and Identity in Afro-American Literature*—fail both to deconstruct such concepts as "originality" and "exceptionalism"

and to show their fundamental Americanness. In trying to emphasize "black difference," such studies, for Warren, ignore black self-difference, while refusing to examine likenesses between Afro-American and "Euro-American" literary and cultural constructions of self, tribe, and history. For Warren, then, as for Sollors, black critical discourse is marred by its misguided examinations of cultural distinctiveness, which force critics to ignore essentially more important, nation-building non-differences. For Warren and Sollors, Afro-Americanist critics are involved in "removing [such] concepts [as originality] from their 'American' locus and relocating them on the 'African' side of the hyphen in African-American" (See Warren, "Delimiting America: The Legacy of Du Bois," *American Literary History* 1 (spring 1989): 172–89. In a response to a condensed version of this essay, which appeared under the same title in *American Literary History* 2 (winter 1990): 581–606, Warren chides me for not being sufficiently attentive to these similarities. See "From under the Superscript: A Response to Michael Awkward," *American Literary History* 4 (spring 1992): 97–103, and my reply, "The Politics of Positionality: A Reply to Kenneth Warren," *American Literary History* 4 (spring 1992): 104–9.

26. For other examinations of this discussion, see Theodore Mason, "Between the Populist and the Scientist: Ideology and Power in Recent Afro-American Literary Criticism; or, 'The Dozens' as Scholarship," *Callaloo* 11 (1988): 606–15; Diana Fuss, "'Race under Erasure? Poststructuralist Afro-American Literary Theory," *Essentially Speaking: Feminism, Nature and Difference* (New York: Routledge, 1989), 77–79, 85–86; and Anthony Appiah, "The Conservation of 'Race,'" *Black American Literature Forum* 23 (1989): 39–41.

27. Harold Fromm, "Real Life, Literary Criticism, and the Perils of Bourgeoisification," *New Literary History* 20 (autumn 1988): 50. Subsequent references to this essay appear in the text in parentheses.

28. Fromm expresses similar reservations in a volume Gates edited, *"Race," Writing, and Differences*, where his ire is directed at Gates and Mary Louise Pratt, a white literary scholar. In that volume, see Fromm, "The Hegemonic Form of Othering; or, The Academic's Burden," 396–99, and Pratt, "A Reply to Harold Fromm," 400–401.

29. In *Black Like Me*, John Howard Griffin says of the motivations for his transracial experience:

> How else except by becoming a Negro could a white man hope to learn the truth? Though we lived side by side throughout the South, communication between the two races had simply ceased to exist. Neither really knew what went on with those of the other race. The Southern Negro will not tell the white man the truth. He long ago learned that if he speaks a truth unpleasing to the white, the white will make life miserable for him.
>
> The only what I could see to bridge the gap between us was to become a Negro. I decided I would do this. (7–8)

30. Quoted in Appiah, "The Conservation of 'Race,'" 50.

31. For Fromm's response to the condensed version of this chapter, see his letter to the Editor, *American Literary History* 4 (1992): 365–66.

32. Foucault, "The Subject and Power" in *Michel Foucault: Beyond Structuralism and Hermeneutics*, 226.

33. Barbara Johnson, "Thresholds of Difference: Structures of Address in Zora Neale Hurston," *A World of Difference* (Baltimore: Johns Hopkins University Press, 1987), 183. Subsequent references to this essay appear in the text in parentheses.

34. Arnold Rampersad, "The Literary Blues Tradition," *Callaloo* 8 (1985): 498. This piece is a review of *Blues, Ideology, and Afro-American Literature*. While I am inclined to believe, with Rampersad, that Baker's work reflects his desire for "a better understanding of the special beauty, dignity, and authenticity of black American" and that "this quest for understanding is taken so seriously that propaganda and defensiveness play little or no part in his enterprise," I am fully aware that my views may, in fact, be influenced by my personal relationship with and fondness for Baker, my mentor and friend, and the most significant influence in my academic life. The task of negotiating the personal in both academic discourse and in the incredibly—and increasingly—small world of the academy is, however, difficult not only for me, but for scores of scholars, and I can only say there that I've tried, in this chapter and elsewhere, to be more responsive to the intellectual than to the emotional challenges presented by his work. Clearly, given its breadth, scope, and plentitude, I cannot ignore Baker's work and still consider myself an adequately engaged Afro-Americanist literary scholar.

35. Case, *Feminism and Theatre*, 95.

36. Ibid., 96.

Chapter Four: Representing Rape

1. Jeff Hearn and David Morgan, "Men, Masculinities and Social Theory," in *Men, Masculinities and Social Theory*, ed. Hearn and Morgan (London: Unwin Hyman, 1990), 11.

2. Ibid., x.

3. The trajectory of my critique of men's studies, as Hearn and Morgan define it, is in some respects quite different from those feminist critiques they include in *Men, Masculinities and Social Theory*. See Jalna Hanmer, "Men, Power and the Exploitation of Women," 21–42; and Joyce E. Canaan and Christine Griffin, "The New Men's Studies: Part of the Problem or Part of the Solution," 206–14. Those critiques are concerned primarily with the misrepresentation and co-optation of feminism by malicious or insufficiently self-critical males. According to Hanmer, men's studies is driven in part by a desire "to misrepresent radical feminism to be about femininity—to conflate feminism, woman, women, femininity—[which] is a theoretical travesty. Co-opting femininity as a strategy by men to meet the criticisms of radical feminism does not begin to come to grips with their arguments" (29). For an extended critique of men's studies and male feminism, see Tania Modleski, *Feminism without Women: Culture and Criticism in a "Postfeminist" Age* (New York: Routledge, 1991).

4. Wiley offered his remarks on ESPN Sports Reporters, 16 February 1992; Tyson's supporters' comments appear in E. R. Shipp, "Church Backing of Tyson Splits Baptists," *New York Times*, 16 March 1992, sec. 1, p. 10; King discussed his distrust of Washington on "Our Voices," Black Entertainment Network, 25 February 1992. Who doubts that King would have read the presence of screams and scratches as *proof* of Washington's pleasure in Iron Mike's lovemaking? Such responses were, of course, not limited to black participants in the debate. For example, an increasingly self-parodic and obviously economically self-interested Donald Trump suggested that, instead of sending Tyson to jail, Judge Gifford should allow him to continue to make a sportsman's extremely lucrative living on condition that he donate his earnings over a specified period to American rape victims.

5. Hanmer, "Men, Power and Exploitation of Women," 27.

6. Catharine MacKinnon, *Toward a Feminist Theory of the State* (Cambridge: Harvard University Press, 1989), 178. Subsequent references to this study appear in the text in parentheses.

7. A number of feminist scholars reject aspects of MacKinnon's theorizing of female sexuality. For example, in *Thinking Fragments: Psychoanalysis, Feminism, and Postmodernism in the Contemporary West* (Berkeley and Los Angeles: University of California Press, 1990), Jane Flax argues that reduction of female sexuality "to an expression of male dominance" is problematic, in part because "such a definition leaves unexplained how women could ever feel lust for another woman and the wide variety of other sensual experiences women claim to have—for example, in masturbation, breast feeding, or playing with children" (180). And in "Disorderly Woman," *Transition* 53 (1991), Judith Butler writes that MacKinnon's work is unconvincing in its "repudiation of the possibility of pleasure under dangerous conditions; they cannot coexist [for MacKinnon], they cannot be formulated in and through one another; pleasure is only pleasure when it is fully free of domination, because it is never free of domination it is never pleasure" (93).

8. Judith Butler has this to say in "Disorderly Woman" about the need to be attentive to varying degrees and manifestations of female domination:

> There is no doubt that subordination is effected, done, and we know by whom, and that the effects of male domination are the way things "are," the second nature produced by a systemic misogynist practice. . . .
>
> What happens when we shift the terms of analysis from domination to power—that is, when we understand domination as one articulation of power, but not the only one? One can make the claim that women are subordinated without claiming that they are unilaterally and deterministically subordinated—that is, that they are *all* subordinated *in the same way*. The view of domination as a causal determinism underestimates the complex routes by which power operates, the inadvertent sites that it mobilizes, the differentiated mechanisms of its deployment. A feminist theory that seeks to establish a cross-cultural analysis of subordination and to interpret multiple forms of class, racial, sexual, geopolitical forms of colonization cannot rest content with a unilateral view of the oppression of women; neither the view of power as domination nor the stability of the gendered terms "men" and "women" is suitable for the complexity of this contemporary political task. (94)

9. Patrick Colm Hogan, *The Politics of Interpretation* (New York: Oxford University Press, 1990), 141.

10. Joyce Carol Oates, "Rape and the Boxing Ring," *Newsweek,* 24 February 1992, p. 60.

11. Michael Denning, "The End of Mass Culture," in *Modernity and Mass Culture,* ed. James Naremore and Patrick Brantlinger (Bloomington: Indiana University Press, 1991), 255.

12. Robert Lipsyte, "From Spark to Flame to a Roaring Blaze," *New York Times,* 12 February 1992, sec. 2, p. 13. Lipsyte offers one of the few analyses I have encountered of the ways in which class might be said to be implicated in the Tyson event. According to Lipsyte, "The Class Warriors will add that only in Tyson's case [as compared with Clarence Thomas's and William Kennedy Smith's] was the woman considerably above the male in social standing" (12 February 1992). If class is involved in the arena, clearly he means not economic class but the possession of a more refined behavioral aesthetics and ethos than he seems ever to display.

13. E. R. Shipp, "Accuser Flirted with Tyson, Witnesses Say," *New York Times,* 7 February 1992, sec. 2, p. 16.

14. Richard Corliss, "In Judgment of Iron Mike," *Time,* 10 February 1992, p. 77.

15. Shipp, "Church Backing of Tyson Splits Baptists."

16. Howie Evans, "Mike Tyson's Team of Lawyers partly to Blame," *New York Amsterdam News,* 15 February 1992, p. 46; Ed Davis, "Black Men, Black Sex—Black Destruction, Black History," *Pittsburgh Courier* 7 March 1992, p. 5, in Larry Hardesty, "Jury Finds Tyson Guilty of Rape." *New York Amsterdam News,* 15 February 1992, p. 48.

17. Shipp, "Court Begins Process of Setting Tyson's Sentence," *New York Times,* 12 February 1992, sec. 2, p. 9 quoted in Manning Marable, "Mike Tyson Is in Jail, but His Public Trial Continues," *Philadelphia Tribune,* 20 March 1992, sec. 1, p. 7.

18. Shipp, "Church Backing of Tyson Splits Baptists."

19. Susan Brownmiller, *Against Our Will: Men, Women, and Rape* (New York: Simon and Schuster, 1975), 212.

20. Lena Williams, "Growing Black Debate on Racism: When Is It Real, When an Excuse," *New York Times,* 5 April 1992, sec. 1, p. 28.

21. Ira Berkow, "The 'Animal' in Mike Tyson," *New York Times* 11 February 1992, sec. 2, p. 11.

22. William Nack, "A Crushing Verdict," *Sports Illustrated* 17 February 1992, 22.

23. Susan Estrich, *Real Rape* (Cambridge: Harvard University Press, 1987), 4.

24. Dave Anderson, "10 Years, 10 Years, 10 Years," *New York Times,* 27 March 1992, sec. 2, p. 7.

25. Before his second fight with Donovan "Razor" Ruddock, in fact, Tyson himself saw physical battery as a means of attaining another's sexual submission; using what one of his biographers terms "jailhouse" discourse, he threatens to beat his opponent so brutally, "I'll make you my girlfriend. . . . I'll make you kiss me with those big lips," in Montieth Illingworth, *Mike Tyson: Money, Myth, and Betrayal* (New York: Birch Lane Press, 1991), 391. Moreover, Washington's accusations suggest the veracity of a statement that the boxer's former friend, Jose Torres, attributes to him (a statement Tyson denies having made): "I like to hear them [women] scream with pain, to see them bleed. It gives me pleasure" (quoted in Illingworth, 327).

26. In Hardesty, "Jury Finds Tyson Guilty of Rape," 48.

27. Published reports of Tyson's relationship with, among other women, model Naomi Campbell suggest that the boxer had on several occasions employed such a bold tactic, and with marked success. In the case of Campbell, his tactics did not prove wholly repugnant because, as reported in *People* magazine, 24 February 1992, "the two later dated" (40).

28. For an astute discussion of black women and nineteenth-century theories of true womanhood, see Hazel Carby, *Reconstructing Womanhood: The Emergence of the Afro-American Novelist* (New York: Oxford University Press, 1987), 20–61.

29. Calvin Hernton, *Sex and Racism in America* (New York: Doubleday, 1965), 139–40.

30. This icon's attitudinal availability could be said to confirm Hernton's reading of the black woman as "the most sexual animal on this planet" and hence serve to explain black masculinist imperatives to maintain a Miss Black America pageant despite the fact that the more established annual Atlantic City event has expanded its notions of female beauty to embrace what used to be called negroid features. Just as important, perhaps, we might see Hernton's mythologizing and sexualizing of a historically conditioned black female attitidunal "rigidity" as encouraging a male response of erection or penile "rigidity."

31. For an engaging discussion of this incident, see Elizabeth Colton, *The Jackson Phenomenon: the Man, the Power, the Message* (New York: Doubleday, 1989), 203–15.

32. Shipp, "Tyson Found Guilty on 3 Counts As Indianapolis Rape Trial Ends," *New York Times*, 11 February 1992, sec. 2, p. 15.

33. Joe Treen and Bill Shaw, "Judgment Day," *People*, 24 February 1992, p. 38.

34. Ibid., 37, 40.

35. Phil Berger, "Tyson's Driver Says Woman Was Dazed," *New York Times*, 2 February 1992, sec. 8, p. 1.

36. Treen and Shaw, "Judgment Day," 37.

37. For popular studies of the consequences of the objectification of the female body, see Susan Brownmiller, *Femininity* (New York: Simon and Schuster, 1984); and Naomi Wolf, *The Beauty Myth: How Images of Beauty are Used against Women* (New York: Morrow, 1991).

38. A vulnerable aspect of MacKinnon's theorizing is her representation of black men's implication in this gendered script. Warner, for example, views as particularly problematic the following passage from an early version of one of her essays: "This does not mean all men have male power equally. American Black men, for instance, have substantially less of it. But to the extent that they cannot create the world from their point of view, they find themselves unmanned, castrated, literally and figuratively." In response, Warner argues,

> Black men, placed opposite white male power, are "unmanned," and therefore not-men, but ones who (in the terms of masculinist psychology) are "castrated," and thus like "women." The use of this circular definition of black-men-as-woman to "defend" black men produces its own ironic effects. Black men's particularity and difference (from white men, from black women, from white women) is reduced, at the very moment, and with the very conceptual terms (the idea of their lack of power), mobilized to protect that difference (from white men). (117–18)

This problem is not evident in MacKinnon's book, however, which profited from "the misunderstandings, distortions, and misreadings of a wide readership" that led her to revise parts of her manuscript and to state explicitly, "This book does not try to explain everything" (xi). MacKinnon acknowledges that her book "does not pretend to present an even incipiently adequate analysis of race and sex, far less of race, sex, and class." Nonetheless, she attempts to "avoid the fetishized abstractions of race and class (and sex) which so commonly appear under the rubric 'difference' and to analyze experiences and demarcating forces that occupy society concretely and particularly—for example, 'Black women' instead of 'racial differences.'" Such fetishizing, in her view, seeks "to evade the challenge women's reality poses to theory, simply because the theoretical forms those realities demand have yet to be created" (xii). Further, she argues that "[m]ale dominance appears to exist cross-culturally, if in locally particular forms" (130).

Warner is right to critique the facile formulations of black male psychic castration that MacKinnon offers (as do many Afro-Americanists and postcolonialists) as a consequence of the fact that oppressed men are denied access to the full range of masculinity's options and objects. He might have been more persuasive, however, had he attempted to deal with the historical and conceptual connections between the denial to black men of hegemonic masculinity and the "literal" castration of members of this group during the ritual of social control called lynching. Further, his critique would have profited from an acknowledgement that MacKinnon's formulation of black males "unmanning" turns on a definition of hegemonic masculinity as possessing the cultural power to "create the world from their point of view," a possibility white male hegemony has in fact worked strenuously to deny black men. Whatever problems exist in MacKinnon's formulations in this regard, they are no more profound than Warner's suggestion that acts of "unmanning"—if, for a moment at least, we can limit our study of male difference specifically to lynching's severing of male genitals—had and have no fundamental impact upon black men's psyches. These racial and gendered rituals were and are profoundly influential, as attested in literary texts otherwise as ideologically disparate as *Native Son* and *Invisible Man*. Both of these novels, as well as many others, figure black male sexuality in the context of fears of racially charged castration. See William Beatty Warner, "Treating Me Like an Object: Reading Catharine MacKinnon's Feminism," in *Feminism and Institutions*, 90–125; Richard Wright, *Native Son* (1940; reprint, New York: Perennial, 1966); and Ralph Ellison, *Invisible Man* (1952; reprint, New York: Vintage, 1972).

39. Diana Scully, *Understanding Sexual Violence: A Study of Convicted Rapists* (Boston: Unwin Hyman, 1990), 27.

40. Treen and Shaw, "Judgment Day," 38–39; the Tyson statement is cited in Corliss, "In Judgment of Iron Mike."

41. Corliss, "In Judgment of Iron Mike," 38.

42. Wendy Lesser, *His Other Half: Men Looking at Women through Art* (Cambridge: Harvard University Press, 1991), 3–4. Subsequent references to this study appear in the text in parentheses.

43. Judith Fetterley, *The Resisting Reader: A Feminist Approach to American Fiction* (Bloomington: Indiana University Press, 1978).

44. Indeed, Lesser appears unwilling to conceive of such a possibility. In the space she reserves for a consideration of male readerly interaction with female-authored texts—the "reverse" of male penetration of the female—she inserts not female artistic penetration to the male psyche but rather the effects on male artists of entering the female imagination.

45. Because of the discrepancy at several points between Lee's published screenplay and the actual film, I have used the following citation scheme: Where no significant deviation from the screenplay exists, I use the screenplay's wording, which appears in Spike Lee, *Spike Lee's Gotta Have It: Inside Guerrilla Filmmaking* (New York: Fireside, 1987), and mark the page numbers in parentheses; where there is significant deviation or where scenes in the movie are not in the screenplay, I use the film words of the film.

46. Hearn and Morgan, *Men, Masculinities*, 11.

47. Lee, *Spike Lee's Gotta Have It*, 137, 140.

48. Lee desires a black film renaissance, but only one in which he will play a central role, as is evidenced by his remark, "I truly believe I was put here to make films. . . . It's not for me to say whether *SGHI* is a landmark film . . . but I do want people to be inspired by it, in particular, black people. Now there is a present example of how we can produce. We can do the things we want to do, there are no mo' excuses" (17). And later in the journal he says, "Yesterday Nelson George and I went to see *The Color Purple*. The movie is weak. We were both disappointed, but that was no surprise. WE, I GOTTA HAVE OUR OWN GODDAMN FILMS. FUCK HAVING THESE WHITE BOYS FUCK UP TELLING OUR STORIES. WE GOTTA TELL OUR OWN AS ONLY WE CAN" (253).

49. Stephen Heath, "Male Feminism," *Men in Feminism*, 4.

50. Lee repeatedly mentions this novel in his journal: "I will get permission to use the

opening paragraph from Zora Neale Hurston's *Their Eyes Were Watching God*. Hopefully I can get the piece free especially since I am dedicating the film to her" (106); "I'm thinking about having the Zora Neale Hurston thing as an actual invocation" (133); and "The scene where Nola is reading a book with Greer it should be Zora Neale Hurston's *Their Eyes Were Watching God*. By the way, I have to tell Tracy [Camila Johns, who plays Nola] to read it" (135).

51. Whatever its other merits, some of which I will speak about below, Michele Wallace's "Spike Lee and Black Women" (*Invisibility Blues: From Pop to Theory* (New York: Verso, 1990), 100–106) falls into just such an interpretive trap in its attempt to assess the significance of Lee's use of the opening paragraphs of Hurston's *Their Eyes Were Watching God* as epigraph. Wallace regards Lees epigraphic use of Hurston as license to argue that the three male lovers in the film are intended as replicas of Janie's husbands:

> Jamie seems most like Logan Killicks, who offers Janie the lackluster security of forty acres and a mule and wants to grade her when she fails to appreciate it. Greer Childs resembles Joe Starks, who becomes the mayor of an all-black town and wants to put Janie on a pedestal. Tea Cake, who offers Janie pleasure and companionship "on the muck" among the "folk farthest down," seems a dead ringer for Mars Blackmon, whose love of fun emerges as a critique of conventional masculinity. (102)

The persuasiveness of these pairings is debatable at best, if only because Nola loves Jamie, not Mars, who, in Wallace's estimation, is intended to assume the role of soul mate that is Tea Cake's in Janie's life. It might be most accurate to say that Lee takes the idea of three lovers from Hurston, but compresses the relationships into a simultaneous rather than sequential figuration in order to reflect aspects of the sexual mores of the historical moment he is recording. Subsequent references to Wallace's essay appear in the text in parentheses.

52. Keith Cohen, "Eisenstein's Subversive Adaptation," in *The Classic American Novel and the Movies,* ed. Gerald Peary and Roger Shatzkin (New York: Ungar, 1977), 245.

53. Zora Neale Hurston, *Their Eyes Were Watching God* (1937; reprint, New York: Perennial, 1990), 178. Subsequent references to this novel appear in the text in parentheses.

54. Even films that heavily employ voice-over narration are characterized invariably by omniscient storytelling, because, in the end, the audience encounters a visual landscape that extends beyond the sight of the intratextual storyteller, if only to include that storyteller literally in the picture. For examples of the inadequacies of film to replicate first-person narration, see *Criss Cross* and *The Prince of Tides.*

55. But for a provocative critique of the overemphasis by Lee and his critics on the realistic nature of his figurations of Afro-American life (and, indeed, the problems implicit in privileging authenticity as a desired artistic goal), see Wahneema Lubiano, "But Compared to What? Reading Realism, Representation, and Essentialism in *School Daze, Do the Right Thing,* and the Spike Lee Discourse," *Black American Literature Forum* 25 (summer 1991): 253–82.

56. Linda Hutcheon, *The Politics of Postmodernism* (New York: Routledge, 1989), 2.

57. Walker discusses the consequences for females of being bereft of a medium of artistic expression in her titular essay in *In Search of Our Mothers' Gardens* (San Diego: Harcourt Brace Jovanovich, 1983), 231–43. For a discussion of how the formulations of that essay bear upon a reading of her most famous novel, see Awkward, "*The Color Purple* and the Achievement of (Comm)unity," *Inspiriting Influences,* 135–64.

58. Nola dreams of being burned in her "loving bed" by Mars's, Jamie's, and Greer's girlfriends. For scenes in Toni Morrison, *Sula* (1973; reprint, New York: Plume, 1982), from which Lee apparently draws in this regard, see 42–48, 75–78, 112–18. Subsequent references to Morrison's novel appear in the text in parentheses.

59. As I have noted, Wallace asserts that Nola serves her male suitors as "a dark continent to be explored and conquered" (103). While I will have more to say below about the meanings of such a representation of Nola's body, it is interesting to note that Rosie Perez, whose bare breasts are prominently featured in a love scene between her character, Tina, and Lee's Mookie in *Do the Right Thing,* has expressed similar feelings about what she regards as the filmmaker's cinematic exploitation of her body. Perez says: "I don't consider that a love scene. It was just an exposing of my breasts. I felt the camera raped me in *Do the Right Thing*"; Tom Green, "Rosie Perez Makes a Fast Break," *USA Today,* 2 April 1992, D1.

60. Useful formulations on these matters are offered in Ellen Carol DuBois and Linda Gordon, "Seeking Ecstasy on the Battlefield: Danger and Pleasure in Nineteenth-century Feminist Sexual Thought," in *Pleasure and Danger: Exploring Female Sexuality,* ed. Carol Vance (Boston: Routledge, 1984), 31–49.

61. Carol Vance, "Pleasure and Danger: Toward a Politics of Sexuality," in *Pleasure and Danger,* 3. Subsequent references to the essay appear in the text in parentheses.

62. Jane Gallop, "Phallus/Penis: Same Difference," *Thinking through the Body* (New York: Columbia University Press, 1988), 132–33.

63. Ibid., 127.

64. In her introduction Vance criticizes both masculinist views of female sexuality which "encouraged [women] to assent that all male sexuality done to them is pleasurable and liberatory" and "the feminist critique [which] emphasized the ubiquity of sexual danger and humiliation in a patriarchal surround" (5). She argues for a different analysis:

> The truth is that the rich brew of our experience contains elements of pleasure and oppression, happiness and humiliation. Rather than regard this ambiguity as confusion or false consciousness, we should use it as a source-book to examine how women experience sexual desires, fantasy, and action. We need to sort out individually and together what the elements of our pleasure and displeasure are. What, for instance, is powerful, enlivening, interesting in our experience? Our task is to identify what is pleasurable and under what conditions, and to control experiences so that it occurs more frequently. (5–6)

Vance's insights support a reading of Lee's film which suggests that Nola has embarked upon the type of self-inventory Vance recommends, and that in her rejection of monogamy she has indeed found a way to "control experience." But clearly, despite the persuasiveness of Vance's pragmatic perspective—and it is a perspective much more appealing to live with and by than, say, MacKinnon's figuration of female sexuality as pure danger—not even the sort of self-awareness of the sources of individual female sexual pleasure that she speaks of can protect the female from the threat of transgressive male behavior. Female self-inventory is limited as a means to achieve "the experience of heterosexuality," given its inability to produce the concomitant male self-reflexivity that MacKinnon demands, and it is for this reason that formulations such as MacKinnon's, despite their problematic rejection of the possibility of gynocentric female sexual pleasure, are still desperately needed in order to assist the radical transformation of our patriarchal society. As a male scholar conversant with feminist ideas and ideals who acknowledges—and strives to resist—the seductiveness of aspects of phallic rule, I suggest that rather than reject views such as MacKinnon's in order to be able to point to pleasurable instances of female sexual expression, we need to recognize the potentially narrow success of Vance's pragmatic politics of sexuality, given the capacity of patriarchy in its present form to co-opt or take full advantage of even the most self-reflexive of female self-inventories.

65. Jamie's interchanges with Opal—including his insistence that because she is "a beautiful woman," he would not have "dreamed she was gay"—suggest that he has absorbed characteristic features of a homophobic mainstream's views of homosexuality.

66. Jacques Lacan, "The Meaning of the Phallus," in *Feminine Sexuality,* ed. Juliet Mitchell and Jacqueline Rose, trans. Rose (New York: Norton, 1985), 81.

67. Audre Lorde, *Sister Outsider* (Trumansburg, NY: Crossing Press, 1984), 64.

68. I do, however, want to note that Coco Fusco, in her review of *She's Gotta Have It* (*Cineaste* 15 [1987]), suggests that Nola's mural is not thoroughly integrated into the film's thematics: "In her spare time she works on a mural in her apartment made up of sketches of famous blacks. Occasionally, she adds a headline clip about violent crimes against them. Though the sentiment is well-placed, these quotations lose much of their impact as it grows clearer and clearer that neither Nola nor her suitors is the least bit concerned with the stories beyond the clips" (24). Though I have tried to demonstrate ways in which the mural can be viewed as being crucial to a comprehension of aspects of Nola's character, Fusco is correct that its significance is neither clearly nor overtly rendered in the film.

69. In her study of convicted rapists, *Understanding Sexual Violence,* Diana Scully argues:

> It is clear that whatever else they may believe, sexually violent men believe the cultural stereotype that, once the rape began, their victims relaxed and enjoyed it. Indeed, 69 percent of deniers justified their behavior by claiming not only that their victims were willing but that they enjoyed themselves—in some cases, to an immense degree. Several men even boasted that they had made their victims' fantasies come true. Additionally, while the majority of admitters used adjectives such as "dirty," "humiliated," and "disgusted" to describe how they thought rape made women feel, 20 percent still believed that their victims, in particular, had enjoyed themselves. (105–6)

70. In *Real Rape,* Susan Estrich speaks derisively of theories of rape that seek to place upon female victims the blame for their own victimization. Estrich cites one such theory as being particularly flawed: "Menachem Amir . . . adapted the concept of the 'victim-precipitated' rape to describe, and implicitly ascribe blame for, just such cases. Amir considered rapes to be 'victim precipitated' where the victim acted in a way that 'could be taken as an invitation to sexual relations'—agreed to drinks, rides, or dates or failed to react strongly enough to sexual suggestions and overtures" (25). This notion of "victim-precipitated" rape supports the view that any nonhostile social behavior on a woman's part can be deemed by a male as sexual invitation.

71. *Acquaintance Rape: The Hidden Crime,* ed. Andrea Parrot and Laurie Bechhofer (New York: Wiley, 1991), offers some of the best research currently available on this complex, prevalent, and underreported crime. For a particularly illuminating discussion of the impact of acquaintance rape, see Christine A. Gidycz and Mary P. Koss, "The Effects of Acquaintance Rape on the Female Victim," 270–83. The authors speak about the fact that

one of the "deleterious consequences for the victim" is that "because the rape victim [often] doesn't believe that what happened to her is rape, she sometimes decides to give her attacker another chance." Such acts of denial contribute to the findings of one study that "acquaintance rape victims were twice as likely as stranger rape victims to be assaulted multiple times by the same man" (277–78).

72. For a fuller discussion of this issue, see Awkward, *Inspiriting Influences*, 15–57.

73. For example, Jamie and Mars are unable to agree about Nola's dependability. According to Mars, Nola, who did not show up for one of their dates, was " 'bout as dependable as a ripped diaphragm" (340), though Jamie, who says she "never gave me a move like that" (341), insists that "many a time she came through for me in the clutch" (342). But minutes before (in film time at least), Jamie was furious with Nola specifically because she was not reliable: she canceled a date to see a movie because, as she put it, "I have to help Mars look for an apartment" (335). Lee's juxtaposition of these scenes highlights the selectivity of memory and, more to the point, the fact that the exhibition of memory's selectivity by both men reflects their psychic states after the relationship as much as it does Nola's behavior. (In a play on her novel's introductory paragraphs, he creates males as capable as Hurston's women of making the dream the truth.) Jamie's act of recollection results from his desire, even after his relationship with Nola has ended, to regard her as his "mythic" (361) soul mate. Conversely, Mars, the beneficiary in this instance of Nola's unreliability where Jamie is concerned, but whose desertion by her threatens his fragile sense of self, is compelled to forget all of her acts of kindness. In effect, Mars reduces Nola to her sexual function: she was "a freak, y'know, freaky-deaky," a woman commendable only because "[t]he sex was def. Nola had the goods and she knew what to do" (290–91).

Chapter Five: "Unruly and Let Loose"

1. See Genevieve Fabre, "Genealogical Archaeology or the Quest for Legacy in *Song of Solomon*," in *Critical Essays on Toni Morrison*, ed. Nellie McKay, (Boston: G. K. Hall, 1988), 105–14; Dorothy H. Lee, "*Song of Solomon*: To Ride the Air," *Black American Literature Forum* 16 (1982), 64.

2. Lee, "*Song of Solomon*: To Ride the Air," 64.

3. Toni Morrison, "Rootedness: The Ancestor As Foundation," in *Black Women Writers, 1950–1980: A Critical Evaluation*, ed. Mari Evans (New York: Doubleday, 1984), 340, emphasis added. Subsequent references to this piece appear in the text in parentheses.

4. The question of behavior, both appropriate and inappropriate, dominates the narrative and discursive action of this novel.

5. Lee, "*Song of Solomon*; To Ride the Air," 64.

6. Julius Lester, "People Who Could Fly," *Black Folktales* (New York: Grove, 1969), 149.

7. Toni Morrison, *Song of Solomon* (New York: Signet, 1977), 341. Subsequent references to this novel appear in the text in parentheses.

8. Lester, "People Who Could Fly," 152.

9. I term Lester's version of the flying Afro-American myth "traditional" because in its setting (black slaves working southern plantation fields) and theme (the possibility for physical and/or psychic escape from white racist dehumanization of the black body) "People Who Could Fly" echoes other recorded versions of the myth. For other versions, see "All God's Chillen Had Wings," *The Book of Negro Folklore*, ed. Langston Hughes and Arna Bontemps (New York: Dodd, Mead 1958), 62–65; J. D. Suggs's "The Flying Man,"

in Richard Dorson, *American Negro Folktales* (Greenwich, Conn.: Fawcett, 1956), 279; and "Flying People," in J. Mason Brewer, *American Negro Folklore* (Chicago: Quadrangle Books, 1969), 309. Hughes and Bontemps's version is in many striking ways similar to Lester's tale; one significant difference, however, is that the male figure empowered with the word in the Hughes-Bontemps text is old; in the Lester version he is young.

10. Morrison's appropriative, transformative intent is signaled clearly by her emphasis on Solomon's failure to bring Jake along with him on his flight to his African origins. That failure is in dramatic contrast to the Hughes and Bontemps version, which begins by introducing a crying child whose birth has weakened the young black mother who represents the tale's initial transcendent figure (63). Kimberly Benston argues that in her appropriation of the epic quest narrative, Morrison delineates "the black male hero [who] experiences no rapture or relation that can hold him from pursuit of a beckoning world that is always elsewhere" (93). For his astute interrogation of Morrison's engagement with inherited epic and Afro-Americanist masculinist narratives, see Benston, "Re-Weaving the 'Ulysses Scene': Enchantment, Post-Oedipal Identity, and the Buried Text of Blackness in *Song of Solomon*," in *Comparative American Identities: Race, Sex, and Nationality in the Modern Text,* ed. Hortense J. Spillers, (New York: Routledge, 1991), 87–109.

11. Rosemarie K. Lester, "An Interview with Toni Morrison, Hessian Radio Network, Frankfurt, West Germany," in *Critical Essays on Toni Morrison,* 54.

12. Alan Dundes, *Sacred Narrative: Readings in the Theory of Myth,* ed. Dundes (Berkeley: University of California Press, 1984), 1.

13. George deForest Lord, *Trials of the Self: Heroic Ordeals in the Epic Tradition* (Hamden, Conn.: Archon, 1983), 1.

14. Richard Slotkin, "Myth and the Production of History," in *Ideology and Classic American Literature,* 70.

15. Ibid., 78.

16. For examples of traditional masculinist Afro-American folklore, see Lester, *Black Folktales,* especially "The Girl with the Large Eyes," 57–61, and "Jack and the Devil's Daughter," 73–90.

17. Gerry Brenner, "*Song of Solomon:* Rejecting Rank's Monomyth and Feminism," in *Critical Essays on Toni Morrison,* 115.

18. Rachel Blau DuPlessis, *Writing beyond the Ending: Narrative Strategies of Twentieth-Century Women Writers* (Bloomington: Indiana University Press, 1985), 5. Subsequent references to this study appear in the text in parentheses.

19. Joseph Campbell, *Hero with a Thousand Faces* (New York: Pantheon Books, 1949), 116.

20. What complicates such a reading of Morrison's feminist encounter with myth, however, is the fact that the traditional Afro-American folktale upon which she bases the Song of Solomon cannot accurately be termed phallocentric. Indeed, as I have demonstrated, the sacred narrative of the flying Africans portrays communal—male and female—flight from a corrupt (American) society. Thus, it is in Morrison's appropriation that the myth can be said to represent an androcentric narrative. This fact suggests, it would appear, that in her "new grounding" of the myth, Morrison wishes to demonstrate the extent to which the Afro-American value system has suffered from corruption by an individualistic and phallocentric Western belief system. Thus, it is not in Morrison's reading of the traditional folktale itself but rather in her transformation of it in the blues lyrics which constitute the song of Solomon, that Du Plessis's formulations concerning a resistant female myth-

ological writer seem appropriate. It is in her response to a version of the myth she herself constructs that we can locate in *Song of Solomon* a tension between critique and affirmation, her apparently bifurcated perspective.

21. Susan Willis, *Specifying: Black Women Writing the American Experience* (Madison: University of Wisconsin Press, 1987), 59–60.

22. Fabre, "Genealogical Archaeology," 106.

23. Ibid., 107. Fabre is not alone in neglecting the full implications of gender in *Song of Solomon*. Philip Royster notes in passing that *Song of Solomon* "is the first of her novels that employs a male protagonist"; "Milkman Flying: The Scapegoat Transcended in Toni Morrison's *Song of Solomon,*" *College Language Association Journal* 24 (1982): 419. He fails, however, to allow this obviously important matter to inform his reading. Similarly, Jane Campbell, *Mythic Black Fiction: The Transformation of History* (Knoxville: University of Tennessee Press, 1986): 137, argues that Morrison has "invested *Song of Solomon* with an epic quality," but she does not consider the significance of gender to the novelist's figuration of what she calls "ancestral quests." However, see Benston, "Re-Weaving the 'Ulysses Scene,'" which provocatively focuses attention upon, among other matters, the implications of Morrison's choice of a male protagonist.

24. See Lee, "*Song of Solomon:* To Ride the Air," 67.

25. Campbell, *Her with a Thousand Faces,* 20.

26. Ibid.

27. Ibid.

28. Lord, *Trials of the Self,* 221.

29. Clearly, Hagar's tragic plight is accelerated by her status as woman in a masculinist plot which insists that a female is nothing without a man. Hagar is unable to find, and, indeed, is not even permitted to search for, in any potentially fruitful locale, the type of significant and sustaining personal and tribal meaning in history and myth, a fact that signals her place outside of the myth's transcendent action. Morrison employs song to contrast the disparate successes of Milkman's and Hagar's quests. The male protagonist finds new life in the cryptic blues lyrics of the song of Solomon. In contrast, the use of song in the concluding scene of chapter 13—Pilate's and Reba's mournful pleas at Hagar's funeral for "Mercy" and Pilate's reenactment of a lullaby ("Who's been botherin my baby?" [322]) she'd sung to her granddaughter "when she was a little girl"—signals the anguish of the female characters at their inability to protect Hagar from the deadly effects of her rejection of Milkman that had "been botherin my baby girl."

30. Benston, "Re-Weaving the 'Ulysses Scene,'" 93.

Chapter Six: "The Crookeds with the Straights"

1. References to the August Wilson texts with which I am engaged in this chapter—*Fences* (New York: Plume, 1986) and "'I Want a Black Director,'" *New York Times* 26 September 1990, sec. 1, p. 15—appear in the text in parentheses; James Greenberg, "Did Hollywood Sit on 'Fences' over Hiring a Black Director?" *New York Times* 27 January 1991, sec. 2, p. 13.

2. George Bluestone, *Novels into Film* (1957; reprint, Berkeley: University of California Press, 1985), 1.

3. Neil Sinyard, *Filming Literature: The Art of Screen Adaptation* (New York: St. Martin's, 1986), 117. A look at two analyses of filmic adaptations demonstrates this tendency within scholarship to minimize the importance of issues such as those Wilson considers

central. Richard Hulseberg argues that "our own biases and predilections, and experience and value of all sorts hover about our dealings with an individual work" and that "many comparisons of novels and films are sensed as moral ones, the idea being that the film-maker has an obligation to 'restate,' in his fashion, the essence of the novel, and that anything less constitutes a kind of vulgar cultural cannibalism, an abuse of the high art of fiction." See Hulseberg, "Novels and Films: A Limited Inquiry," *Literature and Film Quarterly* 6 (1978): 57, 58. Hulseberg locates cultural co-optation not in the exchange between directors and counterhegemonic texts—where Wilson places it—but in American society's simplistic distinctions between high and low art, between the literary text as bourgeois form of consumption and its formally and diegetically unfaithful filmic rendering. Conversely, Donald Larsson focuses at points on contemporary critical notions of ideology, even going so far as to refer to an Althusserian notion of ideology as "the way in which people live the relationship between themselves and the conditions of their existence." See Larsson, "Novel into Film: Some Preliminary Reconsiderations," in *Transformations in Literature and Film,* ed. Leon Golden (Tallahassee: University Presses of Florida, 1982), 79. However, rather than seeing the enactment of ideology potentially as an attempt to neutralize the impact of counterhegemonic ideological energies, Larsson foregrounds historical difference—what he refers to as a "change in lived relationships"—as the primary motivation for tangible differences between originary text and filmic adaptation.

In addition to considering the ways in which historical differences transform the texts we receive from earlier periods, I believe we need a theory of adaptation that encourages our serious attention to the textual transformations which take place *within* historical periods if we want to investigate more fully ideology's continual impact on narrative and form.

For other discussions of filmic adaptations, see Keith Cohen, *Film and Fiction: The Dynamics of Exchange* (New Haven and London: Yale University Press, 1979); and Robert Giddings, Keith Selby, and Chris Wensely, *Screening the Novel: The Theory and Practice of Literary Dramatization* (London: Macmillan, 1990).

4. For discussions of Steven Spielberg's adaptation of Alice Walker's novel, see Jacqueline Bobo, "Sifting through the Controversy: Reading *The Color Purple,*" *Callaloo* 13 (1990), 332–42; Gerald Early, "*The Color Purple* As Everybody's Protest Art," *Tuxedo Junction: Essays in American Culture* (New York: Ecco, 1989), 33–45; and Michele Wallace, "Blues for Mr. Spielberg," *Invisibility Blues.*

5. According to Keith Cohen, "Adaptation is a truly artistic feat when the new version carries with it a hidden criticism of its model, or at least implicit (through a process we should call 'deconstruction') certain key contradictions implanted or glossed over in the original." See "Eisenstein's Subversive Adaptation," *The Classic American Novel and the Movies,* 245. Cohen's contention, I believe, is merely a poststructuralist-inflected articulation of Bluestone's perspective, and is echoed in Neil Sinyard's assertion that

> the best adaptations of books for film can often be approached as an activity of literary criticism, . . . [as] a critical essay which stresses what it sees as the main theme. Like a critical essay, the film adaptation selects some episodes, excludes others, offers preferred alternatives . . . [Film adapters] are also not afraid . . . to take liberties with character and structure when they feel they have more convincing readings to offer than the original, to emphasize some features and disregard others. In other words, they go for intensity of illumination more than a shapeless inclusiveness. (*Filming Literature,* 117)

While we need not accept black filmmaker Warrington Hudlin's view that a white film director inevitably seeks to bracket the ideological thrust or black focus of Afro-American texts because of his inability otherwise "to find an emotional center that he can identify with" (Greenberg, 18), views such as Sinyard's and Cohen's might cause concern for any artist who wishes to see his or her ideas reflected on the screen, particularly authors like Wilson who have what they feel are historically justifiable suspicions about white filmmakers' appropriations of black texts.

6. Greenberg, "Did Hollywood Sit on 'Fences'?" 18.

7. Larsson, "Novel into Film," 80.

8. Michael Omi and Howard Winant,. *Racial Formation in the United States: From the 1960s to the 1980s* (London: Routledge, 1986), 69–69.

9. James Clifford, *Writing Culture: The Poetics and Politics of Ethnography,* ed. Clifford and George E. Marcus (Berkeley: University of California Press, 1986), 19.

10. Ibid., 18.

11. See chapter 3 for my discussion of "A Critique of Pure Pluralism." Sollors's extended discussion of these matters appears in *Beyond Ethnicity: Consent and Descent in American Culture* (New York: Oxford University Press, 1986).

12. As is perhaps most perversely—and tragically—manifested in the murder of black urban youths by other blacks in order to steal expensive court shoes, it is clear that certain trends in Afro-American communities can be regarded as direct responses to the commodification of aspects of black cultural style.

13. I have identified this adaptive process elsewhere as *denigration.* See *Inspiriting Influences,* particularly pp. 8–14.

14. Henry Louis Gates, Jr., *The Signifying Monkey: A Theory of Afro-American Literary Criticism* (New York: Oxford University Press, 1988), xxiii.

15. Indeed, whatever the differences between Wilson's and Miller's family dreams (and they are significant), a recitation of some of the most central of *Fences'* concerns—intergenerational male conflict; the motivations for and far-reaching impact of marital infidelity; the consequences for the patriarchical figure of not achieving the American dream; a wife's victimization and complicity in her husband's self-deluding efforts to maintain a positive sense of self despite evidence of his failures; paternal socialization of male offspring through sports; the thematic centrality of death; and, finally, a concluding requiem in which mother, close male friend, and sons assess the meanings of the patriarch's life just before attending his funeral—suggests that Wilson's play would not have been possible in its present form without the precursorial presence of Miller's canonical white American middle-class family drama.

16. Greenberg, "Did Hollywood Sit on 'Fences'?" 18.

17. Houston A. Baker, Jr., *Modernism and the Harlem Renaissance,* 18. Subsequent references to this study appear in the text in parentheses.

Chapter Seven: "A Slave to the Rhythm"

1. Diana Fuss, *Essentially Speaking: Feminism, Nature and Difference* xii, 1. Subsequent citations to this text appear in parentheses in my text.

2. Marjorie Garber, *Vested Interests: Cross-Dressing and Cultural Anxiety* (New York: Routledge, 1992), 296; Susan Willis, "I Shop Therefore I Am: Is There a Place for Afro-American Culture in Commodity Culture?" in *Changing Our Own Words: Essays on Criticism, Theory, and Writing by Black Women,* ed. Cheryl Wall (New Brunswick: Rutgers Uni-

versity Press, 1989), 184. Subsequent citations of these studies appear in parentheses in my text.

3. Greg Tate, "I'm White! What's Wrong with Michael Jackson," *Flyboy in the Buttermilk: Essays on Contemporary America* (New York: Fireside/Simon and Schuster, 1992), 96, 95. Subsequent citations of this study appear in parentheses in the text.

4. Kobena Mercer, "Black Hair/Style Politics," *Out There: Marginalization and Contemporary Cultures,* ed. Russell Ferguson, Martha Gever, Trinh T. Minh-ha, and Cornel West (Cambridge, Mass.: MIT Press, 1990), 262, 248. Subsequent citations of this essay appear in parentheses in my text.

5. One study of vitiligo, the skin disease from which Jackson allegedly suffers, reports that "the ancient Hebrews considered this affliction a punishment. There was a widespread belief that this disfiguring disease was "not a natural phenomenon but a Divine visitation." Jean-Paul Ortonne, David B. Mosher, and Thomas B. Fitzgerald, *Vitiligo and Other Hypomelanoses of Hair and Skin* (New York and London: Plenum Medical Book Co., 1983), 130.

6. We might consider breast implantation as a specifically gendered and classed act of political intervention and neglect. After years of glamorizing breast augmentation, the press witnessed the fallout in 1992 of such widespread, medically untested procedures. Scores of women who have undergone the procedure have discovered that silicone has begun to leak out of their implants and into their bloodstreams, causing massive and varied internal damage. Both the lengths to which women feel forced to go in order to embody masculinist ideals of beauty and the largely male medical community that has allowed literally millions of these surgeries to take place without testing for possible dangers are clearly manifest in this example of surgical intervention.

7. Abdel Monem el Mofty, *Vitiligo and Psoralens* (Oxford: Pergamon, 1968), 6.

8. Ortonne et al., *Vitiligo and Other Hypomelanoses of Hair and Skin,* 129.

9. Isaac Julien, "'Black Is, Black Ain't: Notes on De-Essentializing Black Identities," in *Black Popular Culture,* ed. Gina Dent (Seattle: Bay Press, 1992), 255.

10. Randy Taraborrelli's biography, *Michael Jackson: The Magic and the Madness* (New York: Birch Lane Press, 1991), contains discussions with two of Jackson's associates, who insist that the purpose of his many plastic-surgery operations has been to minimize his resemblance to his verbally and physically abusive father, Joseph. One associate, Marcus Phillips, is quoted as saying, "Michael was elated about the fact that with the second nose job he looked less like his father. . . . That appealed to him very much. If he couldn't erase Joe from his life, at least he could erase him from the reflection in the mirror" (258). Another associate, "a former girlfriend of [Motown founder] Berry Gordy," claims that Michael "told me . . . himself" that "he would do anything not to look like Joe Jackson. Believe me, the last thing he wants to see when he looks at the man in the mirror is his father. With each operation, he distances himself not only from his father but from his whole family. I'm afraid that's the sad, pathetic point of all the surgery" (422).

Jackson's oedipally driven efforts to erase his father surgically from his face are reminiscent of Richard Wright's energetic utilization of his autobiographical text, *Black Boy* (New York: Perennial, 1945), as a means of psychically transcending his abusive father. Visiting his "sharecropper" father "upon the red clay of a Mississippi plantation" after not seeing him for a quarter of a century, the successful Wright says, "My mind and consciousness had become so greatly and violently altered that when I tried to talk to him I realized that, though ties of blood made us kin, though I could see a shadow of my face in his face, though there was an echo of my voice in his voice, we were forever strangers, speaking a different language, living on vastly distant phases of reality" (42). Wright proceeds to distinguish himself irrefutably from his progenitor. According to a cosmopolitan Wright, his rural, toothless, uncomprehending sharecropper father is "fastened . . . to a crude and raw past, . . . chained . . . to the direct, animalistic impulses of his withering body." (43)

11. An Italian sculptor recently produced a large likeness of Jackson, with its scaffolding still in place in order to suggest, somewhat derisively, the entertainer's status as work-in-progress. See "International Lampoon," *People* 15 March 1993, pp. 46–47. I wish to thank Linda Palmer for bringing this photograph to my attention.

12. "Michael Jackson Talks . . . to Oprah: 90 Prime Time Minutes with the King of Pop," ABC Network, 10 February 1993.

13. Mary Talbot with Charles Fleming, "The Two Faces of Michael Jackson," *Newsweek* 23 February 1993, p. 57.

14. F. James Davis, *Who Is Black? One Nation's Definition* (University Park: Pennsylvania State University Press, 1992), 125. Subsequent references to this study appear in the text in parentheses.

15. James Weldon Johnson, *The Autobiography of an Ex-Colored Man,* ed. William Andrews (1912; reprint, New York: Penguin, 1990), 1, 154.

16. See John Howard Griffin, *Black Like Me* (1961); Grace Halsell, *Soul Sister* (1969); and George Schuyler, *Black No More* (1932; reprint, Boston: Northwestern University Press, 1989). See also Eddie Murphy's "Saturday Night Live" short film on *The Best of Eddie Murphy* and the Hollywood films *Soul Man* and Melvin van Peebles's satirical *Watermelon Man.*

17. One might argue that Jackson's new designation, "King of Pop"—an appropriation of the practice of black musicians' early- and mid-century projections of themselves as royalty—is intended to signify superiority over Prince, the royally designated figure who challenges Jackson's entertaining preeminence.

18. Mercer comments on Hall's term:

> Stuart Hall . . . emphasizes the composite nature of white bias, which he refers to as the "ethnic scale," as both physiological and cultural elements are intermixed in the symbolization of one's social status. Opportunities for social mobility are therefore determined by one's ranking on the ethnic scale and involve the negotiation not only of socio-economic factors such as wealth, income, education and marriage, but also of less easily changeable elements of status symbolization such as the shape of one's nose or the shade of one's blackness. (250)

Mercer refers here to Stuart Hall, "Pluralism, Race and Class in Caribbean Society," in *Race and Class in Post-Colonial Society* (New York: UNESCO, 1977), 150–82.

19. Michael Jackson, "Black or White," *Dangerous* (Epic Records EK45400).

20. Stuart Hall, "What Is This 'Black' in Black Popular Culture?" *Black Popular Culture,* 30.

21. Adrian Piper, "Passing for White, Passing for Black," *Transition* 58 (1991): 30.

22. Ann Powers, "Just What Does Michael Jackson's Story Add up To?" *New York Times,* 21 February 1993, sec. 2, p. 33.

23. I would add further that it is not simply virgins who equate sensuality with "frustration and anxiety" but scores of sexually unsatisfied and/or dysfunctional individuals for whom sexuality and pleasure are not contiguous phenomena.

24. Judith Butler, "Gender Trouble, Feminist Theory, and Psychoanalytic Discourse," in *Feminism / Postmodernism,* 337.

25. "Michael Jackson Talks . . . to Oprah: 90 Prime Time Minutes with the King of Pop," ABC Network, 10 February 1993.

26. Much more extensive discussions than I have space to offer here appear in *Racing Justice, En-gendering Power,* ed. Toni Morrison.

27. For an especially compelling discussion of questions of sexuality, black men, and lynching, see Robyn Wiegmann, "The Anatomy of Lynching," *Journal of the History of Sexuality* 3, no. 3 (1993): 445–67.

28. In the wake of allegations of child abuse against Jackson which came to light after this chapter had been completed, it has become difficult to continue to view him as asexual. His return to the public stage will have to be carefully choreographed if he is to remain a popular entertainer, many of whose fans are young. In particular, it may be wise for Jackson to consider removing crotch-grabbing from his repertoire of stage moves.

Abbott, H. Porter, 74
Acquaintance Rape (Parrot and Bechhofer), 211–12 n. 71
African American Review, 25
afrocentric reading, 25–26, 31, 39
afrocentrism, defined, 25; use explained, 195 n. 5
Against Our Will (Brownmiller), 105
Amir, Menachem, 211 n. 70
Andrews, William, 60
Armstrong, Paul, 16, 194–95 n. 7
Asante, Molefi, 25, 195 n. 5
Attaway, William, 65
authority of experience, the, 28
Autobiography of an Ex-Colored Man, The (Johnson), 180

Bad (Jackson), 176
Baker, Houston A., Jr., 26–30, 35–36, 39–41, 45, 70, 72, 74–77, 81, 82, 87, 164–65, 193–94 n. 8, 197 n. 35, 195–96 n. 10, 197 n. 36, 201 n. 2, 204 n. 34
Baldwin, James, 7, 69, 157
Baraka, Amiri, 7
Baym, Nina, 39
beauty pageants, 100, 107–8
Bechhofer, Laurie, 211–12 n. 71
Benston, Kimberly, 60, 150, 213 n. 10
Bercovitch, Sacvan, 75–77, 80, 202 n. 23
Black Aesthetic, The (Gayle), 59, 62–63
Black Aestheticians, 30
Black Boy (Wright), efforts to distinguish self from father, 217 n. 10
Blackburn, Sarah, 198 n. 23
"Black Culture/White Teacher" (Stimpson), 62, 66–69
Black Like Me (Griffin), 11–13, 81–82
Black Literature and Literary Theory (Gates), 23–25

black male feminism, 5, 18, 19, 48–57, 97
black male identity formation, 51
Black No More (Schuyler), 181
Black on White (Littlejohn), 62–66, 83
"Black or White" (Jackson), 184–86
black phallus, 191
Bloom, Harold, 32–33
Blues, Ideology, and Afro-American Literature (Baker), 29, 76, 84, 87
Bluest Eye, The (Morrison), 143, 153
Bluestone, George, 155–56
Bobo, Jacqueline, 215–16 n. 4
"Body in General, The" (Kennedy), 8
Boone, Joseph, 43–44, 49, 198 n. 1, 198 n. 2
border crossings, 9–11, 18
boundary transgression, 4
boxing, as a masculine endeavor, 100
Brandeis University, 53
breast augmentation, 217 n. 6
Brenner, Gerry, 141
Brooks, Gwendolyn, 65
Brown, James, 188
Brownmiller, Susan, 105
Butler, Judith, 33, 187, 189–90, 193–94 n. 8, 208 nn. 7, 8

Campbell, Jane, 214 n. 23
Campbell, Joseph, 141–42, 147
Canaan, Joyce E., 204 n. 3
Cane (Toomer), 66
Carby, Hazel, 206 n. 28
Case, Sue-Ellen, 60, 87–90
category crisis, 182, 191–92
Chapman, Tracy, 3, 5
Christian, Barbara, 10–11
Clemente, Roberto, 170
Clifford, James, 158–61
Cohen, Keith, 119, 215–16 n. 5
Coleman, Milton, 111